"With a historian's attention to love for both the biblical text and McNutt brings to life the 'forgotten Mary and, in so doing, reminds us that such figures in the Bible were living, breathing people of flesh and blood who have things to teach us today. This is a rich and provocative book that brings the larger biblical narrative to life again."

—**Karen Swallow Prior**, author of *The Evangelical Imagination: How Stories, Images, and Metaphors Created a Culture in Crisis*

"McNutt leaves no stone unturned in her quest for the real Mary Magdalene. As a church historian with biblical and theological training, she disentangles Mary Magdalene's story from the other Marys and unnamed women of the New Testament, work she is uniquely qualified to do. As someone with pastoral experience, McNutt helps us see why Mary's story is critically important for the church today. This book was a joy to read!"

—**Carmen Joy Imes**, associate professor, Talbot School of Theology; author of *Being God's Image* and *Bearing God's Name*

"At a time when we have forgotten so many biblical women, this book calls us to remember one of the most crucial. With remarkable pastoral wisdom and academic expertise, McNutt challenges us not only to see the historic Mary Magdalene better but to understand how she changes the way we see women in the church today. Take up and read!"

—**Beth Allison Barr**, James Vardaman Professor of History, Baylor University; bestselling author of *The Making of Biblical Womanhood*

"It is difficult to praise this book too highly. Jennifer Powell McNutt not only helps us distinguish between the various Marys of the New Testament, she also recovers the voice and example of Mary Magdalene for the church today—and, it must be noted, for men and women alike. Fascinating and accessible, this book is a must-read for anyone who preaches and teaches regularly, but it would also aid anyone who is interested in more deeply understanding the Scriptures. I commend this book to all who want to follow Jesus, especially those interested in the attention, dignity, and tasks of ministry that he gave (and gives) to women in the church. Highly recommended!"

—**Tish Harrison Warren**, Anglican priest, former *New York Times* columnist, and author of *Liturgy of the Ordinary* and *Prayer in the Night*

"Harlot. Sinner. Mystic. Wife. Mary Magdalene has been called many things throughout history. The fanciful story of prostitute-turned-saint makes for good drama, but what does Scripture really say about this Mary? McNutt rightly dwells on what the Gospels teach: her faith and deep devotion to Jesus. This book not only clarifies the woman we forgot but also helps us see more clearly the Messiah who sent her as first witness of the resurrection. McNutt is a gifted spiritual biographer. This was a delight to read."

—**Nijay K. Gupta**, professor, Northern Seminary; author of *Tell Her Story*

The
MARY
WE
FORGOT

The
MARY
WE
FORGOT

WHAT THE *APOSTLE TO THE APOSTLES* TEACHES THE CHURCH TODAY

Jennifer Powell McNutt

BrazosPress
a division of Baker Publishing Group
Grand Rapids, Michigan

Published by Brazos Press
a division of Baker Publishing Group
Grand Rapids, Michigan
BrazosPress.com

Printed in the United States of America

Library of Congress Cataloging-in-Publication Data
Names: McNutt, Jennifer Powell, author.
Title: The Mary we forgot : what the apostle to the apostles teaches the church today / Jennifer Powell McNutt.
Description: Grand Rapids, Michigan : Brazos Press, a division of Baker Publishing Group, [2024] | Includes bibliographical references.
Identifiers: LCCN 2024013552 | ISBN 9781587436178 (paperback) | ISBN 9781587436369 (casebound) | ISBN 9781493446438 (ebook)
Subjects: LCSH: Mary Magdalene, Saint.
Classification: LCC BS2485 .M38 2024 | DDC 226/.092—dc23/eng/20240412
LC record available at https://lccn.loc.gov/2024013552

Cover illustration by Mallory Heyer
Cover design by Paula Gibson

24 25 26 27 28 29 30   7 6 5 4 3 2 1

To my loving mother,
the Rev. Dr. Pamela Powell,

and to my aunt of the heart,
Rev. Karen Berns,

both of whom pointed me to the women of the Bible
and modeled pastoral ministry in the church
from my first memories.

I am honored to walk in your footsteps
with joy and gratitude.

CONTENTS

Foreword

Esau McCaulley

It would be hard for someone to prepare the reader for all the moments of surprise, inspiration, and challenge that await them in the pages of *The Mary We Forgot: What the Apostle to the Apostles Teaches the Church Today.*

Like many Christians, I have a passing knowledge of the story of Mary Magdalene, the disciple of Jesus and witness to the resurrection. As a New Testament scholar, I might even have taken a bit of pride in the fact that I had not confused her with the woman who anointed Jesus's feet with her hair and tears in Luke 7:36–38. Dr. McNutt definitely puts that error to bed and explores many other aspects of Mary's life and legacy.

Nonetheless, I quickly found myself humbled as chapter after chapter taught me much about Mary that I did not know. Dr. McNutt has offered a well-researched and clear case for a recovery of the real Mary Magdalene. I will not spoil it via summary here.

Let me be clear. This book is not just a life of Mary Magdalene that links all the relevant biblical passages. It is closer to a treasure hunt in which Dr. McNutt repeatedly delves into her diverse scholarly tool kit of biblical interpretation, church history, and theology to help us understand the apostle to the apostles. Dr. McNutt switches between close readings of biblical texts, examinations of church history in the East, the West, and the Reformation era, and theological analysis with ease. The result is a clearing away of the weeds and brambles that have grown up around the life of Mary Magdalene so that we can understand the challenge she poses to the church in our day. We also get an opportunity to know something of the author herself as her journey to find the real Mary Magdalene at times takes on the feel of a travelogue or, better yet, spiritual pilgrimage.

This should go without saying, but I will say it anyway because honesty requires a bit of plain speaking. This is a book about an influential female follower of Jesus, and in the pages of this book we meet other women who have also borne faithful witness to Jesus. The misinterpretation and sometimes sidelining of Mary Magdalene is something of a warning to the church of what happens when we neglect the gifts of women in our midst. We are all the poorer for it. But just because this is a book about a woman written by a woman doesn't mean it is only for women any more than a book written by a male about the apostle Paul would be only for men. We can all learn from each other.

In the end, this is a book about a disciple of Jesus who bore witness to his resurrection. Mary Magdalene's story has been too often misinterpreted or neglected. She has been made a harlot or Jesus's wife or simply cast aside. This book corrects that. By helping us find the real Mary, this book does what Mary's own story does. It points us to Jesus, the King and Savior who healed her and changed her life.

Esau McCaulley
Feast of the Ascension 2024

Introduction

Mary Magdalene Superstar

Broadway came to Lubbock, Texas, while I was in high school, and it was big news. My parents arranged for me and a group of friends to see the show. Rarely did the Bible Belt receive the likes of Broadway (at least in the 1990s), and they did their best to fit in by bringing Jesus along for the ride. It was the time of the West End London revival and a resurging interest in the musical *Jesus Christ Superstar*, which was all the rage. It was not a version of Jesus I had ever seen.

That evening, the curtain lifted to a colorful and audacious telling of the Jesus story interpreted as a rock opera. Andrew Lloyd Webber's musical reveled in anachronisms and a retro-modern telling of Christ's life. Embodying a 1970s ethos and color palette, Jesus was in every way a superstar. Judas surprised audiences by taking center stage in a bold precursor to antihero shows like *Breaking*

Bad. An unexpected grouping emerged—not Jesus with Peter, James, and John, as in the transfiguration of Jesus as recorded in Scripture; nor the crucified Jesus with John and the Virgin Mary at the foot of the cross, as often depicted in the history of art—but Jesus, Judas, and Mary Magdalene. Judas is depicted as controlling and anxious about money, politics, power, and appearance (some of this resonates with the biblical text). Mary Magdalene, meanwhile, is the former prostitute falling for Jesus.

At the time, I didn't know how much the Western Christian tradition had shaped the portrayal of Mary Magdalene as the penitent prostitute. I was a teenager only scratching the surface of understanding the women of the Bible. Growing up while both my parents served as pastors meant a lot of discussion about Scripture and a lot of time at church. I was drawn, even then, to learn more, and I was curious about Mary Magdalene. Who was this woman who traveled with Jesus and showed such devotion to him? She seemed both indispensable and taboo.

As I watched the show, the more she leaned into Jesus with confused, romantic feelings for him, the more I felt like leaning the other way in my seat. When Webber's Mary Magdalene sang "I don't know how to love him," I cringed (though the song is otherwise lovely). Through the eyes of faith, I registered the importance of Jesus eating with tax collectors, prostitutes, and sinners, but I was bothered that Mary Magdalene's commitment to Jesus had been reduced to her love for a man rather than love for God or even the God-man, as Jesus is described by the earliest theologians of the church.[1] Wasn't it possible that she was drawn to the truth of Jesus's preaching and message just as the male disciples were? Here was a musical written and performed at the historical intersection of the women's rights movement and the sexual revolution, but what if her actual story differed entirely? After all, didn't Jesus call his followers "friends" (John 15:14–15)? Didn't he describe himself to his followers as a "brother"?[2] As she sang "He's a man. He's just a man," I wondered: didn't she know that Jesus wasn't *just* a man?

A Vanishing Figure

Decades have passed since that evening, and yet the difficulty of knowing Mary Magdalene persists—when she is remembered at all. I am struck again and again by how often her story has been forgotten or mistaken in both the church and the public square. She is conflated or confused with other women in the Gospels, undervalued as the first witness to the resurrection, and overlooked, particularly in the Western church, as the "apostle to the apostles."

Her story has too often been shrouded in distortion and controversy, making it tricky to bring her up in church; big feelings cling to the mention of her name. Consider the striking dissonance between how the church has remembered the Virgin Mary but forgotten or distorted Mary Magdalene. While Jesus's mother Mary has been elevated to immaculate birth and bodily ascension in the Roman Catholic tradition, Mary Magdalene has been painted as a prostitute in many Western retellings from the sixth century onward. The label of prostitute has continued to dog her name from modern theater such as Webber's musical to modern movies such as Martin Scorsese's film

The Last Temptation of Christ. Even in the popular series *The Chosen* she is associated with prostitution. Consistently, both women have been caught in church politics and by cultural evaluations that root their value in their sexuality (one elevated as virgin and the other demoted as prostitute), even to the point of diminishing what the Bible says about them.

Sorting out Mary Magdalene is far from simple.

My husband and I lived for a cherished season in Cambridge, England, early in our marriage. We became frequenters of the marvelous Fitzwilliam Museum near our favorite café, Fitzbillies (I still miss their violet cakes!). The museum houses several depictions of the crucifixion scene. One piece especially captures the dilemma of looking for Mary Magdalene and her place in Jesus's ministry according to Scripture. The painting is called *Crucifixion*, and it comes from thirteenth-century Italy. Its straightforward title masks a complicated subject.[3] Two figures are seen standing together at the foot of the cross: the disciple John and Mary, the mother of Jesus. But there is a third who is barely visible.

Centuries of decay have weathered the painting so that the figure is nearly absent; only hands and the outline of a body can be faintly seen at the very bottom of the cross near Jesus's feet. Art history instructs us that the depiction follows the tradition of a repeated triad based on John 19:25–26 (though not exact since the artistic tradition leaves out a third Mary who is not depicted here)—John, Mary the mother of Jesus, and Mary Magdalene.[4] We know her not by her features but by the elusive outline of her actions. She is the humble disciple, grief-stricken and grasping the feet of Jesus. Her placement at the foot of the cross associates her with the anointing stories found in the Gospels (Matt. 26:6–13; Mark 14:1–9; Luke 7:36–50; John 12:1–11), with learning at Jesus's feet (Luke 10:39), weeping at his feet (John 11:32), and gripping the feet of the risen Jesus on Easter morning (Matt. 28:9; John 20:17).[5]

But in this particular painting, the inclusion of Mary Magdalene is almost completely missing. Even though she hasn't been entirely erased or flaked away, the casual onlooker would easily miss her presence. She is literally vanishing from the painting before our very eyes.[6] She is the forgotten Mary.

Just as in the painting, Mary Magdalene's impact on, presence in, and contribution to Christ's ministry has too often been missed, overlooked, and even erased. But what does the church lose when we forget Mary Magdalene at the foot of the cross, at the empty tomb, and before the risen Christ?

Feasting on the Whole of Scripture

Over the course of this book, we will probe the biblical text together in the hopes of remembering the forgotten Mary. We will sort through how Mary Magdalene's conflation with other women in the Gospel accounts has confused our perception of her. We will see how she was admired, distorted, and forgotten in church history. We will grapple with important questions and plausible answers regarding the continuation of her ministry through the traditions of Eastern and Western Christians. We will journey to the south of France to explore the remembered traces of her story there. We will consider tools of hermeneutics and theology to think more deeply about the significance of Mary Magdalene in the Christian faith. We look back in order to look ahead more clearly and faithfully.

At the heart of this book is my hope to retrieve Mary Magdalene for the church and for faith formation and discipleship today, and there is no better time to pursue this. In recent years, scholars of the Bible, church history, and art history have turned their attention to the enigma of Mary Magdalene and her legacy so that a treasure trove of insights is within reach.[7] And yet the opportunity before us offers much more than simply seeing Mary Magdalene rightly.

Searching for Mary Magdalene in the biblical account challenges the whole church, both men and women, to take to heart the whole of Scripture, including Mary Magdalene's story and example. Perhaps you come from ecclesiastical spaces where the church's attention to women in the Bible is too easily reserved for women's ministry rather than the shared space of Sunday morning worship. That kind of practice, whether intentionally or not, bifurcates Scripture's teaching on discipleship that divides up the Bible and disconnects stories that should be interconnected for brothers and sisters in Christ. We might find ourselves avoiding certain portions of the Bible as we filter out those passages that we think don't apply to us, at least not in a foremost way. But even the apostle Peter reminds us that there is no separate gospel for men and women: "They [women] are joint heirs of the gracious gift of life" (1 Pet. 3:7). When we pick and choose, partitioning off some stories of Scripture for some Christians and other stories for other Christians, we do ourselves a disservice. We act like finicky eaters who choose only a few things at a feast when the whole bounty of the feast has been given to nurture and fill us (Ps. 36:8). We should feast on the whole of Scripture since all of it is for all of us.

I am reminded of the beloved film character Indiana Jones, who searches for ancient artifacts and often declares, "This belongs in a museum!" Over and over, he risks his life seemingly due to this primary conviction that human history is shared across civilizations and should not belong to one person or group alone. Similarly, to discover Mary Magdalene in the biblical text is to declare, "She belongs in our church!" Each one of us can and should connect to her story of following Jesus.

The whole Bible is meant for the whole church, which requires us to grapple with the whole of God's revelation both from the passages that easily resonate with us as well as from the passages that we find hard to understand and even harder to receive. A close reading of even the hardest texts is rewarding and enriching to the church body, though they must be handled with care.[8] Even Peter acknowledges that some portions are hard to understand (2 Pet. 3:16). But when we pay attention to where Scripture is directing us, we come to learn more about ourselves and more about God. In her case, to see her story is to see a God who calls a woman to proclaim that Jesus Christ has risen. It has often been said that Scripture functions as a type of mirror through which we can come to see ourselves more clearly and accurately while simultaneously revealing God to us more clearly. John Calvin, the sixteenth-century French Protestant Reformer, used the metaphor of Scripture as a pair of glasses that helps us see rightly.[9] And so the search for Mary Magdalene in the biblical account is a chance for the whole church to read Scripture more deeply, fruitfully, and faithfully.

For those up to the task, reflecting on Mary Magdalene in the Bible requires us to use our theological muscles (yes, you have them!). As we root ourselves in the text, her story can become a vehicle for considering the depths of who God is and what God has done for us. Clearly seeing Mary Magdalene's inclusion in Christ's ministry and in the gospel message allows us to see something more than her. Through her story, we encounter a God who surprises us by who he calls and sends. We witness God's unflagging commitment to healing, calling, and sending ordinary and unexpected people for the extraordinary mission of salvation through Jesus Christ.

Ultimately, Mary Magdalene's legacy is not as a penitent prostitute but as the first apostle. She was saved from seven demons by Jesus, and she turned around to travel with him and contributed to the funding of his ministry. She encountered the risen Lord and was called and sent to proclaim the good news to the disciples. Through her story, we may discover how Christ's command to "go and tell" (Matt. 28:10) was not only for her but for us all. Across generations the body of Christ shares in the drama of God's act of salvation through Jesus Christ. The work of one member of the body is connected to the work of other members of the body so that the whole story is our story (1 Cor. 12). Mary Magdalene's story as an eyewitness connects the whole body of Christ to the unprecedented claims of the Christian faith about what God did at the rugged cross and in the empty tomb. Remembering her presence helps us read Scripture more closely, grow in our understanding of the triune God, and be more faithful disciples in the mission and ministry of Christ's church.

After that moment of encounter with the risen Christ in the garden, Mary Magdalene ran to the disciples to tell them, "I have seen the Lord" (John 20:18). What would happen if we ran with her?

ONE

The Women of Scripture and a Hermeneutic of Surprise

The Sequoia

In 1864, President Abraham Lincoln signed legislation to set aside Mariposa Grove—home to many giant sequoia trees in the Sierra Nevada mountain range—as protected federal land for the public, now part of Yosemite National Park. The sequoias of Mariposa Grove are all magnificent, some growing as tall as a twenty-six-story building, but one stands out from the rest.

This particular sequoia started to grow before the time of Christ. Some three thousand years later, the Grizzly Giant is the oldest tree in the grove and is truly a wonder: immense, awe-inspiring, and irreplaceable. In July 2022, when wildfires threatened the grove, firefighters worked around the clock to ensure that this tree was not lost. Why go to such great lengths to save a tree? Giant sequoias are the longest living things on earth and the largest trees by volume. Though durable, they have their vulnerabilities. They require an exact balance of conditions, from temperature to altitude. Their roots must dig deep enough to prevent them from falling over, since they become so top-heavy. Sequoia cones, meanwhile, depend on heat to spread their seeds. Their resilience offers a rare glimpse of enduring life in the natural world. While visiting the grove, our family marveled at the height and girth of the Grizzly Giant the summer after the fire. Although the damage from the fire was still visible, she was continuing to stand tall.

Like the Grizzly Giant, Mary Magdalene stands tall in the grove of biblical witnesses.

To draw out her significance entails no twisting of the text. Scripture directs our attention to Mary Magdalene, who rooted herself deeply in the life and ministry of Jesus. Her presence, inclusion, and contribution to the flourishing of the grove turns out to be irreplaceable. She is no addendum to Jesus's story. She is a towering, resilient sequoia that requires our focus and attention for all that she contributes to our faith in Christ.

What's in a Name?

Mary Magdalene is mentioned in the Gospel accounts nearly as much as Jesus's mother, Mary (Mary of Nazareth), and more than most of the disciples. Consider

Matthias, who replaced Judas Iscariot among the twelve in Acts 1. Matthias is said to have been present with Jesus throughout his ministry but is never mentioned by name in the Gospels, though he was likely part of the seventy (or seventy-two) sent by Jesus. This is not a competition, of course, but by comparison, it tells us that Mary Magdalene's participation is notable not only for what she sees and hears but for what she does. The fact that only two hundred women are named in all of Scripture out of three thousand figures means that these odds could easily have gone the other way.[1] We are directed to know her by the simple fact of the inclusion of her name *and* by its repetition across the Gospels.

The Gospels invite us to remember her in three critical ways: as being healed from demons, as a financial supporter of Jesus's ministry, and as the first apostle called and sent by Jesus at the resurrection (not by title but by Christ's authority and her qualifications). Highlights include her support of Jesus's preaching and healing ministry (Matt. 27:55–56; Mark 15:40–41; Luke 8:1–3), her witness at the cross, and her return to the tomb, which she finds empty (Matt. 27:55–28:10; Mark 15:40–16:8; Luke 24:1–12; John 20:1–18).

Her prominence is further indicated by the fact that she is named first among the groups of women that the Gospels mention from Jesus's ministry, first among the women at the cross (except for John's account, where Jesus's mother takes first place), and first among those who visited Jesus's tomb. Every Gospel recounts Mary Magdalene's presence at the empty tomb, and in two of the Gospels she is either the first or one of the first witnesses to Jesus's resurrection.

For all the variation in these accounts, there is no question or disagreement about Mary Magdalene's inclusion at that pivotal turning point. Her presence and prominence at the tomb and as a witness to the resurrection is not contested by the church. In these crucial ways, Mary Magdalene is a towering presence in the Gospels.

Scripture also sets her apart by applying the moniker "Magdalene" to her name, which helpfully distinguishes her from among a sea of Marys. No doubt you've noticed and perhaps experienced the confusion that comes with trying to sort out the Marys. It's a common experience! Even *Saturday Night Live* has drawn attention to the humor of there being so many Marys.[2] You could probably guess that Mary was the most common name for Jewish women in first-century Palestine.[3] As a Jennifer growing up in the early 1980s, I can relate. Each year, we-the-many-Jennifers would scramble on the first day of school to claim the preferred version of our name. During the first half of my life, I was called Jenny, but more and more, I'm identified with my given name. Even now, at work or among other moms, there can be a sort of negotiation to claim the preferred distinction. Otherwise, greeting one another is like a scene out of Greta Gerwig's *Barbie* movie: "Hi, Jennifer!" "Hi, Jennifer!" "Hi, Jennifer!"

Thankfully, Scripture sorts this out for us by identifying this Mary with "Magdalene," and there are several layers as to what that could mean.[4] Magdalene is commonly thought to be a reference to her place of origin, the city of Magdala or Migdal.[5] This is notable because women were typically identified in association with the men of their lives rather than their place of origin. The fact that her identity is linked to a place may have meant that she had no husband, father, or son, or was even disinherited.[6] An added dynamic to her geographical association is that for many centuries, Magdala was believed to have been a humble, lowly village, which in turn caused Mary Magdalene to be considered humble and lowly. But scholarly consensus based on recent archaeological excavations has shifted and now points us to an understanding of Magdala as a large, bustling town on the west shore of Galilee.[7] This location stands just a few miles from Capernaum, Jesus's home base for ministry. Although the text does not reveal the story to us, Jesus's first encounter with Mary Magdalene could have taken place simply due to this proximity.[8]

Meanwhile, scholars recognize the meaning of Magdala in Aramaic as "the tower," which is presumed to be a reference to the tower connected to the city's port.[9] Acknowledging this layer of meaning has caused Mary Magdalene's name to be associated more readily with strength, rather than lowliness.[10] Some recent scholarship questions whether there is a geographical link in her epithet, instead favoring it as an honorific title.[11] By this thinking, she is herself a "tower" of faith, even if she didn't come from Magdala. Perhaps both dimensions—the geographic indicator and reference to her character—are being affirmed somehow. Is she "Mary of the place of the tower" in more ways than one?

Scripture can function in layered ways, with meaning grounded in the literal sense while also having additional spiritual implications.[12] What is literally true (she is from the place Magdala) can also hold figurative or metaphorical meaning—namely, that she is a person of strength.

Holding these two things together recognizes that the Bible is a historical text (reflecting the way that she was identified in the group) and that Gospel writers can, at the same time, highlight details that are meaningful in other ways. The honorific need not be something that we have imposed on her but something that is intended and included after the events have taken place. After all, puns or plays on words are noticeable in the Gospels. Peter's name as meaning "the rock" is evidence that Jesus enjoyed giving nicknames to certain disciples. As one scholar points out, "Magdalene may also have been a pun, indicating that Mary was from Magdala while simultaneously depicting her as a tower of strength."[13] Women were rarely given nicknames at that time, so this would point to Mary's immense significance in Jesus's group, seeing her through his eyes. Whether we can compare Mary's naming with Peter's is debated,[14] but the association of Mary with a "tower" has historic roots.[15]

Relating Mary's name to a tower of faith may seem like a paradigm shift for many in the church today, but this is not the first time that the church has identified her as such. Though latent in the record of church history, the church has already thought about Mary Magdalene's name in a multidimensional way beyond just geographically. Five hundred years ago, Martin Luther interpreted the significance of Mary Magdalene's name as a "good strong castle" or a "strong tower" as a reference to her faith.[16] And long before Luther, the early church father Jerome (who translated the Bible into Latin in the fourth century, which came to be known as the Vulgate) claimed the importance of this moniker, pointing out, "Mary of

Magdala, called 'of the tower' because of her earnestness and ardent faith."[17] The tower imagery is, by his interpretation, associated with her exemplary faith. As Jerome drew a connection to Mary Magdalene's name and the strength of her faith through the tower pun, Augustine of Hippo allegorized the strength of Mary Magdalene's faith by claiming she symbolized the church.[18] These brief examples illustrate how she was already more than her geography to the early church fathers. Yet even with that early understanding, her significance was often caught in a web of assumptions and cultural perceptions pertaining to women. In the same breath that Luther recognized her strength, he also described her as the "fool Mary Magdalene" who did not realize that Jesus was going to be resurrected. We also need fresh eyes to see her today.

We can step through this haze by acknowledging that something undeniably special is happening in the biblical text when it points us to Mary Magdalene—to her geography, to the Christian virtue that she exemplifies, and to the role she plays in the salvation story. But this requires us to think first about what Scripture is doing when it points us to women in the text at all.

Women Called by Name

Christianity stands out from other faith traditions and cultural contexts for how it remembers and dignifies women and, in many cases, includes their actual names. This practice is received from the Hebrew Scriptures and Jewish faith: the very first chapter of Genesis affirms that humanity is made in the image of God, both men and women, and blessed by God (Gen. 1:27). Twice in Genesis, Eve is described as *ezer* (Gen. 2:18, 20), a term used sixteen times in the Old Testament to describe God to mean "strong helper" or "warrior."[19] Scripture does not shy away from attributing strength to women and rooting their place alongside men in the good creation. Mary Magdalene fits right into this trajectory of Scripture.

Beginning with the Old Testament and throughout the New Testament, Scripture points us beyond remarkable women, such as the Queen of Sheba, to examples of everyday women such as the servant Rhoda (Acts 12:12–15). We can see this happening in the New Testament with Jesus's genealogy in Matthew. I'm guessing it's not your usual devotional reading, but how Jesus's lineage is recounted matters. The inclusion of four named women—Rahab, Ruth, Bathsheba (or "Uriah's wife"), and Mary the mother of Jesus (Matt. 1:5–6, 16)—would have been a surprise at the time, a break with custom. By this, Scripture is signaling that something different is happening with Jesus and because of Jesus. Women—even Gentile women at that—are being honored by name along the way that leads to Christ.[20] Biblical scholar Jeannine Brown points out that Matthew's Gospel draws our attention to women as "positive" contributors shaping the church by their "examples of persistence, faith, and faithfulness."[21] Moreover, the diversity of the women themselves captures a vision of God's coming kingdom "rich with ethnic distinctiveness" so that "in Matthew's narrative world, the richness of the reign of God includes people of Canaanite, Moabite, Roman, and, of course, Jewish descent."[22] To read past their names would be to read over the message.

Naming women in Scripture matters immensely for how we understand the kingdom of God that is being forged through the person and work of Jesus Christ.[23]

Nineteenth-century Korean church history beautifully illustrates how Christianity can offer dignity to women in ways that upend cultural norms.[24] Women became indispensable in the evangelism of Korea since male missionaries were prevented from speaking directly with Korean women or accessing the *anbang*, a private room for women in a Korean home. This dilemma opened up an unexpected opportunity for missionary wives, who became instrumental in women's ministries, and for Korean female evangelists called "Bible women."[25] Consider the conversion of Kim Gang.

At fifty years old, Kim Gang received the preaching of Jesus Christ as freedom from the bondage of Confucian patriarchy. With her baptism in 1899, which she describes as the "happiest day of my life," she received the biblical name of Dorcas (named after the woman in Acts 9:36–43 who is raised back to life after Peter's prayer and who is described in the text as a "disciple").[26] Before that moment, she had never been called by her name; she had been known by her father's, her husband's, and then her son's names. She recounts the joy that she experienced when in Christ she was noticed and dignified with her own name.

Dorcas was given a preaching circuit of 1,450 miles of mountainous territory. As she walked it, she was verbally attacked, refused food by local people, and once imprisoned. Today, she is regarded as one of the great evangelists of Korea, and we know her name.[27]

Jesus, in fact, calls women by their names.[28]

"Mary!" Jesus said to Mary Magdalene, and with that name, with those words, and by that voice she knew so well, Mary recognized the risen Lord in the garden (John 20:16). Though it might not readily seem like it, there is a good word here for us that Jesus called her by name and that John included that exchange in his Gospel.

As Hagar experienced and knew to be true, our God is the God who sees even the most humble and destitute of women (Gen. 16:13). God speaks to women.

The Hermeneutic of Surprise

In seeking to recover the forgotten Mary from the biblical text, we should consider that not every moment with Jesus is recorded in Scripture. John explains that Jesus did other signs in the presence of the disciples, who witnessed these things, that were not included in the Gospel (20:30). At the end of his Gospel, John writes, "There are also many other things that Jesus did; if every one of them were written down, I suppose that the world itself could not contain the books that would be written" (21:25). Scripture tells us that we don't have the full story of Jesus's every interaction. What we do have has been cultivated, but not in the way that you would expect.

We live in an age of social media where appearances can be deceiving. With the right angle and filter, we can all too easily cast out the real from real life. But the Bible avoids the Instagram temptation of self-hagiography. Time and again the ignorance of the disciples and their many blunders are prominently shown. Scripture avoids putting on a front, as though everyone were abiding by every cultural nicety, law, and expectation. On the contrary, the Gospels feature some of the most unlikely people.

Some interpreters employ a "hermeneutic of suspicion" toward the biblical text, rooted in the expectation that self-interest shapes the biblical text and its interpreter.[29] There is a tendency to read the text with skepticism, expecting distortion or alteration. There can be an assumption that the biblical writers are bound to their cultural context and expectations alone. There may be little room for revelation in these cases, not to mention surprise. Rather than mere suspicion, I invite us to read the women in the text through a "hermeneutic of surprise." Scripture, in fact, can point us to God's truth and goodness through unexpected avenues that lean contrary to first-century polite society and authorial self-interest. The dissonance between the text and its context can clue us in to the greater purpose at work.

A coherent thread of surprise runs throughout Scripture from Genesis to Revelation. God uses unexpected people in their time to do remarkable things that bring glory to God. Discerning surprise in the text can help us make sense of those who followed Jesus during his earthly ministry, particularly women and pointedly Mary Magdalene.

Consider the nature of Scripture itself. On the one hand, the Bible reflects its times. The human biblical authors wrote from their own background, experience, and context, which modern readers can find difficult to understand apart from helpful resources that reveal history, culture, and the original language.[30] In Christian theology, we recognize the necessity and goodness of our inadequacy. We are creatures, and thus we are contingent on God's gracious, accommodating revelation to us. Part of God's goodness to us is manifest in the fact that God knows us and wants to be known by us. We therefore require revelation from God to know God, since this truth does not come from within us but outside us.

And yet the biblical writers were not robots or ChatGPT programs. Christian doctrine across the traditions denies that Scripture came about by dictation. The inspiration of Scripture does not erase the context of it even as God seeks to transform the human context (2 Tim. 3:16).

Reflect for a moment on our situatedness as humans. For example, climbing a mountain is challenging even with proper equipment, training, and wherewithal, not merely because of the terrain but also because of the air and altitude. The 1997 bestselling book by Jon Krakauer, *Into Thin Air*, is a lesson in the human body's demand for oxygen to the point that an oxygen mask becomes essential when climbing Mount Everest. More recently, the documentary *Free Solo* tracks the unbelievable story of climber Alex Honnold scaling Yosemite's El Capitan without a rope (it's really something to see!). For most people, this would be an experience so far outside of their usual situatedness that a built-in safety mechanism in their brain would not allow this kind of risk-taking.

These challenges are navigated not only at the height of mountaintops but in the depths of the sea. I recently went snorkeling (I know, not scuba diving), and it was a lot. I dove down to get closer to the schools of fish and the corral, but the pressure on my mask and my ears at just a few feet was more than I could ignore. I ended up getting seasick from all the rocking on the surface. It reminded me just how delicately positioned we are on this earth. To move our bodies across several time zones can be physically unsettling. We thrive when we live into our circadian rhythm, our natural body cycle. Take us out of the squeeze of gravity and our bodies languish. I'm reminded of a 2019 study by NASA where one identical twin stayed on earth and the other lived for a year in space. There were significant effects on the twin who lived in space.[31] The (unseen) protective layers of the earth may be more expansive than we realize, perhaps extending more than 391,000 miles beyond the planet's surface (or twice as far as our moon).[32] If true, that would mean humans have never actually left the earth's atmosphere. Earth is truly a precious and protective home.

In these ways and more, humans are contextual creatures, and not just in our bodies and limitations. Scripture, too, comes to us as a narrative within the context of space, time, and place as we know it. When Scripture surprises us with the unexpected, when it acts contrary to its context or upends its own social norms—when it lives outside its own situatedness—we need to take extra notice. I am speaking here not about the surprise we might experience in trying to understand Scripture through our modern eyes but about the surprise that's already embedded in the text within its own time. That can be a clue.

Sometimes something can be so out of place that it draws our attention. By this principle, every time Scripture names a woman or includes a woman as an exemplar, we should pay attention. Scripture surprises us by going against the grain of its context. We can see this happening when women are named but not for their association with men, as with Mary Magdalene.[33] Though some churches and leaders may speak more about the Jezebels than the Deborahs, the scales don't often tip that way in the biblical text.[34] In the Gospels, women are frequently mentioned as faithful examples of an obedient life, not cautionary tales.

Mark 12:41–44 is one example. Here, Jesus criticizes the rich who give to God out of their "large sums" of money while wearing their grand robes and holding the best seats at the synagogue and the place of honor at banquets. They enjoy being greeted and praying long prayers for the sake of being seen. Instead, Jesus redirects the disciples' attention to an unremarkable woman. Not only is she a woman but a poor woman, and a poor, widowed woman at that. She puts two small copper coins in the treasury, worth nothing more than a penny. Jesus watches her, and he calls his disciples around to observe and teach them. Her faithfulness is a hidden devotion that Jesus calls attention to as an opportunity not to shame her but to elevate her. She is a worthy example in Christ's eyes: "Truly I tell you, this poor widow has put in more than all those who are contributing to the treasury. For all of them have contributed out of their abundance, but she out of her poverty has put in everything she had, all she had to live on" (vv. 43–44).

Did you see what he did there?

Imagine Jesus beckoning the twelve around him, then saying "Look!" with admiration and love in his eyes. Surprisingly, they are invited to learn from her example. He is preparing them, perhaps planting the seeds to ready them to listen to Mary Magdalene to whom he will later command, "Go and tell." When we encounter this story, we too are beckoned to notice that poor widow, not for pity's sake and not in a judgmental way, but as a source of admiration. We are being prepared to listen to Mary Magdalene.

There is a pattern of surprise throughout Scripture that involves both men and women, including Mary Magdalene, who defied the expectations of their time as God worked through them (and sometimes despite them) toward the fulfillment of his purposes. Once you see this pattern in Scripture, you cannot unsee it, and it doesn't just apply to Jesus's female followers.

Marvel at the Ordinary

In a first-century context, it would have been expected for Jesus's innermost circle of disciples to be men. Yet even here, there is surprise. In this case, the surprise stems from the fact that they aren't the kind of men one would choose for the work that Jesus had in mind. Fishermen as orators in the Greco-Roman world? Nice try. And yet, that is exactly what Jesus orchestrated.

Acts 1 recounts the followers of Jesus waiting prayerfully for the Holy Spirit, just as Jesus had instructed before his ascension. The faithful group includes Peter and other male disciples as well as Jesus's mother Mary and his brothers and "certain women" (1:14). When the Holy Spirit arrives as tongues of fire and the disciples begin to speak in other languages, Peter declares the fulfillment of Joel's prophecy (Joel 2:28–29). The crowds are amazed not merely at what is being said but *who* is saying it: "Are not all these who are speaking Galileans?" (Acts 2:7). The inauguration of Christ's spiritual kingdom on earth invites a priesthood of all believers, and Peter in a particular way represents the new dawning. He and John are described as boldly preaching Jesus Christ by the power of the Holy Spirit as more and more come to believe.[35] Their arrest in Jerusalem quickly follows as the priests and Sadducees take issue with the content of their teaching. Yale theologian Willie James Jennings writes, "The table is being turned over, an upside down world is being turned right side up in these words of Peter."[36] By teaching the people, they are an affront to those in power.

Peter is no Levite. By the understanding of the Jewish authorities, he is off base, presumptuous, and out of his league. And so it is striking when Peter, a fisherman, is brought before Annas, the high priest, and leaders from the high-priestly family. Standing before the descendants of Aaron, the keepers of the priesthood, Peter and John are described as "uneducated and ordinary" (Acts 4:13). But this perception also leads their audience to be "amazed." How are these lowly men able to do what they have done? The authorities can't explain it, and Peter and John are warned to stop teaching about Jesus. Later, Peter and John are brought back before the council for their ongoing ministry. A turning point comes when Gamaliel the Pharisee declares to the council, "Keep away from these men and *let them alone*, because if this plan or this undertaking is of human origin, it will fail; but if it is of God, you will not be able to overthrow them—in that case you may even be found fighting against God!" (Acts 5:38–39).[37]

To see Mary Magdalene in the fullness of the story, we must become attuned to the ways that Scripture points us to the surprising faith of the ordinary, to see their proc-

26

lamation of Jesus bear fruit according to God's calling. God is at work through the unexpected and invites us to see and receive the unexpected. *Let them alone* so we can marvel at what God is doing.

Mary Magdalene's journey of discipleship sometimes parallels, sometimes contrasts with, and sometimes intersects with Peter's. Peter dropped his nets at Christ's invitation to follow him, while Mary was freed from the bondage of demon possession to follow him. Both were zealous in their affection for Christ. Mary wept for Jesus from the cross to the tomb, then ran to tell the disciples the good news. Peter ran to the empty tomb, and then he jumped out of the boat (fully clothed!) to greet the risen Christ on the beach. Both became part of Jesus's inner circles (especially clear in the Gospel of Luke) and were key witnesses to Jesus's ministry. Both were commissioned by Christ to proclaim his resurrection. Mary's faithfulness in particular kick-started the work that all Christians are to accomplish from Pentecost on, including Peter and those in our own day. Together, Mary and Peter reflect how God calls, equips, and sends ordinary people, both women and men, for his extraordinary mission to the world. *Let them alone.*

But there are also important differences between how Scripture portrays Peter and how it depicts Mary Magdalene. Scripture readily details the faults and failures of Peter, who denied Jesus three times and wept at his own betrayal of Jesus (Matt. 26:33–35, 69–75; Mark 14:29–31, 66–72; Luke 22:31–34, 54–62; John 13:36–38; 18:25–27; 21:15–19). His many blunders—from initially refusing when Jesus offers to wash his feet to awkwardly speaking out of turn at Christ's transfiguration to drawing a sword at Jesus's arrest to cut off the ear of a soldier—give us a realistic, raw, and honest look at an unlikely leader of Christ's disciples. These hard realities also draw our attention to God's glory and mercy and power despite our weakness.

In surprising contrast, the Gospels speak only of Mary Magdalene's faithfulness.[38] She comes into focus in the text both healed and present. We know little about her past except that she is a new woman no longer bound to demons. She is devout and undeterred. Scripture forms our remembrance of her around her care for Christ and contributions to his ministry. She bears witness to the resurrection, the culminating point of Christ's earthly ministry. And this too is intentional.

According to Greek culture, the mistakes of one woman could implicate her entire gender.[39] Where Scripture is loose with Peter, it treads carefully with Mary Magdalene for good reason. Biblical scholar Craig Keener helpfully explains, "Women play significant roles in the Gospel, sometimes shaming the male disciples by the women's positive contrast with them."[40] While Peter deserts Jesus at the eleventh hour, Mary Magdalene does not, and God blesses her faithfulness in a marvelous way.

The word "marvel" holds a lot of cultural cachet these days, such that the term has been recast completely. Today, it is next to impossible not to associate the word with Stan Lee's Marvel Cinematic Universe (MCU) and that universe within American culture. The remarkable novel *Everything Sad Is Untrue* traces the journey of author and refugee Daniel Nayeri from Iran to America following his mother's conversion to Christianity. The impact of the MCU on the cultural narratives of America is not lost on young Daniel, who is trying to find his way in Edmond, Oklahoma. For Daniel, while J. R. R. Tolkien is the epitome of British literature and Alexandre Dumas the greatest French author, Lee's work is what helps Daniel gain insight into his new country, and he identifies with Wolverine, an immigrant (from Canada) who can heal from anything.[41]

In the MCU, enhanced humans with special powers and advanced machines face botched scientific experiments and diabolical villains and engage in the endless struggle between good and evil. Acts of self-sacrifice tend to lead to the unintentional destruction of lives and cities, and collateral damage is treated as an inevitable, unavoidable consequence of wielding power. Like the Greco-Roman gods before them, these superheroes are more human than god. Though there is imperfect self-sacrifice—as the character of Iron Man reveals—as the layers of power peel back through the stories, we see how the strongest powers too often succumb to the temptations that come with possessing total control or clamoring for it. The all-good, all-powerful, and perfect triune God of Scripture who self-sacrifices and conquers death for the redemption of humanity would be unrecognizable in the MCU, where Kang the Conqueror holds court behind the curtain. What would it mean to reclaim the word "marvel"? What if we adopted Scripture's lens to direct us toward the marvelous?[42]

The New Testament uses the Greek word for "marvel," "astonish," or "amaze" (*thaumazō*) most often to describe people's responses to Jesus's teachings and miracles. He, too, this carpenter from Nazareth, is not what is expected!

As Nathanael asks Philip, "Can anything good come out of Nazareth?" (John 1:46). Witnesses are amazed as Jesus calms storms (Matt. 8:27; Luke 8:25), exorcises demons (Matt. 9:33; Mark 1:27; Luke 4:36; 11:14), and heals the sick (Matt. 15:31; Mark 2:12; 5:42; Luke 5:26). Amazement is reported at the events of his birth (Luke 2:18, 33), at his responses to difficult questions (Matt. 22:22; Mark 12:17; Luke 20:26), and when he foretells his death and resurrection to the disciples (Mark 10:32). Later, at his trial, Pontius Pilate marvels at Jesus's silence in the face of accusation and capital punishment (Mark 15:15). In Luke's words, which summarize people's reactions to Jesus, "everyone was amazed at all that he was doing" (Luke 9:43).[43]

In only two cases do the Gospel writers describe Jesus as the one who stands amazed. Both concern the faith (or lack of faith) that others have in him. In Mark 6:6, Jesus is amazed at the extent of the unbelief in his hometown. Their rejection of him comes in part from their familiarity with his family and the fact of his profession: "Is not this the carpenter?" (6:3). Jesus the carpenter from their hometown is not what they expected.

In the second case, Jesus marvels at the strength of one individual's faith: a Roman centurion. The inclusion of this story is itself amazing, considering that there was no love lost between Rome and Israel at that time. Nevertheless, Matthew recounts, "when Jesus heard him, he was amazed and said to those who followed him, 'Truly I tell you, in no one in Israel have I found such faith'" (Matt. 8:10 // Luke 7:9). Matthew was writing his Gospel after the destruction of the temple in Jerusalem (70 CE), so

30

the immediate readership would have known people who died at the hands of the Romans or would have witnessed members of their community being enslaved.[44] The fact that Roman soldiers participated in the pagan religious oaths required by the "divine" emperor further amplifies how significant it is for Jesus to stand amazed at the faith of a Gentile (and no one else!). It is an unexpected precursor of what is to come—namely, that the good news of Jesus Christ is for everyone: Jew and Gentile, rich and poor, slave and free, men and women.

Amazement is also reserved for the events of Jesus's resurrection. The women are amazed at the words of the angel in the empty tomb (Mark 16:8), and Peter stands amazed at the empty tomb (Luke 24:12). The testimony of the women, including Mary Magdalene, is also the source of amazement according to Jesus's followers on the walk to Emmaus: "Some women of our group astounded us. They were at the tomb early this morning, and when they did not find his body there they came back and told us that they had indeed seen a vision of angels who said that he was alive" (Luke 24:22–23). In these ways, Scripture invites us to marvel at Jesus, to marvel at the faith that he inspires, and to marvel at the testimony of the women pointing us right back to Jesus Christ.

Like the disciples on the walk to Emmaus, Mary Magdalene's story inspires all of us to stand amazed and to marvel at God's unexpected work. Ultimately, we turn our eyes to Mary Magdalene because Scripture directs us to her name and to her role in Jesus's ministry. But the goal is not just to look at her. Rather, we are directed to see *with* her, to see the one she sees, to look at the risen

Lord, and to run to share the news. Her proclamation is
Christ (2 Cor. 4:5), and he is marvelous.

The Sycamore[45]

Like many of us, my adult life has been consistently
marked by the terrorist attacks of our era. I was out of
college and in my second year at Princeton Theological
Seminary when the Twin Towers were attacked on 9/11 just
an hour train ride away. Later, as a doctoral student living
and working in Cambridge, I experienced the heartache
from the environs of London during the July 7 bombings
in 2005. Ten years later, I was in Paris on a research trip
when the 2015 terrorist attack took hold of the city, and a
close friend of mine lost their best friend in the attack. I
never imagined adulthood would be this way.

The year 2021 was the twentieth anniversary of the
9/11 attacks. To mark the anniversary, Wheaton College
alumna Lisa Beamer spoke in chapel.[46] She is the widow
of alumnus Todd Beamer, who had bravely rallied resis-
tance to terrorists on United Flight 93. Her message has
continued to be one of resilience. The Christian faith, she
maintained, offers "ordinary people, extraordinary courage" even in times of terror because it is a faith rooted in
the God who willingly suffered and died on our behalf
and who defeated death to give us bodily life with God
forever.[47] Even though towers may collapse, the tower of
faith need not.

Perhaps you have heard of the remarkable story involving St. Paul's Chapel in New York City on that day. Across
the street from the Twin Towers stood a sycamore tree.

Sycamore trees are among the oldest and largest trees on earth. Some can reach to 100 feet tall and 10 feet wide. As the debris from the towers fell, that sycamore tree shielded the chapel so that not even a single window was broken.[48] Because the chapel was protected, it served for months as a place of refuge for rescue workers who found shelter, rest, food, medical care, and prayer. To many, the sycamore has become a symbol of God's unexpected provision through the ordinary, an unlikely show of strength in the face of devastation. Who could have imagined that a sycamore tree would have such a significant impact?

The surprise of the gospel is not in *what* God has promised to us—namely, abundant life with him forever. That promise has been with us since creation. In the providence of God, it cannot be lost or shaken, even by the sin of Adam and Eve. It is the faithful promise of a good God who does not change, who loves justly and rightly, and who offers mercy and friendship to those who believe in his Son. We count that promise as revealed, not hidden, and we have carried it with us since God's revelation to us began.

But what is often a surprise is *how* God brings about the work that he has promised. In Ephesians 3, Paul grapples with the complexity of the hidden and the revealed as he unpacks the "mystery of Christ," saying, "In former generations this mystery was not made known to humankind, as it has now been revealed to his holy apostles and prophets by the Spirit: that is, the Gentiles have become fellow heirs, members of the same body, and sharers in the promise in Christ Jesus through the gospel" (3:5–6). Simply put, God does not always call upon the people that we expect in the ways we expect.

We don't expect God to speak through a burning bush to Moses, who was "amazed" at the sight (Acts 7:31). We don't expect God to instruct Noah to build an ark. We don't expect a young shepherd boy to defeat a giant on behalf of a king. We don't expect a young virgin to bear and birth the incarnate God, Jesus Christ. We don't expect a ministry to launch at a wedding by turning water into wine. We don't expect a Jew to transform the life of a Samaritan woman in order to proclaim good news to a people otherwise scorned. We don't expect a Pharisee who zealously and violently persecutes those who follow Jesus to dedicate his life to converting Gentiles to the very cause that he deemed heretical. We don't expect death on a cross, a criminal's death for an innocent man. We don't expect bodily resurrection. We certainly don't expect Jesus to reveal himself first to a formerly demon-possessed woman and then tell her to proclaim to his male followers the most important message that has ever been delivered. There is no universe in which we expect Mary Magdalene. But that's actually the point, right?

Mary Magdalene is not an oddity in this story. She is no anomaly. She is no more unexpected than Abraham, Moses, Peter, and all the others called by God. Once we see her surprising thread in the tapestry of God's handiwork, we see that this is exactly as it should be. She is an unexpected part of *how* God did what he had promised to do. She is a strong tower that deserves our remembrance. But do we remember her *rightly*?

TWO

Will the Real Mary Magdalene Please Stand Up?

A Royal Chrism

In 2023, Charles Windsor was crowned King Charles III of England. People around the globe were able to watch every moment of the ceremony—except for one.[1] Behind the screen at Westminster Abbey, the archbishop of Canterbury anointed Charles's hands, chest, and head with consecrated oil, known as chrism, using a golden spoon. Anointing a monarch with chrism is a Judeo-Christian practice and an English tradition going back to the eleventh century. Charles chose the fragrant spices added to the oil in a rare opportunity to contribute his own take on a historic and religious moment. The chrism was prepared by Greek Orthodox monks and blessed at the Church of the Holy Sepulchre by the Orthodox patriarch of Jerusalem and the Anglican archbishop. The olives used to make the oil, meanwhile, were harvested from the Eastern Orthodox Monastery of the Ascension and the Monastery of Mary Magdalene located on the Mount of Olives in Jerusalem, near the garden of Gethsemane.

The Christian tradition has consistently remembered Mary Magdalene as anointing Jesus. An anointment is a weighty act that often carries a twofold purpose: (1) preparation for burial and (2) the coronation of kings. A sacred anointing is a priestly act, as it was with King Charles's coronation. Within the Bible, anointing was performed by a priest, as when Samuel anointed David as king of Israel (1 Sam. 16:13), though it would take some time for him to assume the throne (2 Sam. 2:4). For Christians, both purposes find their fulfillment in Jesus Christ. In fact, the term Messiah and its Greek equivalent, Christ, mean "anointed one" or "chosen one." To think of Mary Magdalene as a priest may be a far cry from current sensibilities, but her anointing ministry is part of the tapestry of her remembrance, giving her a priestly role. In fact, Klagenfurt Cathedral holds one of the earliest depictions of Mary Magdalene and the oldest stained-glass window in Austria (Magdalenenscheibe), dating back to 1170. She is depicted wearing priestly vestments and holding the censer or incense burner.[2]

But did she actually anoint Jesus? The question gets at the heart of the issue of correctly identifying and remembering Mary Magdalene.

In remembering Mary Magdalene today, we must not only recognize her place in the biblical narrative but also untangle the convoluted history of interpretation, which has often conflated Mary Magdalene with other women, especially the other Marys. Intentionally or not, interpreters in the Western church have often confused Mary of Bethany's anointing with the sinner woman of Luke 7 and then both with Mary Magdalene. In the Eastern church, her place in the story has sometimes been replaced with Martha.[3] At one level, the confusion is understandable. There are so many Marys and there are several similar anointing stories. And also how does Mary Magdalene relate to Mary and Martha of Bethany? But reading Scripture faithfully means dealing with all its complexities. Examining who did and did not anoint Jesus can help bring clarity to this issue.

So, did Mary Magdalene anoint Jesus?

No and yes.

Anointing Jesus, Conflating Mary

In the Western church, Mary Magdalene came to be formally associated with the anointing stories of Jesus by influence of Pope Gregory the Great in the late sixth century (ca. 540–604). But there is more to the story. Gregory codified threads of other Bible stories that were slowly becoming associated with Mary Magdalene through the interpretive tradition before him. He formalized the belief that Mary of Bethany and Mary Magdalene were the same person, who was also the same person as the "sinner" woman of Luke 7. The muddle of the anointing stories led to what has been described as a muddle of the Marys.[4]

If, as Gregory suggested, Mary of Bethany and Mary Magdalene were the same person, that linked Mary Magdalene's life to a whole other sequence of accounts and associations in Jesus's ministry. It would make her the one who sat at Jesus's feet and learned from him while her sister Martha was distracted by household tasks (Luke 10:38–42). Mary Magdalene would have been the sister of Lazarus, whose death she lamented before Jesus raised him from the dead (John 11:1–45). Most importantly, John records Mary of Bethany as the one who anointed Jesus's feet with perfume and wiped them with her hair (John 11:2; 12:1–8). It would give Mary Magdalene that anointing story and open the door to *all* the anointing stories, particularly the unnamed "sinner" woman of Luke 7.

How did it get to that point? A brief look at the early Christian fathers illustrates the complex threads that were woven together to create this pattern.[5]

Irenaeus to Tertullian

Centuries before Gregory arrived on the scene, the early Christian fathers had already begun to determine the place of Mary Magdalene in Christian theology and exegetical history. The Greek bishop Irenaeus references "Mary" in his treatise *Against Heresies* (ca. 180), describing her as "the first to see and to worship Him" according to John 20:17.[6] He gives attention to her in order to respond to the Gnostic denial of Jesus's bodily resurrection, pointing to Mary Magdalene's encounter. His recognition of her as the first witness and first worshiper of Jesus Christ served as a foundation of both Western and Eastern Christian interpretation relating to Mary Magdalene, though differences arose. In this early period, the passages that related to her were often shaped by the conversation of Christian apologetics.

Tertullian, an apologist theologian from second- and third-century Carthage in North Africa, is often considered the first to conflate Mary Magdalene. He discusses the anointing woman of Luke 7 in response to the Gnostic Marcion. There he stresses how the woman of Luke 7 touches the actual body of Jesus rather than a "phantom body."[7] To Tertullian, she models the true expression of repentance, but he does not equate her with Mary Magdalene.[8] Instead, Tertullian groups the "sinner" woman of Luke 7 and the Samaritan woman (whom Tertullian labels as a "prostitute") as examples of how Jesus favored sinners.[9] Any allusion to Mary Magdalene is absent. Meanwhile, a hint of conflation *might* be present between the sinner woman of Luke 7 and Mary of Bethany's anointing story in John 12. Tertullian interprets the act in Luke 7 as preparation for Jesus's burial, which is the reason given for Mary of Bethany's anointing story and not for that of Luke 7. The fact that all the anointing stories (Matthew, Mark, and John), apart from the Luke 7 passage, interpret the anointing as preparation for burial leaves room for uncertainty. By attaching that reason to the Luke 7 anointing, a conflation between all the anointing stories—including Mary of Bethany's—emerges.[10] By the fifth century, reading Mary of Bethany as the woman of Luke 7 would become more explicit. And so, these initial complexities involve keeping the multiple anointings straight rather than keeping the multiple Marys straight.

Does Tertullian mix up Martha and Mary Magdalene? Though it has been claimed that he attributed the John 12 confession, typically associated with Martha, to Mary Magdalene, evidence points to the contrary in his *Against Praxeas*, where he directly mentions "when Martha in a later passage acknowledged Him to be the Son of God."[11] It is also frequently repeated that Tertullian associated Mary Magdalene with the woman caught in adultery (John 7:53–8:11), but, in fact, he never engages with that story at all because it was likely unknown in Carthage at the time.[12] Although he does open the door for conflating the Luke 7 anointing with *all* the anointing stories, including Mary of Bethany's, in the limited cases we have, Tertullian seems to maintain Mary Magdalene as her own person and evaluates her example positively, much in the spirit of Irenaeus.

In Tertullian's reading of John 20, he includes the full name "Mary Magdalene" and compliments her as "so faithful a woman."[13] Her faithfulness is evident in her desire to touch Jesus "out of love," which he contrasts with Thomas, who touches out of doubt in the same chapter.[14] Tertullian, importantly, does not read blame into Jesus's avoidance of Mary Magdalene's touch, which would become a later interpretation revolving around Mary's unworthiness as a sinner.[15] Instead, the exchange between Mary Magdalene and Jesus served Tertullian's purposes of setting the record straight over the Trinity (namely, that Jesus is distinct from the Father).

But Tertullian does not always consider Mary Magdalene individually. At other points, he reads her story through the larger group of women who ministered to

Jesus. No doubt the anti-Christian philosopher Celsus informed this tendency. Celsus claimed that Jesus appeared secretly to one woman, and in response, early Christian theologian Origen (a contemporary of Tertullian) stressed that Mary Magdalene was certainly not the *only* witness to Christ's resurrection, citing Matthew's Gospel and "the other Mary" in support.[16] There was a concerted effort at the time to counter accusations of secrecy and to highlight the broad base of witnesses to Christ's resurrection.

When Tertullian references the women of Luke 8 (where Mary Magdalene is introduced by name) who provide for Jesus financially, he does not single out Mary Magdalene. She is embedded in the larger group of women who fulfill a prophecy from Isaiah, and he describes them first as "disciples" and then as "assistants and helpers."[17] Mary Magdalene is neither ignored nor undervalued nor defamed. She is treated as a disciple among the group of women or as her own person, depending on the text.

Overall, from these early Christian fathers there are hints of conflation that involve mixing up the anointing stories, which is understandable given their complexity. Attention to Mary Magdalene's texts served as an opportunity to respond to early Christian heresy and accusation, to emphasize the resurrection, and to clarify theology pertaining to Christ and the Trinity rather than to focus on her specifically. Though Mary Magdalene is ancillary to Tertullian's main focus on Jesus, she is nonetheless regarded as a faithful disciple and first witness and worshiper. Given that Tertullian is prominently remembered for calling Eve, and therefore all women by his understanding, the "devil's gateway," his appreciation for Mary Magdalene is perhaps understandably overlooked.[18] The challenge arose for Mary Magdalene when she became too closely tied to Eve.[19]

Ambrose to Chrysostom

A change becomes evident when fourth-century theologians such as Ambrose, the bishop of Milan, began treating Mary Magdalene as a new Eve (though Hippolytus of Rome had previously developed that interpretation in the East).[20] The early Christians—and indeed still today!—were trying to understand why Jesus appeared to women first and gave them the good news first. How could this be? For Ambrose, Mary Magdalene's disposition provided an answer. Because she worshiped Christ when she encountered him in the garden (Matt. 28), she was rewarded, in Ambrose's words, as "the messenger of the Resurrection to the apostles."[21] Ambrose treated Mary Magdalene's act of faithful worship as bringing absolution to Eve's sinfulness in the garden, saying, "And rightly is a woman appointed [as messenger] to men; that she who first had brought the message of sin to man should first bring the message of the grace of the Lord."[22] The idea of a new Eve was not new but was initially applied to the Virgin Mary rather than to Mary Magdalene (the Virgin Eve was linked to the Virgin Mary).[23] Ambrose attributed Mary Magdalene's sinfulness to her being a daughter of Eve (a woman)—in that regard, she served as a lesson in the abounding grace of Christ.[24] The idea of Mary Magdalene as a new Eve proved to be a shared emphasis between Western Christianity and Eastern Christianity, as expressed by Gregory of Nyssa along with Ambrose in the fourth century followed by Cyril of Alexandria in the fifth century.[25]

Ambrose also looked critically on Mary Magdalene in his *Exposition of the Faith*, where she serves as a cautionary tale for those who search for Christ among earthly things. Jesus's command to Mary Magdalene to not touch him (John 20) was treated by Ambrose as a metaphor for those who are barred from entrance to the kingdom by the true gate of Christ.[26] Ambrose even draws a parallel between "Mary of Magdala" and the Arian heretics of his day (those who denied Christ's full divinity): just as Christ sent Mary to the apostles, so too the Arians must return to the right teaching of the apostles in order to enter the true door to salvation (a kind of apostolic tradition).[27] Ambrose meanwhile uses this scenario to elevate Peter as the "everlasting door" to the true church, an allusion to Peter's exchange with Jesus in Matthew 16 and an immensely important reference used by Western Christianity to formalize its church structure around Petrine succession in Rome.[28] Although Ambrose avoids conflating Mary Magdalene with Mary of Bethany and with the woman of Luke 7, associating her with Eve and general sinfulness opens the door for identifying her with particular sexual sinfulness in the generations to come.[29]

Similarly, John Chrysostom, the fifth-century archbishop of Constantinople, does not associate the sinner woman of Luke 7 (indicated by his labeling of her as a "harlot") with Mary Magdalene. Instead of drawing a parallel between Mary Magdalene's tears at the tomb with the tears of the anointing woman, a later interpretive connection, Chrysostom chooses to reflect on Hannah's tears before God in 1 Samuel 1:7, 10.[30] In fact, Chrysostom admires the tears of the "harlot" as the evidence of her sincere and admirable repentance. Rather than read with blame, her actions should be celebrated, he explains. For just as she weeps, so too does Christ.[31] Chrysostom importantly does not associate the other three anointing stories of the anonymous women with Mary of Bethany,[32] which counts him among a number of early Christian theologians who distinguished the women from each other and consequently distanced Mary of Bethany from prostitution.[33] Nevertheless, some issues do creep in.

When Chrysostom considers Mary Magdalene among the group of women at the cross and then at the tomb in Homily 88, he makes much of a reversal that God enacts through them. Because they do not desert him, they are blessed, and this is a blessing to their sex in general. He writes, "They had followed Him ministering to Him, and were present even unto the time of the dangers. . . . The sex that was most condemned, this first enjoys the sight of the blessings, this most shows its courage. And when the disciples had fled, these were present."[34] The compliments are profuse; they are admired for their courage, affection, generosity with money, and nobility. These exemplary women are presented as examples even for men to imitate: "Let us men imitate the women; let us not forsake Jesus in temptations."[35]

Chrysostom honors Mary Magdalene for her "loving affection" and "zeal" rewarded by God with seeing first what the disciples did not see.[36] And yet this quality is also tied in his estimation in an essentialist way to being a woman: "Full of feeling somehow is the female sex, and more inclined to pity."[37] As Amanda Kunder summarizes, "Her zeal, however, comes from the nature of the female sex, which is predisposed to feeling more and to pity."[38]

The pieces were slowly settling into place for a gendered reading of affection and a general association of women with sinfulness through Eve contributing to the next tide of theologians, who conflate the anointing stories of both affection and sinfulness more explicitly to the Mary who encounters Christ at the tomb.

Augustine to Jerome

Ambrose baptized Augustine, the fourth- and fifth-century theologian who became the bishop of Hippo in North Africa. Augustine is the one who identifies Mary of Bethany, who anoints Jesus in John 12, as the unnamed sinful woman who anoints Jesus in Luke 7.[39] This conflation of anointings opened the door for the next conflation of Marys.

It's worth recognizing that Augustine's interpretation of the Gospels is informed by his goal of harmonizing them. Consequently, differences between the Gospel stories can, to him, be resolved with the explanation that the same Mary anointed Jesus on two different occasions (the first represented by Luke and the second by Matthew, Mark, and John). Since Mary of Bethany is the only named woman among the anointing accounts in the Gospels, Augustine came to describe Mary of Bethany as a former "notorious sinner" transformed by Christ's forgiveness born out of her deep love for him.[40] We might forgive him for perhaps reading his own life story, detailed in the *Confessions*, through hers in this way. There is surely no condemnation in Augustine's characterization but rather a recognition of his own

45

experience of God's saving grace. Nevertheless, the explicit conflation of the anointing stories around Mary of Bethany becomes a significant step toward conflating the Marys.

Jerome, Augustine's contemporary and translator of the Bible into Latin, added to the complexity. Undoubtedly, Jerome elevated Mary Magdalene in significant and enduring ways. He celebrated the humility of the one who washed his disciples' feet, conversed with the woman of Samaria, discussed the kingdom of heaven "with Mary at His feet," and revealed himself "first to some poor women."[41] Jerome appreciated the irony of God's plan that fishermen teach the wise. Out of this paradigm we should read his comments pertaining to Mary Magdalene in his letter to Principia (412):

> The unbelieving reader may perhaps laugh at me for dwelling so long on the praises of mere women; yet if he will but remember how holy women followed our Lord and Saviour and ministered to Him of their substance, and how the three Marys stood before the cross and especially how Mary Magdalen—called the tower from the earnestness and glow of her faith—was privileged to see the rising Christ first of all before the very apostles, he will convict himself of pride sooner than me of folly. For we judge of people's virtue not by their sex but by their character, and hold those to be worthy of the highest glory who have renounced both rank and wealth.[42]

Mary as the "tower" of the Christian faith speaks of her strength as well as her identification with the church.[43]

At the same time, Jerome does not shy away from criticizing Mary Magdalene, which would come to be repeated and echoed in the interpretive tradition, sometimes with a harshness that he may not have intended. His assessment that she and the women should have expected to encounter the resurrected Jesus at the tomb meant to Jerome that Jesus's refusal to be touched was a punitive measure taken against Mary. Rather than associate the encounter with the ascension, according to Jesus's explanation, Jerome concludes that Mary Magdalene is "not worthy to touch, as risen, one whom you suppose still in the tomb."[44] Nevertheless, Jerome describes Mary Magdalene as "privileged to see the rising Christ first even before the apostles."[45]

What we have is a game of pinball. From the pen of the man who celebrated the strength of Mary's faith as a tower also comes the impugning of her worthiness and specifically her touch. What could have been a commentary on the position of us all, reaching out to Christ unworthily in the weakness of our faith, too easily became a direct indictment on Mary Magdalene. What might have been a general critique of female unworthiness— because females are human and all fall short of the glory of God—too easily slipped into an essentialist accusation of unworthiness. As the woman of Luke 7 can attest, it has been easy in the church's reading of Scripture to assume that female sin must be sexual sin, which brings us to Pope Gregory the Great.

Gregory I

In the basilica of San Clemente in Rome on September 21, 591, Pope Gregory I preached a sermon that introduced, in the words of Katherine Ludwig Jansen, "a new Magdalen for western Christendom."[46] The associations,

47

of course, had been building over time. With a gloss heard round the world, Gregory linked Mary Magdalene with the act of anointing Jesus by conflating her with both Mary of Bethany and the unnamed "sinner" woman (Luke 7:36–50) who washes Jesus's feet with her tears, costly perfume, and kisses. He declares, "We believe that this woman [Mary Magdalen] whom Luke calls a female sinner, whom John calls Mary, is the same Mary from whom Mark says seven demons were cast out."[47] Because Luke's description of her as a "sinner" was interpreted as a euphemism for prostitute,[48] drawing that story into Mary Magdalene's biography led the church to incorrectly associate Mary Magdalene with prostitution. Although the church's reading of the Luke 7 text has continued to favor Gregory's interpretation, Luke's intended meaning is disputed today. Biblical scholar Lynn Cohick points out that Luke does not use the Greek word for "prostitute" in that story, though he does use that term in the parable of the prodigal son (15:30). So if the woman of Luke 7 were a prostitute and since Luke did use the word for "prostitute" elsewhere in his Gospel, the fact that he doesn't use the term in this case is significant. More likely, Cohick suggests, Luke associates the anointing woman with the "tax collectors and sinners" referenced in 7:34.[49]

When the church has read Mary Magdalene through the lens of Luke 7, she has been treated as the epitome of both a sinful life and, conversely, a penitent one. Even Gregory compliments her fervent love and faithfulness. The sinful past life, though, is hard to shake. In the history of the church, she has been imagined and depicted with very long hair, a reference to the anointing passages in which both Mary of Bethany and the unnamed woman wipe their tears and perfume from Jesus's feet with their hair. Long hair in the case of Mary Magdalene became a way for the church to allude to past promiscuity.[50] By absorbing Mary of Bethany into Mary Magdalene's story, Mary Magdalene's name became identified honorably with Lazarus's family and dishonorably with prostitution. Interestingly, even that kind of baggage could not keep Mary Magdalene from being remembered as a preacher during the medieval period (as we will see in chap. 3).

Certainly, Scripture elevates Mary Magdalene's story as a surprising model, but is it a model of repentance from prostitution? True, Scripture indicates Mary Magdalene's reception of Jesus's teaching, but was it at the home of Martha? Scripture also stresses Mary Magdalene's tender care of Jesus and weeping, but was it at Lazarus's home and his tomb or was it at the cross and Jesus's tomb? What do we make of these anointing passages? Perhaps some clarity is possible amid the interpretive confusion.

Sorting Out the Anointings

Jesus was anointed by a woman (Matt. 26:6–13; Mark 14:1–9; Luke 7:36–50; John 12:1–11). All four Gospel writers are clear on that. But was it the same event or different events? Was it the same woman or different women? Was it Mary Magdalene? Sorting out the anointings requires some careful reading.

Although the accounts include similarities, they are not identical. While the Synoptic Gospels recount Jesus being anointed by an unnamed woman, John's Gospel names

TABLE 2.1

The Anointing Passages

Scripture	Matthew 26:6–13	Mark 14:1–9	Luke 7:36–50	John 12:1–11
Location	Bethany, Simon's home (former leper)	Bethany, Simon's home (former leper)	Unknown, Pharisee's home	Bethany, Lazarus's home
Anointing woman	Woman	Woman	"Sinner" woman	Mary of Bethany
Anointing object	Perfume (alabaster jar)	Perfume (alabaster jar)	Tears, perfume, kisses, hair	Perfume (jar, pure nard), hair
Jesus's anointed/ washed body part	Head	Head	Feet	Feet
Purpose of anointing/ washing	Preparation for burial	Preparation for burial	Expression of love, faith	Preparation for burial
Text	"Now while Jesus was at Bethany in the house of Simon the leper, a woman came to him with an alabaster jar of very costly ointment, and she poured it on his head as he sat at the table" (vv. 6–7).	"It was two days before the Passover and the Festival of Unleavened Bread. . . . While he was at Bethany in the house of Simon the leper, as he sat at the table, a woman came with an alabaster jar of very costly ointment of nard, and she broke open the jar and poured the ointment on his head" (vv. 1, 3).	"One of the Pharisees asked Jesus to eat with him, and when he went into the Pharisee's house he reclined to dine. And a woman in the city who was a sinner, having learned that he was eating in the Pharisee's house, brought an alabaster jar of ointment. She stood behind him at his feet, weeping, and began to bathe his feet with her tears and to dry them with her hair, kissing his feet and anointing them with the ointment" (vv. 36–38).	"Six days before the Passover Jesus came to Bethany, the home of Lazarus, whom he had raised from the dead. There they gave a dinner for him. Martha served, and Lazarus was one of those reclining with him. Mary took a pound of costly perfume made of pure nard, anointed Jesus's feet, and wiped them with her hair" (vv. 1–3).

Mary of Bethany (see table 2.1). None of the accounts name Mary Magdalene, but her association with the anointings would come by way of confusing the anointings as well as confusing the Marys. In two Gospels, Jesus's head was anointed (a priestly act), and in two Gospels his feet were washed. Other differences include the location of the act and the purpose or meaning of the act. Since the Gospel writers draw our attention to this encounter in Jesus's life and ministry, what do the anointing passages mean, and how do they relate to Mary Magdalene?

Luke's Gospel recalls when an unnamed "sinner" woman washes Jesus's feet. The event serves as an expression of her hospitality and gratitude for the forgiveness of her sins and to the shame of the host, Simon the Pharisee, who did not offer Jesus that same welcome. Her presence is unwanted and troubles the religious leaders who have already scoffed at Jesus's fellowship with tax collectors and sinners (Luke 5:30). Jesus points to her care of him to counter the host's treatment of him. She is exemplary in her faith-filled response to forgiveness.

Meanwhile, Matthew, Mark, and John present the anointing of Jesus as primarily a display of tender care toward Christ's body in preparation for his burial. This foreshadowing of what awaits Jesus elevates the belief and discipleship of each woman in each account. The act is prophetic.

In John 12 specifically, Mary of Bethany's anointing or washing of Jesus's feet with expensive perfume is presented in juxtaposition to the unbelief of the Jewish council and the plot to kill Jesus.[51] Despite Judas's protests, her act of washing Jesus's feet with perfume is a mark of her model discipleship. It echoes her kneeling at his feet and her pleading with Jesus at Lazarus's death (11:32), and it anticipates Jesus's own act of kneeling to wash his disciples' feet (13:1–20).[52] Biblical scholar Marianne Meye Thompson notes that Mary of Bethany glorifies Jesus with her lavish gift of perfume, though it is not considered a messianic anointing (since oil is not used, it is not poured on his head, and the Greek verb for "messianic anointing" is not used).[53] Rather, Mary of Bethany exemplifies the necessary servant's heart and humility befitting a follower of Christ. She washes the feet of the one about to enter Jerusalem.[54] Thompson makes the claim that the aroma of perfume may even anticipate resurrection in striking contrast with the stench associated with the raising of Lazarus's body.[55]

Mary of Bethany's act is presented in John as exemplary in a notable manner. We are invited to see her washing of Jesus's feet as a pair with Jesus's own act of washing his disciples' feet that follows (John 13:1–17). While Jesus's example is rightly interpreted as an example of his countercultural love, it can also be interpreted as an act that dignifies Mary of Bethany (and the woman of Luke 7 by extension). If foot washing was regarded in its context as a necessary but menial task of hospitality typically fulfilled by slaves or freed women (whether servants or wives),[56] a radical turnabout was in the works. Jesus is not merely dignifying the act of a servant but the act of a woman's hospitality as well, since women might wash the feet of guests as either slaves or wives.

Jesus's response to the anointings is a point of continuity across all four Gospels. In each case, Jesus warmly receives the devotion of anointing women. His response stands in striking contrast to that of the onlookers, whether the disciples, guests, Simon the Pharisee, or Judas Iscariot. They wrinkle their noses at the humility and tender devotion of a woman (Jesus describes it as "great love" in Luke 7:47), but Jesus publicly honors her with no hint of embarrassment or disgust. In each account, he accepts the costly tears and perfume, and in the one case, even the kissing of his feet. The text depicts him as being unconcerned by what others think of him or that she will render him ritually impure. Her touch is not rejected. Instead, he defends her, saying, "Why do you trouble the woman?" (Matt. 26:10) and "Let her alone" (Mark 14:6; John 12:7) when her devotion is denigrated.

Each account calls out the behavior of church authorities by elevating the worth of the woman treated as inferior.[57] By foreshadowing Jesus's death, the prophetic act of these women is a gift to the church. In the demonstration of love, a surprising archetype of disciple gains prominence. Like the centurion in the same chapter (Luke 7:1–10), the "sinner" woman of Luke 7 is the unlikely, unexpected, and faithful follower.[58] Like Jesus's onlookers, we might not expect him to receive her with such dignity. Her label as a "sinner" might lead us to overlook, undervalue, or even reject her completely. Like the onlookers, we might be repulsed by her behavior,[59] while Jesus affirms her faith, forgives her sins, assures her of salvation, and sends her in peace (Luke 7:44–50). The story is valuable for drawing out a pivotal question of the Gospels: Who is this man who forgives sins? (Luke 7:49). Once again, we find ourselves surprised by Jesus's ministry toward women.

Sojourner Truth (born Isabella Baumfree) was a nineteenth-century emancipated slave of New York who became a well-known public speaker and itinerant preacher. She was a six-foot-tall illiterate woman who overcame unimaginable hardship. She forged a new life under a new name, making an extraordinary impact for her time and beyond. Her story connects with well-known names such as Frederick Douglass, Harriet Beecher Stowe, and Abraham Lincoln. In 1851, she delivered her most famous speech, "Ain't I a Woman?," at the Women's Rights Convention in Akron, Ohio. In the speech she roots the dignity of women in Jesus's treatment of them, saying, "[Jesus] never spurned woman from him!"[60] The speech was printed in the *Anti-Slavery Bugle* and widely circulated. It is considered one of the most significant speeches in American history, and at its heart is Jesus's treatment of women. To Sojourner, the fact that Jesus was even willing to be born of a woman at all was remarkable. And look at the tears that he wept at the pleading of Mary and Martha over their brother, she noted. Across the centuries, it seems, Jesus's reception of the devotion of women astounds.

But where does this leave Mary Magdalene?

There are a number of good reasons to question Mary Magdalene's identification with the Gospel's anointing passages, if for no other reason than that she is never named by Scripture in those accounts. Continuing with our focus on Luke, it seems unlikely that Luke would tell Mary Magdalene's story through an unknown, anonymous woman immediately before he names her in the very next section as someone who was previously healed from seven demons (8:2).[61] The Gospel authors were writing after the events had taken place, and they therefore knew what a significant role Mary Magdalene would play as witness to Christ's ministry, including his death on the cross, the empty tomb, and his resurrection. Importantly, Scripture names Mary Magdalene in all four Gospels multiple times, but she is never introduced as a prostitute or with the descriptive "sinner." For these reasons and perhaps more, it is unlikely she is the woman in Luke 7.

In addition, prostitution tends to reflect a financial disadvantage that does not fit Luke's characterization of Mary Magdalene, who like "many others . . . ministered to them out of their own resources" (8:3). She evidently had economic means or else she would not have been able to provide patronage for Jesus's ministry. And her identification with the city of Magdala indicates that she traveled, according to Cohick, perhaps on business.[62] Magdala (or Taricheae) was economically flourishing at this time. The image of an impoverished prostitute does not line up well here, especially when we recognize that prostitution was often bound to slavery.[63] As Cohick explains, female slaves most often had nothing, and they were treated as "economic tools" that profited their owners or other male authorities, who had legal control over them.[64] The Gospels do not direct us to remember Mary Magdalene this way.

And yet to deny that Mary Magdalene was a prostitute is not to say that Christ cannot transform such a life. In the case of the Luke 7 woman, whatever her sinful past might have been, the text instructs us that the unnamed anointing woman shouldn't be forgotten or overlooked. In two of the accounts, Jesus prophesied that his followers would remember her: "Truly I tell you, wherever this good news is proclaimed in the whole world, what she has done will be told in remembrance of her" (Matt. 26:13; Mark 14:9). What a striking way to honor this woman. We, too, are invited to receive the anointing women with the same acceptance that Jesus showed. Even so, it does not mean that she should be equated with Mary Magdalene. It matters how Scripture does and does not identify Mary Magdalene.

When we muddle people and passages, we miss what Scripture is saying to us. We become like the baker popularized in church sermons, who was instructed to print 1 John 4:18 on a wedding cake ("There is no fear in love, but perfect love casts out fear") but by accident prints John 4:18 ("For you have had five husbands, and the one you have now is not your husband"). Both passages are found in Scripture, but that doesn't mean they are interchangeable.

Mary Magdalene should not be regarded as interchangeable with the "sinner" woman who anointed Jesus *before* his death. Different followers have different roles in the narrative of Jesus, and the Gospels direct us to remember Mary Magdalene as someone who is healed from demons, as a faithful disciple and financial contributor, and as the first witness to the resurrection or among the first group to witness the resurrection.

But even that does not mean that the anointing, priestly Mary Magdalene has no place in the right remembrance of the church. As we will consider, Mary Magdalene and the other women *did* intend to anoint Jesus's dead body with spices and ointments (Mark 16:1; Luke 23:55–56) but instead discovered the empty tomb and encountered the risen Lord. In a way, instead of anointing Jesus the King with chrism, they anointed him with recognition, joy, fear, faith, and worship (Matt. 28:8–9). As the Gospels close, Mary Magdalene offers Jesus what even religious leaders were unwilling or unable to offer: an anointing from the heart (Mark 7:6–8). This anointing of belief in the resurrected Christ is in fact the whole trajectory of Christ's kingdom in the first place.

But there is another "Gospel" account linked to Mary Magdalene that requires our consideration if we are to remember her rightly.

Gospel or "Gospel"?

Although our understanding of Mary Magdalene has been largely confused due to her confusion with other Marys and conflation with the sinful woman of Luke 7, important texts outside the accepted canon of Scripture have also added to the Mary Magdalene mix.

Some readers may be surprised to learn that other "Gospels" existed before the early church formally clarified the canon of Scripture. One such Gospel is commonly known as the Gospel of Mary Magdalene, though it is self-titled as simply the Gospel of Mary. It is the only "gospel" to be named for a woman, and it was popularized by Dan Brown's *The Da Vinci Code.* The text itself is often counted among the New Testament apocrypha that emerged from the regions of Syria and Egypt sometime around the second and third centuries. These texts have never been considered fully trustworthy accounts in the history of the church, but they are magnets for speculation and are valuable for revealing important context among early Christians of the time. They are reminiscent of accepted Scripture but can also distort the teachings of Christianity in specific ways.

Many of these texts stem from Gnosticism, a second-century movement that presented a different version of Christianity. At the core of Gnosticism is a dualistic teaching (spirit is good, matter is bad) that denies some of the primary and central teachings of orthodox Christianity: namely, that God directly created the material world and that Jesus Christ actually took on flesh, suffered, died in his body, and rose again from the dead. Early Christians knew that, as Paul said, "if there is no resurrection of the dead, then Christ has not been raised, and if Christ has not been raised, then our proclamation is in vain and your faith is in vain" (1 Cor. 15:13–14). To deny this was to deny the good news of Jesus Christ, and to associate Mary Magdalene with that stream of "Christianity" also denies what Scripture says about her role at the resurrection event. But stick with me for a moment more since the texts also reveal something about their own time.

Much of what we know about Gnosticism comes from an early Christian theologian and defender of the faith, Irenaeus of Lyon, in his work *Against Heresies*. Discoveries of ancient documents over the last century or more have also extended that knowledge. In 1896, the Gospel of Mary was found in Akhmim, Egypt, in a fifth-century papyrus codex that was written in Sahidic Coptic. In 1945, a farmer uncovered twelve leather-bound codices in a sealed clay jar in the desert at Nag Hammadi, Egypt. The jar included, among fifty-two Gnostic texts, the Gospel of Thomas and a partial translation of Plato's *The Republic*, which helped to confirm and expand our understanding of Gnosticism in its diversity as well as shared themes and teachings. The Gospel of Mary (known as the Berlin Codex because it was taken to Berlin) was translated and published for the first time in 1955. There are some notable family traits shared across Gnosticism worth mentioning that relate, though in moderation, to the Gospel of Mary.[65]

Gnosticism taught that salvation was achieved through hidden or secret gnosis or "inner knowledge," which leads to the ascent of the soul.[66] That theme is at work in the Gospel of Mary when Peter asks Mary to share "whatever you remember of any words he told you which we have not yet heard." She agrees, the texts continues, to share "of that which has not been given to you to hear."[67] What proceeds is instruction that she received from Jesus through a vision rather than an in-person conversation. How might we evaluate this?

According to the canonical Gospels, Mary Magdalene did have a direct encounter and exchange with Jesus in the garden. This was not a vision or revelation, but the text claims an actual, historical encounter. Moreover, the Gospels indicate that immediately after she encountered the risen Lord and he sent her to tell the disciples, she did not waste a second. The text describes how she "went and announced to the disciples, 'I have seen the Lord,' and she told them that he had said these things to her" (John 20:18). This is an important difference between the Gospel of Mary and John's Gospel. In the latter, Mary Magdalene willingly shared the good news with the disciples, not because they pleaded with her to share but because Jesus *sent her* to them (more on that later).[68]

In further contrast to Gnosticism's hidden path to salvation, the canonical Gospels emphasize that Jesus *publicly* taught crowds of people (e.g., see Matt. 4:25; 5:1; 7:28; 8:1; 9:36; 13:2; 14:13; 15:30; 19:2; 21:11; 22:33; 23:1). Even his private teaching moments involved both the twelve and the women. In Luke's Gospel, for example, when the women encountered the angels at the empty tomb, the angels direct them to "remember how he told you . . . ," which prompts them to remember his words. Luke takes note of specific women (Mary Magdalene, Joanna, Mary the mother of James, and the other women) who directly go and tell the eleven and the rest (Luke 24:6–10). The Gospels repeatedly stress that Jesus did not hide his teachings on salvation, though he was sometimes overwhelmed by the crowds to the point of withdrawal (Mark 2:2; 3:9). Even when he spoke in parables, he still offered explanations afterward, which have been passed down (Matt. 13:10–11). Though he concealed his identity as Messiah on occasion (Matt. 16:20; Mark 8:29–30), it may be the worst kept secret of all time. According to 1 John 1, all that is needed to be known from eyewitness accounts has been faithfully passed on:

> We declare to you what was from the beginning, what we have heard, what we have seen with our eyes, what we have looked at and touched with our hands, concerning the word of life—this life was revealed, and we have seen it and testify to it and declare to you the eternal life that was with the Father and was revealed to us—what we have seen and heard we also declare to you so that you also may have fellowship with us, and truly our fellowship

is with the Father and with his Son Jesus Christ. We are writing these things so that our joy may be complete. (1 John 1:1–4)

Paul, too, hands on what he received (1 Cor. 15:3), and even when he teaches about the secret and hidden wisdom of God, he couples that teaching with the gracious and loving decision of God to bring revelation by the Spirit (1 Cor. 2:7–10). The author of Hebrews summarizes, "It was declared at first through the Lord, and it was confirmed for us by those who heard him" (Heb. 2:3). The early Christian church father Irenaeus of Lyon would come to describe this as "apostolic tradition." He stressed that the true teaching of the apostles, received from Christ, was indeed handed on. And so we can see how the Gnostic "Gospels" elevate secrecy while the apostolic Gospels insist on sharing revelation. The reason that Mary Magdalene's story is even included in the Gospels is because she is known for sharing, not hiding, her encounter with Jesus at the empty tomb.[69] In fact, we are told that she *ran* to tell the disciples (Matt. 28:8; John 20:2).

Mary Magdalene versus Peter?

Another relevant question emerges from the New Testament apocrypha: Was there any animosity or competition between Peter and Mary Magdalene? Several Gnostic texts (the Gospel of Thomas and Pistis Sophia) describe such a tension. In the Gospel of Mary, after Mary shares her insights that focus on the progression of the soul in knowledge and out of sin, Andrew responds, "These ideas are too different from those we have known."[70] Thanks, Andrew, for saying what we were all thinking.

The Gospel of Mary then recounts a conflict that erupts not only over the content of Mary's teaching but the issue of listening to a woman at all. In the text, Peter asks, "Must we change our customs, and listen to this woman? Did he really choose her, and prefer her to us?"[71] As Mary begins to weep and plead that she is not lying, Levi gets at the heart of the matter saying, "He loved her more than us."[72] They are like children vying for the attention of a parent, though this window into a struggle for authority is mild compared to the third-century Gnostic text Pistis Sophia, which records Mary Magdalene as fearful of Peter and outright accusing him of misogyny.[73] What can we make of the hostility and jealousy between the male disciples and Mary Magdalene?

First, we should recognize that the canonical Gospel accounts also describe tensions between the disciples over their status in the group. Early Christian texts reflect a struggle for authority that is also evident in canonical Scripture. In fact, they *did* pose questions to Jesus about who would be the greatest in the kingdom of heaven or who would sit at his left and right side in the kingdom (Matt. 18:1–14; Mark 10:35–41; Luke 9:46–48; 22:24). These exchanges illustrate the disciples' immaturity as well as their inability, at the time, to grasp the true nature of Jesus's ministry and mission. Jesus responded by placing a child in their midst as an exemplar, a remarkable and surprising response that illustrated just how out of step the disciples were with Jesus during his ministry with them. So, yes, tension was there, but did it involve tension between Mary Magdalene and Peter?

Scripture records an incident of animosity between Judas and Mary of Bethany over the cost of perfume that she used to anoint Jesus (John 12:4–6). The account predisposes the reader to take the side of Mary of Bethany by disclosing Judas's forthcoming betrayal as well as other hidden sins of stealing and hypocrisy. Mary of Bethany is also featured as a source of frustration—this time to her sister, Martha—when she chooses to learn at Jesus's feet rather than serve as hostess alongside Martha (Luke 10:38–41). Since Scripture presents Mary of Bethany as a different person from Mary Magdalene, perhaps the composite Mary is the culprit here once again. Guilty by association (or conflation). But regardless, according to Scripture, Peter was not involved in either incident. Mary of Bethany's actions causing antagonism with a fellow follower of Jesus perhaps carried over to the composite Mary.

Some have pointed to mild competitiveness between Peter and John insofar as John designates himself as "the disciple whom [Jesus] loved" (19:26; 20:2) and includes the detail that he outran Peter to the empty tomb (20:4). The New Testament also mentions that Peter and Paul experienced tension and conflict over whether Gentiles had to abide by Jewish practice in order to follow Christ, which led to the first council of the church in Jerusalem (Acts 15). Peter elsewhere describes Paul's theology as less than clear in a number of places, saying, "So also our beloved brother Paul wrote to you according to the wisdom given him, speaking of this as he does in all his letters. There are some things in them hard to understand, which the ignorant and unstable twist to their own destruction, as they do the other scriptures" (2 Pet. 3:15–16).

These human elements in Scripture are welcome, even if we cringe, chuckle, or perhaps worry about their place in the narrative. They are not to be overlooked or undervalued. They humanize the disciples and further validate the authenticity of Scripture. Exposing the conflict is a backhanded compliment to everything that Christ accomplishes, and it reinforces our need for a Savior and for the inspiration of the Holy Spirit. Even so, nowhere does canonical Scripture record a dispute between Mary Magdalene and Peter. Moreover, as soon as Mary Magdalene discovered the empty tomb, the first thing she did was run directly to tell Peter and John (John 20:2).[74] That little detail, however small, signals that she recognized the leaders from among the twelve and sought their help. There is no begrudging here as far as Scripture shares.

Even so, witnessing the empty tomb and encountering the risen Lord *does* ignite conflict between the male and the female disciples. When the women share the news that the tomb was empty and that Jesus had risen, the male disciples' response falls short: "These words seemed to them an idle tale, and they did not believe them" (Luke 24:11). But there is one notable exception. Peter seems to believe enough that he runs to the tomb to verify what they shared (Luke 24:12; Peter and John in John 20:3). It is a faith-seeking-understanding moment, and it further complicates any apocryphal treatment of Peter. The witness of Mary Magdalene and the women is promptly validated by Christ's own appearance to the twelve. Their words are found to be truthful and trustworthy. Scripture hides neither the immediate failure of the remaining twelve to believe nor the ultimate faithfulness of the women to go and tell. There is a kind of equalizing at work regarding which parts of the story are included. In this instance, a case can be made for agreement between the Gospel of Mary and canonical Scripture insofar as Mary Magdalene's teachings should not be rejected simply because she is a woman.[75]

In the end, canonical Scripture features the faithfulness of *both* Mary Magdalene and Peter, giving both prominence in the story and on differing occasions in Jesus's ministry. For Mary Magdalene, she is a witness at the cross, at the empty tomb, and of Christ's resurrection: "I have seen the Lord" (John 20:18). For Peter, after his denial of Christ, he is restored while eating breakfast on the beach with the resurrected Jesus and offers a threefold declaration of love as an act of repentance: "Yes, Lord; you know that I love you" (John 21:15–17). Mary's faithfulness to fulfill her commission by Christ is linked to Jesus's Great Commission to his followers (more on that later). Peter's faithfulness leads to his preaching at Pentecost (Acts 2). Both are the foundation of a global mission that continues to this day, wherein God's kingdom is continually advanced through the participation and contributions of both women and men. While Gnosticism all too easily revels in dualism, canonical Scripture invites us to observe pairings and partnerships. But what do we make of these bonds formed with and through Christ?

Jesus as Friend, Brother, Lord, and . . . Lover?

There is another troubling aspect of the Gnostic "Gospel" to consider that continues to strain the legacies of both

65

Mary Magdalene and Jesus. Modern media has zeroed in on the idea that Mary Magdalene and Jesus forged a romantic bond.[76] Stories from *The Last Temptation of Christ* to *Jesus Christ Superstar* to *The Da Vinci Code* give the impression that she was like a wife to Jesus. In the Gospel of Philip, the theme is pronounced, with Jesus often kissing Mary Magdalene. The Gospel of Mary only alludes to a special relationship by claiming, "Peter said to Mary: 'Sister, we know that the Teacher loved you differently from other women.'"[77] These texts reflect an important question that was present then and today: How should this close bond between Jesus and Mary Magdalene be understood?

Scripture indeed emphasizes the intimacy between Jesus and his followers. Biblical metaphors point to Christ as groom and the believer as the bride, with both men and women standing in the position of the bride (Matt. 9:15; 25:1–13; Rev. 19:7). The medieval church, especially in the mystical traditions, put special emphasis on Jesus as the lover of the soul of the believer. This view is influenced by readings from the Song of Songs. Unlike the modern twisting of this theme, which can stress a crude physical, material exchange, the medieval tradition revels in the allegory of our true union with Christ as believers. Grace Hamman's work illumines Jesus through medieval eyes and the theme of Jesus as the lover of souls.[78] In our union with Christ, we experience vulnerability as we become fully known. Our soul is naked before him. We are invited to make our home in that love (to abide!) according to Jesus's teachings in John 15. This love also demands sacrifice. Hamman writes, "In becoming Christ's faithful lover, we take up our cross of human vulnerability in giving our heart. . . . In loving Jesus as our lover, we become more human, like the Son of Man himself. As Jesus says, as we make our home in his love, we are more touched by others' pain and joy. We are more open to the vulnerabilities and glories of being embodied souls (John 15:9–17). The way of the Lover is the way of the cross. Beyond the cross are resurrection and the mystery of true union."[79] This is the medieval tradition exemplified by mystics such as Mechthild of Magdeburg. We can see echoes of it even today in the 1993 song "Jesus, Lover of My Soul," by Hillsong. Yet, importantly, Jesus's teachings on love in John 15 are framed by the relationship of disciple and friend. So how might we think about Jesus's relationship with Mary Magdalene according to the Gospel accounts?

Jesus tested the cultural and religious boundaries of his time, such as healing on the Sabbath (Mark 2:23–3:6) or traveling to Samaria to convert the Samaritan woman at the well (John 4), but that did not mean that his close followers misunderstood their relationship with him. On more than one occasion, he himself set the expectation, for example, by calling the disciples his "friends" (John 15:14).[80] Jesus also employed familial language to define the parameters of his community. Because of the ways that Jesus spoke, we can consider his relationship to Mary Magdalene through the lens of sibling love and friendship.

During Jesus's ministry on earth, he envisioned for his followers a togetherness in faith and ministry as siblings in a spiritual family: "Whoever does the will of God is my brother and sister and mother" (Mark 3:35; see also Matt. 12:46–50 and Luke 8:19–21). As scholar Willie

James Jennings has pointed out, this belonging together became the basis for their boldness: "Of course each disciple can and must be bold, but their boldness is always a together boldness, a joined boldness, a boldness born of intimacy."[81]

My middle brother and I spent cherished years together after high school, through graduate school, and before we each got married. We overlapped at college and shared the same professor mentor. We looked out for each other, prayed, laughed, bickered, teased, and cried together. Many a day was spent discussing theology and faith and listening to music. He was just ahead of me at seminary, in ordination, and in ministry. When he married my best friend, my cup too overflowed. After he became a pastor, he invited me to lead worship one Sunday with him at his church in Texas, where we both grew up in the faith and where our father had served as senior pastor decades prior. That moment was a kind of marker in my life. Who knew that faith, friendship, and ministry could be shared by siblings this way? More often than not, the shows we grew up with (*Back to the Future* or *Honey, I Shrunk the Kids*) depicted siblings in vicious verbal conflict with one another. But maybe there was another way?

The familial bond was no throwaway line for Jesus when we consider that Jesus's flesh-and-blood family members were also prominent in his ministry. John the Baptist, his cousin, baptized him. Jesus's mother Mary never deserted him from the annunciation of his birth to the inauguration of his earthly ministry to his death on the cross (even his aunt was at the cross, John 19:25).[82] Acts 1 declares that Jesus's mother Mary along with his brothers (a reference to his family members, not the disciples) prayerfully waited in the upper room before Pentecost (v. 14). Jesus's earthly family was faithful to him, even after his ascension, but his family was meant to be greater than just them.

When Jesus teaches the disciples to pray, he instructs them to begin with "*Our* Father . . ." Not just *his* Father. By this, he honors and includes in the family all who believe in him. He fosters a holy, sibling camaraderie that thrives by the nourishment of daily bread, the forgiveness of sins, God's deliverance of our family from evil and temptation, and above all, our homecoming to be with our Lord forever. Even in conversation with Mary Magdalene, Jesus describes himself as a "brother" to his followers (Matt. 28:10; John 20:17).[83] Biblical scholar Marianne Meye Thompson points out, "Through his death and resurrection, Jesus gathers together the children of God who are brothers and sisters to each other and to him, and the claims of this family outweigh biological claims."[84]

Beyond the Gospels, Hebrews 2:11 teaches that Jesus is not ashamed to call us brothers and sisters.[85] In fact, he willingly took on flesh and blood, what makes us creatures, so that he could save us: "Therefore he had to become like his brothers and sisters in every respect, so that he might become a merciful and faithful high priest in the service of God, to make a sacrifice of atonement for the sins of the people" (2:17). By his act, we "all have one Father" (v. 11). The idea of Jesus as the generous older brother who shares his father, his name, his inheritance with his siblings powerfully echoes Paul's teaching that we are the adopted children of God. "He destined us for adoption as his children through Jesus Christ, according to the good pleasure of his will, to the praise of his glorious grace that he freely bestowed on us in the Beloved" (Eph. 1:5–6). A glorious inheritance awaits us, Paul assures us, with all the saints (vv. 11, 18). In fact, more than any other description, Paul uses the Greek root for "sibling" to describe the relationship between the followers of Christ.[86]

Jesus as brother is a lens through which we can understand his relationship with Mary Magdalene. What might it mean for Jesus to act as brother to Mary Magdalene given that she is one of the few women in the New Testament who is not associated with any male family member? The fact that she is already set apart by location and character rather than male relation further connects her to this new family being formed by Christ. In the first century, older brothers were expected to respect their sister, defend her, and protect her name and honor. Emotional closeness and devotion often resulted. We see a sister's reciprocal care for her brother with Mary Magdalene's financial support of Jesus's ministry as well as her devotion to his body from the cross to the tomb. Scholar Reidar Aasgaard has shown that "the sibling relationship was by far the most lasting of all family relationships."[87]

Of course, Jesus was not just Mary Magdalene's friend and brother. As the Messiah, the Anointed One, he was also her Lord and Savior. She showed devotion to Jesus the Christ, though we have no reason to believe that she was the sinful woman who anointed him with tears, perfume, and kisses. And though we also have no reason to believe that she was the unnamed woman who anointed his head in Simon the leper's home, she is explicitly named as the one who was sent by Jesus to tell the disciples the good news of his resurrection. In fact, when the risen Christ encounters Mary Magdalene in the garden, he sends her to his "brothers," and she becomes an unexpected agent for the time.[88] She is instructed not only to proclaim the resurrection and coming ascension but to do so in a way that reflects the familial bond forged by Christ: "my Father and your Father, to my God and your God" (John 20:17). These words of familial adoption were given to Mary Magdalene to proclaim. Do we see her in the story?

Recovering the forgotten Mary presents many challenges because she has so often been obstructed by misunderstandings. The Western tradition has made her indistinguishable from other Marys and the unnamed, sinful woman. There are also noncanonical, apocryphal texts to value and grapple with. Though Scripture includes her, names her, and elevates her story as a faithful follower of Jesus, even so, the church has inconsistently received and interpreted passages that explicitly relate to her and those that do not, adding another layer of complexity to remembering her significance. What can we recover when we look at Mary Magdalene through the eyes of church history?

THREE

Mary Magdalene and Her Church Interpreters

Let There Be Light

On Christmas Eve 1968, while in lunar orbit, the crew of Apollo 8 gave a live television broadcast from space. Apollo 8 was the first manned spacecraft to orbit the moon and return to Earth. As they approached the lunar sunrise, astronaut Bill Anders addressed the world, saying, "For all the people back on earth, the crew of Apollo 8 has a message that we would like to send to you." During the most watched television broadcast ever for its time, they read from Genesis 1. One billion people watching the broadcast heard the words, "In the beginning, God created the heavens and the earth . . ." Leading up to that moment, the astronauts had been preparing to see Earth emerge above the lunar horizon. On their fourth rotation, the startling view of Earth's rising had Anders scrambling again for his camera. Partly visible, partly hidden, Earth's vibrant rising out of darkness set stunning image to scriptural words spoken: "God said, 'Let there be light'; and there was light. And God saw that the light was good; and God separated the light from the darkness."[1]

The following year, the US Postal Service commemorated that moment with a stamp featuring the Earthrise image along with the words from Genesis. My husband's grandfather (Elmer Jett) had worked on the Apollo 8 project as an aeronautical engineer at Lockheed in Burbank, California, so this moment is a proud one for their family. In the years since, our world has grown so familiar with Apollo 8's view of Earth that it's easy to forget there was a time when such an image was unimaginable. Seeing Earth through Apollo 8's lens has indelibly shaped how we perceive our world today and our place in the universe. We traveled all that way, it seems, just to look back and see ourselves more clearly: brimming with life, color, beauty, and vibrancy in the vast darkness of the universe from the barrenness of the moon.

When it comes to Mary Magdalene, we need another reality-altering image. Though imperfect, the church's own history can help us. In looking back, we'll see patterns of reading that echo through the ages even when interpreters do not recognize each other. We'll see ways in which the biblical text is illumined through attention to her. And yet, like viewing Earth's rising from the moon, half visible and half shrouded in darkness, we will discover places forgotten or hidden that have prevented us from receiving the full biblical picture of her story and the significance of her place in God's salvific work. Through the centuries, the church has entangled Mary Magdalene's story in confusion. The Mary we forgot has been buried in the archives of church history. Reaching into that history is a bit like traveling into space and around the moon in order to see Earth from a different vantage. Let's see if we can bring her to light.

The Golden Legend

Christians have been playing a game of telephone with Mary Magdalene's story across time, and it shows. As word of mouth travels among the cacophony of voices, the muddle grows. Elaborate and convoluted accounts add, remove, alter, conflate, and overextend her story. As the church has passed down its recollection of Mary Magdalene over the centuries, it has sometimes omitted the specific and powerful moments that Scripture identifies with her by name. We can miss the weight of those stories when we forget or expand her identity, losing sight of who she was from Scripture. Although Mary Magdalene was not ignored by the early church, it was a highly influential medieval text that has played an outsize role in shaping our perceptions: perhaps no other link in the telephone chain has had a greater impact in drawing attention to Mary Magdalene while also complicating her story for the Western tradition than that text, Jacobus de Voragine's *The Golden Legend* (*Legenda Aurea*).

This bestselling, influential medieval text is a rich repository of biblical references and theology and theologians, as well as a complex history of the saints. It has come to shape Christian understandings of Mary Magdalene for generations. She is presented in a variety of roles: penitent sinner, dynamic preacher-apostle, beloved prostitute, desert hermit, and mysterious mystic. The medieval church stretches her story to fit different purposes, and in the process, it both elevated her and contributed to the church's forgetting of the biblical Mary.

The Golden Legend weaves together three distinct traditions surrounding Mary Magdalene's life. The earliest account remembers Mary Magdalene as a hermit and ascetic in the wilderness (called the Vita Eremitica tradition, which reaches back to the ninth century). She is identified with Mary of Egypt, a fourth-century saint described as a reformed prostitute. This is the Eastern version of Mary Magdalene's association with prostitution believed to have been brought to the West by Greek monks fleeing Byzantium.[2] Accordingly, she is named in *The Golden Legend* as "Mary the Egyptian, who is called the Sinner."[3] The reference cements her association with the woman of Luke 7. Meanwhile, *The Golden Legend*'s depiction of her as roaming the desert naked (though covered in hair) and solitary for forty-seven years has contributed to her depiction as naked in the history of art.[4] This ragged Mary Magdalene, subject to the elements and covered in animal skins, has been best memorialized in the Western mind by Donatello's sculpture *Penitent Magdalene* housed at the Opera del Duomo Museum in Florence. Seen through the lens of Mary of Egypt, Mary Magdalene became further associated with a past life of prostitution, this time through an Eastern inheritance.

The Golden Legend does also interact with the biblical text, though the conflation with Mary of Bethany and the sinful woman of Luke 7 quickly obscures the account. By weaving together the three biblical figures into Mary Magdalene's life, the *Legend* reflects not only the formalization of that interpretation by Pope Gregory, as we already saw, but the normalization of that reading thanks to the influence of Odo of Cluny in a sermon attributed to him, "*Vita Evangelica*."[5] Odo is considered the first to reconcile these different pieces of the gospel narrative into one account as well as the first to use the term "prostitute" (or meretrix) in reference to Mary Magdalene.[6] Finally, a third influence is also present, which remembers Mary Magdalene as a preacher and evangelist in Rome to Tiberius Caesar and in France starting in Marseille. Numerous pieces in the history of art depict Mary Magdalene as a preacher, which is a shared understanding between the Roman Catholic and Eastern Orthodox traditions.[7] We will return to this theme of remembering her as apostle-preacher-evangelist in the coming chapter.

When we enter into the text, we notice almost immediately how *The Golden Legend* identifies the two Marys of primary importance as Jesus's mother Mary and Mary Magdalene. From the outset, they are placed in a kind of tug-of-war for honor so that any opportunity to elevate Mother Mary entails humbling Mary Magdalene. Although Scripture highlights the faithfulness of the women, including Mary Magdalene at the foot of the cross, *The Golden Legend* claims that only his mother Mary did not abandon him.[8] At the same time, and not necessarily with coherence, Mary Magdalene is also presented as the woman of Luke 7, a prostitute, saved by her fervent love of Jesus and his forgiveness. In the text, which also reflects medieval perception, Mary Magdalene becomes the representative of "all repentant sinners."[9] But what does this mean for her witness to the resurrection?

Christians have long puzzled over how to make sense of the women at the empty tomb, and *The Golden Legend* reflects that tension. Why would the risen Christ first appear to Mary Magdalene rather than his mother? The matter is resolved in the text by replacing Mary Magdalene as the first witness to the risen Christ with the Virgin Mary: "But perish the thought that such a son would fail to honor such a mother by being so negligent!"[10] Surely, reasons the text, Jesus would not neglect his own mother since he was quick to console others. The early church father Ambrose is mentioned to verify claims that the Virgin Mary saw and believed in the risen Lord first.[11] And yet, according to *The Golden Legend*, the Gospel writers were in a bind. It did not suit for a mother to be the first witness of the resurrection, the thinking goes. If the other women were doubted, certainly Jesus's mother would be.

It's interesting to observe how this priority to elevate Mother Mary as witness to the resurrection extended beyond the pages of *The Golden Legend*. Katherine Ludwig Jansen has shown that, during the twelfth century, the intensifying of Marian devotion led to an increase of claims that the Virgin Mary was the first to encounter the risen Lord. For some medieval preachers, the Virgin Mary, instead of Mary Magdalene, came to be described as apostle to the apostles and evangelist to the evangelists, which adds to the confusion.[12] Nevertheless, *The Golden Legend* also identifies Mary Magdalene as the "apostle to the apostles" because the risen Christ first appeared to her.[13] Herein lies an important and accessible example of the Western tradition's attribution of that title to her as well as the tension at play in sorting out how to honor both Mother Mary and Mary Magdalene.

In other places, a shadow extends over Mary Magdalene's story as *The Golden Legend* identifies her as a former prostitute, building on theological and biblical readings from that perspective. The text associates her story with Jesus's words in Matthew, "Truly I tell you, the tax collectors and the prostitutes are going into the kingdom of God ahead of you" (Matt. 21:31).[14] Her lowliness is further illustrated in Matthew by grasping Jesus's feet as a mark of affection. Only a woman would do such a thing, reasons the text ("as women do"!).[15] She is the forgiven prostitute, whose name "Mary" means "bitter sea" while "Magdalene" means "remaining guilty."[16] Her tears mark her penance for sin.[17] Echoing the teachings of early church fathers, she is presented as the bookend to Eve, as *The Golden Legend* explains: "Woman had been the messenger of death, so a woman should be the one to announce life."[18]

There is also tension with Peter in the text. Mary Magdalene loses pride of place on several occasions during a time when the medieval church was seeking to elevate Simon Peter, whom it regarded as the first pope. The fact that John outran Peter to the empty tomb is explained away: he might have gone a different way, the text reasons. *The Golden Legend* recalls that after denying Christ, Peter fled to a cave and "wept for three days." Jesus appeared there to comfort him. Without any hint of irony, the text instructs that Peter represents the "obedient" and even that his name means "obedient."[19] Peter is boosted as the

Vicar of Christ, especially when set side-by-side with Mary Magdalene as repentant sinner, even though, unlike Peter, she never denies Christ.

Things get even more complicated when Mary Magdalene is conflated with Mary of Bethany. *The Golden Legend* presents her as the sister of Lazarus and Martha, the one who learned at the feet of Jesus, who responded, "Mary has chosen the better part" (Luke 10:42). License is taken to extend this pronouncement to Mary Magdalene as choosing the better part of penance, holiness, and contemplation—an egregious stretch, considering that the Bible doesn't make these connections. To be sure, we should recognize that medieval church teachings regularly combined saints and biblical figures who shared the same name. Even male saints with the same name could be grouped in this way. For example, three men from three different historical periods with the name Dionysius are venerated as one saint at the abbey of St. Denis in Paris.[20] The practice aided in remembrance, conveyed legacy, and affirmed the communion of saints across generations. While such groupings may explain Mary Magdalene's conflation with Mary of Bethany, they do not cohere with her association with the unnamed sinner woman of Luke 7. This game of telephone is falling apart.

Like other medieval texts about the Christian saints, *The Golden Legend* provides an elaborate backstory for Mary Magdalene that identifies her with wealth and royal lineage. Attributing wealth as well as beauty to Mary Magdalene explains her supposedly dissolute lifestyle. Access to riches led her to become dedicated to "sensuous pleasure." In this rendering, she becomes not a prostitute in need of money but a woman corrupted by wealth who has turned to prostitution. The text also attempts to explain the glaring question, If Mary Magdalene were indeed the woman of Luke 7, why was her name not included in that account? *The Golden Legend* claims that her sensual sins were so great that "her proper name was forgotten and she was commonly called 'the sinner.'"[21] By this reasoning, Mary Magdalene was unnamed in Luke 7 because she was just that sinful.

Although *The Golden Legend* includes the biblical witness, those points of contact are muted. Mary Magdalene is identified not only as the one from whom seven demons are cast out (Luke 8) but also as the sinful, anointing woman *and* Mary of Bethany. Instead of seeing Jesus supporting women on many different occasions, it is as though his energy is focused *only* on Mary Magdalene. Jesus is described as her defender when she is called "unclean" by the Pharisees or "lazy" by her sister Martha or "wasteful" by Judas, even though none of these biblical stories name Mary Magdalene in their accounts. *The Golden Legend* also conflates various New Testament stories in how it depicts Martha the sister, who is identified as the bleeding woman in one case and a dragon-slayer in another.[22] Because Jesus cares so deeply for Mary Magdalene, he therefore heals her sister Martha from her bleeding and brings her brother Lazarus back from the dead. In this rendering, Mary of Bethany is not a separate person; she and Mary Magdalene are one. The bleeding woman is not a separate person; she is Martha. Finally, even when *The Golden Legend* recognizes that Mary Magdalene joined Jesus in his traveling ministry, she is described as

Jesus's house cleaner ("had her do the housekeeping on his travels")![23]

Reading *The Golden Legend* serves as a valuable window into the complex reception of Mary Magdalene that has shaped our remembrance today. All too easily the layers of interpretation actually obscure what she did in Christ's ministry according to Scripture. Through her treatment, we can see a tendency to flatten important women of Scripture into feminine tropes and archetypes and absorb them together in a way that obscures the actual people who ministered alongside Jesus. This treatment of the women of the Bible and women of the church has a long trajectory that manifests even in the life of our churches today.

Unfortunately, the practice of presenting a composite, extrabiblical Mary Magdalene extended well beyond the medieval period and into the twentieth century. Among a superabundance of examples from the historical record, we might look to someone like Dorothy L. Sayers (1893–1957). Sayers was an extraordinary English Anglican novelist, playwright, and lay theologian, and one of the first women to receive a degree from the University of Oxford.[24] Popularly, she's known for her series of detective stories featuring Lord Peter Wimsey, and she was a remarkable woman who enjoyed friendship with C. S. Lewis, J. R. R. Tolkien, and other members of the Inklings.

In *The Man Born to Be King*, which was originally a series of plays written for the radio, Sayers presents her own version of the composite Mary Magdalene. In writing to her producer Val Gielgud, she notes, "I don't care if the critics have said that Mary Magdalen and Mary of Bethany were different people—Church tradition has always made them the same, and [we] can't have all these hopelessly disconnected characters."[25] At another point, Sayers grapples with how best to present Mary Magdalene to children, saying, "Mary Magdalen presents difficulties for the Children's Hour; but since we *must* have her for the Resurrection, I hope the suggestion that she was 'a dancing-girl or something' will sufficiently intimate a reckless way of life to the juveniles; and the grown-ups can supply their own gloss."[26]

Even someone like Sayers struggles to communicate how Mary Magdalene fits into Scripture's redemption story, and this comes from a woman who deeply recognizes the profound care that Jesus showed to women in the Gospel accounts. Lest we forget, Sayers is also celebrated for saying,

> Perhaps it is no wonder that the women were first at the Cradle and last at the Cross. They had never known a man like this Man—there had never been such another. A prophet and teacher who never nagged about them, who never flattered or coaxed or patronized; who never made arch jokes about them, never treated either as "The women, God help us!" or "The ladies, God bless them!"; who rebuked without querulousness and praised without condescension; who took their questions and arguments seriously, who never mapped out their sphere for them, never urged them to be "feminine" or jeered at them for being female; who had no ax to grind and no uneasy male dignity to defend; who took them as he found them and was completely unself-conscious.[27]

Sayers is right that the resurrection means we cannot set aside Mary Magdalene no matter how much discomfort her presence creates. Yet, even so, how do we solve a problem like Mary Magdalene? Conflating her with other biblical characters might have made for clearer radio plays, but these decisions also further obscure the women of the biblical story. Over and over again, the church has needed to return to the sources.

Mary Magdalene and the Reformation

The success of Apollo 8 opened the door for Apollo 11, which included Neil Armstrong's moonwalk. As with Apollo 8, the Christian faith shaped those moments before stepping on the moon, though few knew it at the time. Alongside Armstrong on that mission was astronaut and Presbyterian elder Buzz Aldrin. His pastor at Webster Presbyterian Church in Houston allowed him to bring communion elements with him into space. In the first moments after they landed on the moon on Sunday, July 20, 1969, Aldrin showed his gratitude to God by reading Scripture. Then, as he recounts, "I reached into my personal preference kit and pulled out the communion elements along with a three-by-five card on which I had written the words of Jesus: 'I am the vine, you are the branches. Whoever remains in me, and I in him, will bear much fruit; for you can do nothing without me.' I poured a thimbleful of wine from a sealed plastic container into a small chalice, and waited for the wine to settle down as it swirled in the one-sixth Earth gravity of the moon."[28] Even as he was on the brink of embarking into an unimaginable new frontier of human discovery, Aldrin sought first the foundation of Jesus Christ and the words of Scripture.

He was, in a sense, looking back before stepping out in faith into a new world.

An array of Christians across the generations have worked to draw to light the biblical significance of Mary Magdalene despite the confusion surrounding her. They have looked back at Scripture to sort out her story from the mosaic that formed over the centuries of the Christian tradition.[29] The Protestant Reformation that took place in sixteenth-century Europe played an especially significant role in looking back in order to move ahead.[30]

The same year that Martin Luther published his Ninety-Five Theses and controversy erupted over the Roman Catholic Church's selling of papal indulgences (certificates offering forgiveness of sins), controversy erupted over Mary Magdalene. Renaissance humanism and its commitment to go back to the sources of knowledge (*ad fontes*) had begun to disrupt accepted understandings of Scripture, theology, and Christian practices. Along with that came a disruption in the Western church's understanding of Mary Magdalene.

In France, the study of the Bible was advancing under the pen of Renaissance scholar, theologian, and Bible translator Jacques Lefèvre d'Étaples. He soon began to question the church's reading of Mary Magdalene. Daringly he concluded, in opposition to the Gregorian hermeneutical tradition, that she was not Mary of Bethany nor the sinful woman of Luke 7 nor the unnamed adulteress of John 8. In 1517, the same year Luther nailed his list of grievances on the church door in Wittenberg, Lefèvre published a treatise that sought to remove the extrabiblical legends surrounding Mary Magdalene.[31] He intended to get back to her story as one of the first followers of Christ and a witness to his resurrection. Persecution and censorship followed him thereafter. From that point, two traditions began to emerge in the Western branch of the church on the issue of Mary Magdalene: one Protestant, which distinguished her from the other Marys of the New Testament; and the other Roman Catholic, which persisted in conflating her story with that of others.[32]

Luther, for his part, echoed fifth-century church father Jerome, claiming that Magdalene's name meant "tower" and celebrating her for her strength of faith.[33] Luther went so far as to describe Mary Magdalene as "more valiant than Peter."[34] While preaching, he took time to sort out her story in the Bible, denying that she was the unnamed bride at the wedding of Cana (some had claimed that she married John the Evangelist there).[35] But, as with other parts of his theology, some aspects of the medieval readings of Mary Magdalene persisted for Luther. In 1544, he delivered a sermon on Mary Magdalene's day using the traditional scriptural reading of Luke 7. There he acknowledged (while both tipping his hat to the prescribed lectionary and raising the question) that Mary Magdalene *might* have been the sinful woman who washed Christ's feet with her tears at the banquet.[36] Unconcerned by the lack of clarity, he continued to stress the value of the woman's example of penance and forgiveness of sins "whatever her name is."[37]

By the second wave of the Reformation, Geneva's Reformer John Calvin did not even entertain the idea that Mary Magdalene was connected to the sinful woman of Luke 7. Calvin instead stressed Mark 16's and Luke 8's accounts of Mary Magdalene being saved from seven demons. In Calvin's *Institutes*, military imagery frames the conversation. Demonic activity against Christians is described as combat, ambush, and invasion.[38] Calvin draws on the story of Mary Magdalene. Her freedom from demon possession serves as a counter to the terrible wickedness of the devil, whom Calvin identifies as "God's adversary and ours."[39] He notes that Mary faced the worst evil in being possessed by seven demons, citing the significance of the number seven in reference to Matthew 12:43–45. Lest we think Calvin is singling out Mary Magdalene here, he continues by pointing out that Paul too was harassed by demons, which in Calvin's words are "common to all children of God."[40] He stressed the power of her faith in Christ to resist the devil, who he notes is described in 1 Peter 5:8 as a "roaring lion" prowling in pursuit of someone to devour.[41] To a church that faced persecution in France, many of whose members had fled as refugees to Geneva, Calvin taught that such perseverance was possible only by God's help since faith in Christ alone is what protects souls from Satan's rule.[42] Faith, too, delivered Mary Magdalene by Calvin's estimation.

For the Protestant Reformers, Mary Magdalene came to be celebrated as a model of justification by faith through grace alone. In 1529, when Luther preached about the women at the empty tomb,[43] he described them as pious yet weak. To Luther, their attention to perfumes and ointments for Jesus's body was not so much a mark of their devotion but a reliance on good works rather than listening to Jesus's teaching that he would be raised from the dead. Their actions perfectly illustrated the need to cling to Christ's teachings above works.[44] The women at the tomb came to embody the theology of justification for the Reformers in an accessible way for all Christians.

Nevertheless, both Luther and Calvin grappled with the fact that Christ revealed himself first to Mary Magdalene and the women before the male disciples. In their eyes, this served to shame the male disciples for their lack of faith. Luther draws attention to the unexpected turn of events: "What absurdly foolish men, that this treasure should be preached [first] to the weakest vessel."[45] At the same time, Luther contrasted the physical weakness of the women with the strength of their faith and also described them as "disciples." This was the context for his claim that Mary Magdalene's name means "good strong castle" or "strong tower."[46]

For Calvin, Mary Magdalene's apostolicity gains some credibility.[47] What brought honor to the women (being the first to witness Christ) brought shame to the men, who did not hurry to the tomb like the women. Calvin reasons that Christ commissioned the women "to announce the gospel to the apostles, so as to become their instructors."[48] He explains elsewhere that it was necessary that the apostles, called to proclaim the gospel throughout the world, had first to go to "the school of women."[49] Calvin teaches, as a result, that the women received an apostolic office (though a temporary one) in place of the men: ". . . bestowed on them distinguished honour, by taking away from men the apostolic office, and committing it to them for a short time."[50] This provided a lesson in virtue formation for the male disciples to embrace humility and set aside pride by "submitting to receive the testimony of the women."[51]

Finally, Calvin saw Mary Magdalene's evangelistic commission as "an astonishing instance of goodness."[52] He marvels that God used a woman once possessed by seven demons for such good news.[53] These women may be temporary apostles by his view, but their message was not temporary. When it came to the women's testimony at the empty tomb and before the resurrected Jesus, Calvin taught that submission to the women's testimony was nonnegotiable. Although Calvin did not depict Mary Magdalene as a prostitute, he (along with Luther) did emphasize her lowliness as a way to highlight the power of God. To the male Reformers, God's calling of the lowliest communicated the priesthood of all believers.[54] The constraints on female preaching nonetheless remained in place, even with recognition of Mary Magdalene's temporary apostolicity.

In a sermon on Pentecost (1531), Luther clarifies and acknowledges that "this text truly sets up a new priesthood, that does not depend so much on the person."[55] Yet he continues that, while women may prophesy, console, and teach, they may not preach in public. Calvin similarly declares, "Although women have not authority to teach, and they are not in public office, nonetheless, since God *once wanted* to do it this way—that our Lord Jesus Christ sent them His angel and He especially commanded [the women] to go and proclaim His resurrection to His disciples—let us humble ourselves."[56] For Calvin, the witness of the women was akin to the earthquake that shook when the angel appeared and rolled aside the stone (Matt. 28:2). God was testifying to God's own power, and God's power alone, to resurrect; God was not establishing a new order for the leadership of the church.

But that's not how the women of the Reformation regarded the importance of Mary Magdalene.

Mary Magdalene and the Women Reformers

For the women Reformers, Mary Magdalene was much more than a model of justification by faith and more than a temporary apostle. She gave permission for women to preach the gospel at a time when the male Reformers were still sorting out the implications of their teaching on the priesthood of all believers.[57]

You may not have heard of Marie Dentière before. She was a Reformer's wife and a Reformer in her own right in the city of Geneva during the Reformation. In fact, she is the only woman named on the Reformation wall in Geneva today.[58] Dentière was a woman of noble birth who left her role as abbess at the Augustinian convent in Strasbourg to embrace the Protestant faith in the early 1520s. She became a widow with five children, but remarried, joining her husband in embracing the reform that Geneva started in 1535. In a 1539 letter to Queen Marguerite of Navarre (the godmother of her daughter and sister to the King of France), later given the title *Very Useful Epistle*, Dentière wrote to encourage women to be bold and not fear exile from country and family for the sake of God's Word and the gospel of Jesus Christ.[59] She recounts the state of women in the church before the Reformation, saying, "For until now, scripture has been so hidden from [women]. No one dared to say a word about it, and it seemed that women should not read or hear anything in the holy scriptures."[60] But when she looked to the women of the Bible, she saw a different story.

Dentière included Mary Magdalene among a slew of female biblical paragons in the epistle's defense of women, including Sarah, Rebecca, the mother of Moses, Deborah, Ruth, the Queen of Sheba, and Jesus's mother Mary.[61] There she stressed that the women of Scripture should not be written off for being too bold in God's salvation story. Dentière emphasized that Mary Magdalene was commanded by Jesus himself to preach, and she grouped her in the company of the Samaritan woman, the greatest of women preachers, "who was not ashamed to preach Jesus and his word, confessing him openly before everyone."[62] She stressed the women's faithfulness, though imperfect, saying, "No woman ever sold or betrayed Jesus."[63] Dentière is provocative and bold in identifying the double standard at work: "Do we have two Gospels, one for men and another for women?"[64] She notes, there is only "one mediator, Jesus Christ alone . . . without wavering nor seeking anyone but him, in whom resides all wisdom, prudence, generosity, and virtue."[65] The parable of talents is an interpretive key for her: "For what God has given you and revealed to us women, no more than men should we hide it and bury it in the earth."[66] Herein lies the call to faithful action for reforming women.

Citing female biblical exemplars, Dentière claimed the right for women to engage with Scripture, teach, and preach—openly and to everyone, though at the very least to other women.[67] For Dentière, Christ authorized women to preach, meaning that Mary Magdalene's sending was not temporary. Geneva's leadership did not take kindly to her reading of the biblical text and quickly seized and censured copies of the letter. But there has been a reconciliation of sorts through her inclusion on the Reformation wall.[68]

Another example from the Reformation era deserves our attention. Katharina Schütz Zell was the wife of Strasbourg Reformer Matthew Zell, making her a prominent pastor's wife in the region. After grappling with the sorrow of numerous miscarriages and coming to terms with the hard truth that she would not be able to bear children, Schütz Zell claimed a vocational calling and title of "church mother" for her life of ministry.[69] At her husband's funeral in January 1548, following his thirty-year pastorate, she delivered a sermonic eulogy, which eyewitnesses described as a sermon.[70] She recounted her husband's life and character before including an exposition of the basics of the faith, filled with theology and Scripture. What is most interesting is how she claimed authority to speak at his funeral.[71]

Through the example and precedent set by Mary Magdalene, Schütz Zell pleaded with her listeners, saying, "But first I ask you not to take it wrongly and not to be irritated with me for what I am doing, as if I now wanted to place myself in the office of preachers and apostles: not at all! But it is only as the dear Mary Magdalene without any prior thought *became an apostle* and was charged by the Lord Himself to tell His disciples that the Christ was risen and was ascending to His father and our Father. So I also now speak."[72] She was therefore speaking according to the command that Christ gave to Mary Magdalene and through her authority as the pastor's wife, not to elevate herself but to proclaim the good news: "And so I say today, with and in the place of my dear husband, with Mary

Magdalene, 'The Lord is truly risen and lives for us all! And on the contrary the devil and eternal death have died and are dead to us all and have no further power over all those who are in Christ Jesus.'"[73] In these ways and more, the women Reformers saw the significance of Mary Magdalene's story differently from their male counterparts.

For them, Mary Magdalene's example gave them authority to speak and minister in their communities even as they navigated the boundaries of that ministry in their time. The women of the Bible became especially important for the women of the Reformation in providing permission, insight, and precedent for pushing boundaries. While the male Reformers viewed Mary Magdalene as an exception to the rule or a model of justification by faith,[74] the female Reformers regarded her as a preacher and apostle specifically sent by Christ. The female Reformers serve as a kind of bridge between the medieval celebration of Mary Magdalene's preaching and the Protestant messaging about the inclusion of women among the priesthood of all believers. They were, in fact, walking in the footsteps of their forerunners, the Waldensian women of the thirteenth century who claimed the same and faced the vitriol of the Inquisition for it.[75] By associating their actions with Mary Magdalene's actions, they extended her example to them, beyond just the New Testament. In their view, Mary Magdalene set a precedent ordained by Jesus himself for the enduring life of the church that should be transformative for women evermore. Perhaps the most buried and controversial reading of the legacy of Mary Magdalene came from the women of the Reformation.

When we pay closer attention to the history of women biblical interpreters in the church, we begin to see that the female Reformers' reading of Mary Magdalene extended into the modern era, though often without awareness of that earlier contribution. During the seventeenth century, the cofounders of Quakerism, Margaret Fell and George Fox, both regarded Mary Magdalene as justification for women's public preaching.[76] Later, Harriet Livermore (1788–1868), the daughter of a US congressman and granddaughter of a US senator, was allowed to preach to Congress four times over the course of her itinerant ministry. She referred to Mary Magdalene as a model for female preachers, since she was the first to see Jesus after his resurrection and the first to proclaim that he was risen from the dead.[77]

Though too often forgotten, the apostolicity of Mary Magdalene has been recognized and even appealed to as a basis for women preachers across generations of Christians in Western Christianity. For Protestants who emphasize the authority of Scripture above all, it has proven difficult that Paul doesn't include Mary Magdalene when he recalls the early Christian kerygmatic resurrection in 1 Corinthians 15:3–7. Her absence from that passage is a source of much discussion to this day. Yet, because the Protestant tradition underscores the priesthood of all believers as well as individual Bible reading and evangelism, Mary Magdalene's place in the list of apostles is a live question. Whether her call to preaching Christ gives women the freedom and authority to be called to preach in the church's pulpits is not a new question but an old one.

Meanwhile, shedding Mary Magdalene's connection to prostitution has been difficult. Although the Protestant Reformation sought to untie these threads, the association ran deep and thus continued. During the Victorian era, "Magdalene" became a term for a fallen woman, and evangelicals of the nineteenth century led the Magdalenist movement to rehabilitate prostitutes.[78]

Protestant efforts to distinguish Mary Magdalene from the composite tradition led to the Roman Catholic reinforcement of the traditional legends and grouped biblical readings of Mary Magdalene.[79] Although she had been celebrated as a preacher in the late medieval period,[80] the Catholic Church during the Reformation sought to downplay her apostolicity and preaching role, just as the women Reformers were embracing it. Historian Margaret Arnold explains, "The saint's legendary preaching would become problematic given the dangers opened up by evangelical uses of Mary Magdalene as a figure of divinely empowered lay ministry."[81] As the Catholic Church worked to enclose convents, it began to shy away from emphasizing Mary Magdalene as apostle to the apostles and chose to stress her character as a penitent sinner.

But the year 1969 proved to be a turning point. It was the year not only when humanity first landed on the moon but also when Pope Paul VI reformed the Roman Catholic liturgy surrounding Mary Magdalene through the revision of the General Roman Calendar. Two new frontiers became possible that year. Both held the potential for a new perspective on life and new opportunity, one by retrieving clarity from the past and the other forging ahead to the future. No longer treated as the penitent prostitute, Mary

Magdalene was freed to be celebrated first and foremost as a witness to Christ's resurrection.

On June 3, 2016, Pope Francis elevated Mary Magdalene's day of remembrance or memorial to the ranking of feast day on par with the other apostles. With his words, she was affirmed as "first witness" of the resurrection and "first evangelist" as well as "Apostle to the Apostles" in the tradition of Thomas Aquinas. The liturgy reflects these affirmations by adding a special preface entitled "Apostle to the Apostles" to the Mass: "He appeared in the garden and revealed himself to Mary Magdalene, who had loved him while he was alive, seen him dying on the Cross, sought him as he lay in the tomb, and was the first to adore him, newly risen from the dead. He honoured her with the task of being an apostle to the Apostles, so that the good news of new life might reach the ends of the earth."[82] Five years later, Pope Francis clarified the relationship between Martha, Lazarus, and Mary of Bethany as three siblings deserving to be remembered together on July 29 (prior to his decree, Martha alone was remembered).[83]

The Eastern tradition, meanwhile, has walked a different journey with Mary Magdalene.

Tracing the "Apostle to the Apostles" in the East

There are important points of continuity between the Eastern and the Western traditions when it comes to Mary Magdalene. Both traditions remember her as a preacher and evangelist post-resurrection. Both traditions have recognized her apostolicity, though not always unanimously or consistently. Both traditions have experienced some level of confusion or conflation over her identity. At the heart of the complexity for both the East and the West is the relationship between Mary Magdalene, Mary of Bethany, and Martha.[84] While sorting out Mary Magdalene in the West has historically required understanding her association with or distinction from Mary of Bethany, in the East the question has involved her association with or distinction from Martha. The so-called muddle of Marys is more a muddle of Marys *and* Martha when we look to the Eastern side of the story.[85] Why? Because the East claims Martha's apostolicity as well.

Martha the Apostle?

Although the canonical Gospels do not name Martha among those present at the empty tomb on resurrection morning, a surprising number of early Eastern Christian texts (including early hymns, a sermon, and an Easter liturgy) emphasize Martha's presence.[86] Martha is even typically named first among the Christ anointers (called "myrrhophores") and therefore also associated with apostolicity at the tomb. There are at least seven early Christian images that represent Martha among the anointers. The tradition is evident in Palestine, Asia Minor, Syria, Egypt, and Ethiopia, ranging from the second to the sixth century and beyond. Martha is prominent in Eastern remembrance in a way that does not just add her to the list but elevates her position among the canonical women.[87]

The earliest claim to Martha's remembrance at the tomb of Jesus is found in the *Epistula Apostolorum*, which is an anti-Gnostic text that dates around the early to mid-second century and survives today in a Coptic and Ethiopic extant

97

version, though originally in Greek.[88] Martha is joined by Mary and Mary Magdalene in the *Epistula*; the order of the names, in this case, bears meaning.[89] Biblical scholar Allie Ernst explains: "The tradition of Martha among the women at the tomb might be as ancient as some of the traditions known from the New Testament. Since the four canonical Gospels differ both in the number and the names of the myrrhophores, it is hardly inconceivable that there were further versions circulating, or that one or more such versions should name Martha among the women."[90] Certainly Martha was present at Lazarus's tomb, but was she at Jesus's tomb? Hippolytus of Rome and a wide range of other early Christian texts thought so.

Hippolytus's *Commentary on the Song of Songs* is regarded as the earliest surviving Christian commentary on Scripture, dating from the second to early third century.[91] He describes "Martha and Mary" as the first witnesses of the resurrection.[92] The Mary in this case is thought to be Martha's sister Mary rather than Mary Magdalene, but that is a point of disagreement.[93] Hippolytus gives prominence to Martha by attributing the anointing of Christ to her and identifying her and Mary as primary witnesses of the resurrection to the apostles and therefore "apostles to the apostles."[94] The two were sent to the apostles by Jesus, in the words of the text: "I who appeared to these women to send them also as apostles to you."[95] What can we make of this aspect of the Eastern tradition?

There has been a tendency to downplay the claim of Martha's presence[96] by wondering whether Hippolytus was working from a corrupt text that included Martha at the tomb, whether Martha was being conflated with Mary

Magdalene, or whether the Mary mentioned was actually Mary Magdalene (without the full moniker).[97] As Western biblical scholarship increasingly questions why Martha was given the kerygmatic confession of John 11:27 at all ("Yes, Lord, I believe that you are the Messiah, the Son of God, the one coming into the world"),[98] perhaps there are answers here in this early Eastern textual evidence written at the same time as John's Gospel. As Ernst's work has shown, to keep Martha—the one who comes to be known in the tradition as a "second Peter"[99]—in the margins carries a cost and a loss for understanding early Christianity that requires careful consideration.[100] Though Martha continues to be celebrated and honored in the East as one of those who came to the tomb to anoint Jesus, Mary Magdalene's prominence would prove to be the most significant point of connection between the two branches of the church.

The Orthodox Mary Magdalene

In the Eastern Orthodox tradition, Mary Magdalene comes to be remembered for traveling to Rome after Christ's ascension and Pentecost, where she evangelized Tiberius Caesar.[101] Paul's mention of a "Mary" in Romans 16:6 has been interpreted as a post-Pentecost biblical reference to Mary Magdalene.[102] The prominence of this tradition is evident in Sergei Ivanov's nineteenth-century painting of Mary Magdalene "preaching" to Tiberius that hangs above the iconostasis at the Russian Orthodox Church of Saint Mary Magdalene located on the slope of the Mount of Olives in the Garden of Gethsemane.[103] She holds a red egg, signifying the new life of Christ's resurrection, which turns red in her hand to prove the truth of her testimony while declaring, "Christos Anesti!" (Christ is risen!). The practice continues today in the breaking of the Lenten fast so that she is celebrated among the myrrhophore *and* is preacher-evangelist of the gospel. To mark her importance, Greek Orthodox prayers on Mary Magdalene's feast day of July 22 refer to her as "equal-to-the-apostles."[104]

The Eastern Orthodox tradition recounts the traveling ministry of Mary Magdalene after Pentecost as well as her final days in Ephesus.[105] Her connection to Ephesus traces back to Gregory of Tours in the sixth century and is recounted in the *Synaxarion of Constantinople* (tenth century), which lists the feast days and saints for the Eastern Orthodox Church.[106] It is claimed that Mary Magdalene traveled there with John the Evangelist where she lived out the remainder of her days alongside the Virgin Mary.

In the West, the pairing of Mary Magdalene and John the Evangelist was commonplace. *The Golden Legend* taught that Mary Magdalene was engaged to John the Evangelist when Jesus called him to abandon his wedding.[107] A kind of scorned-lover scenario unfolds, leading Mary Magdalene to abandon herself to dissolute living. By the Reformation, Martin Luther reflects on the teachings of Bonaventure that the bride and bridegroom at the wedding at Cana were Mary Magdalene and John the Evangelist.[108] Both traditions recognize the way in which John's Gospel seems to elevate the presence and role of Mary Magdalene and try to define her relationship to John directly as a result. If Bonaventure was right, John would have been writing about his would-be wife!

Meanwhile, the Orthodox church marks her burial at the entrance to the cave of the Seven Sleepers according to Modestos, the seventh-century patriarch of Jerusalem.[109] Tradition tracks the transference of her relics in the tenth century to Constantinople at the monastery of St. Lazaros.[110] And this is where it gets interesting.

Surprisingly, a range of evidence indicates that Mary Magdalene did not truly gain prominence in the Byzantine church until the late twelfth century.[111] Before then, her life had been excluded from a popular collection of saints' lives (*Metaphrastian Menologion*); churches were not dedicated to her memory in the Byzantine empire; portraits of her were either limited or lacking; and the presence of her relics in Constantinople during the Crusaders' sack of 1204 went undocumented. Scholar Vassiliki Foskolou makes the case: "It is clear that the Magdalene did not play a particularly important role in the religious life of Constantinople in the middle Byzantine period, either as saintly figure or on account of her relics. . . . She seems to have remained a rather obscure saint in Byzantium."[112] What changed?

Nikephoros Kallistos Xanthopoulos, a cleric of the patriarch in Constantinople during the thirteenth and fourteenth centuries, wrote an important homily dedicated to Mary Magdalene. Not coincidentally, this occurred as Western Christendom was elevating her memory and claiming her relics. A tug-of-war over Mary Magdalene's relics and therefore apostolicity ensued. Xanthopoulos was seeking to reclaim and revive the cult of relics that had been plundered by Western Christians after the Fourth Crusade.[113] And so the Orthodox Mary Magdalene was born, intentionally fashioned, it seems, to differentiate from the Western tradition's composite Mary Magdalene.[114] Constantinople's recapture from Western Crusaders was the setting and Mary Magdalene the contested ground.[115]

Continuity, meanwhile, is seen across traditions, with the belief that Mary Magdalene was on the move after Christ's ascension. Xanthopoulos describes her apostolic missions and travel to Ephesus. Other traditions followed, linking her to the Greek island of Zakynthos, France, Italy, Egypt, Phoenicia, Syria, and Pamphylia.[116] As will be seen in the next chapter, the Roman Catholic tradition would claim that Mary Magdalene left Jerusalem for Roman Gaul, or modern-day France, to preach and evangelize the people there. In this version, she is joined by Lazarus and Martha and believed to have lived out the remainder of her life in southern France as a holy recluse. Both traditions have understood that being an apostle included first serving as a witness and then bearing witness. To the church, it has been important not only that she proclaimed Jesus's message to the remaining disciples but that she continued to preach that message beyond. Join me in France!

FOUR

France's Beloved
Preacher and Evangelist

An Apostolic Lineage

One summer, our family lived in Provence in the south
of France. As you might suspect, our time there was less
celebrity yachts and Cannes film festival premieres (as in,
not at all!) and more library archives, churches, historical
sites, and lavender fields.[1] We loved every second. Coming
from America, we reveled in the region's many layers of
history. As it turns out, one of the prime destinations for
celebrity sightings, fashion, and luxury vacations remains
a touchstone for some of Western Christianity's earliest
history. Paris alone is enough reason to head to France,
but is Mary Magdalene another compelling reason? Few
of us outside the country would associate her with France.

But Mary Magdalene matters immensely to France,
in the south especially. She is remembered as the first

evangelist of France, and by that account, she represents France's claim to apostolic succession. To this day, she is so well ingrained in the cultural memory and identity of southern France that if you mention Mary, they will assume you mean Mary Magdalene rather than the Virgin Mary.

The importance of apostolic lineage was first developed by the early Christian bishop Irenaeus of Lyon in his effort to strengthen the church against early Christian heresies (such as Gnosticism). He contended that faithful teaching of the church was passed down directly from Jesus to the apostles and on through the succession of bishops. It is a historical claim that declares, in a manner of speaking, What we have received from him, we pass on to you.[2] Irenaeus is remembered as a disciple of Polycarp, who was a disciple of John the apostle, Jesus's disciple.[3] Interestingly, John's first epistle also stresses the importance of eyewitness accounts in rooting the claims of Christianity (1 John 1:1–3). The reference talks about seeing Christ, hearing Christ, and touching Christ. In France's case, Mary Magdalene became that apostolic link who saw, heard, and touched Christ.

Many churches worldwide have traced their Christian origins and legitimacy back to an early traveling evangelist. Christians in India, for example, attribute their apostolic lineage to the apostle Thomas. The Mar Thoma Syrian Church claims this heritage in southern India to this day. This practice recognizes the ways in which regional churches' biblical roots of authority reach back to Christ, and such claims are certainly plausible given the expansive geographical reach of the Roman Empire and the routes of travel available at the time. In France's case, association with Mary Magdalene deserves our attention and consideration, especially given that both the Eastern and Western traditions remember Mary Magdalene at this juncture as a missionary traveler, preacher, and evangelizer. Christ's sending of her, in the church's mind, was more than delivering a message but embarking on a mission as a witness to the good news.[4] Where did she go? Was her departure linked to Pentecost? The biblical text does not specify.

Luke's Gospel indicates that it was not just a few or some but "many" women (Mary Magdalene the first of several named) who traveled with Jesus from Galilee to Jerusalem (Luke 8:3). Luke 24 recounts how Mary Magdalene and the other women returned to tell the eleven and others about Christ's resurrection (vv. 9–10). While they were gathered together (v. 33 specifies "the eleven and companions"), Jesus appeared and declared to them that they are the "witnesses of these things" and to await the coming of the Holy Spirit (24:48–49). Luke continues the account in Acts 1. Later, Paul echoes this account in his sermon from Antioch in Pisidia, declaring, "For many days he appeared to those who came up with him from Galilee to Jerusalem, and they are now his witnesses to the people" (Acts 13:31).[5] And Mary Magdalene was prominent among them.

That's probably why it is surprising that she is not named in Acts 1:14 as present in the upper room prior to Pentecost (though Jesus's mother Mary is named). Mary Magdalene is possibly assumed to be among the "certain women" recognized as present. We would certainly expect her to be there, but we would also expect her to be named. Biblical scholar Beverly Gaventa explains how Luke's specific wording that "these all were persisting together" (Acts 1:14) was a repeated phrase he used to emphasize the unity of the Jerusalem community, which included the women from Galilee.[6] Acts 1–2 attests to the presence of the women and as equal recipients of the Holy Spirit in fulfillment of the Joel 2 prophecy. The circles of preaching, healing, gathering, and ministering in Jesus's name gain momentum after Pentecost, fueled by the Holy Spirit. Mary Magdalene is remembered by the church as part of that expanding geography and demography of Christ's post-ascension ministry, despite questions surrounding her presence at Pentecost.[7]

Mary Magdalene's departure from Jerusalem is not hard to imagine as there was certainly a flurry of travel among Jesus's followers after Pentecost. Given her role at the resurrection and the importance of her testimony, she would have been a target of persecution. She was, after all, ridiculed by second-century Greek philosopher Celsus for bearing "hysterical" witness to the resurrection, which signals that her significance became widely known and recognized early on.[8] The Eastern church identifies Paul's mention of a Mary in Romans 16:6 as a reference to Mary Magdalene, which would place her among those ministering in Rome. Importantly, both branches associate her with missionary travel, but the Western tradition situates the postbiblical portion of her life in France.

The eighth-century church contributed to the formalizing of Mary Magdalene's remembrance in Western church life. Venerable Bede's martyrology, for example, established her feast day on July 22 (observed to this day), according to the Byzantine tradition.[9] Liturgy, prayers, and sermons began to fill medieval worship. During the ninth century, a biography emerged from Charlemagne's court attributed to scholar Rabanus Maurus, who traced details of Magdalene's expulsion from Jerusalem and travel to the south of France with Martha and Lazarus.[10] He recounts them preaching, converting, and performing miracles. Mary Magdalene's withdrawal to an ascetic, contemplative life in the environs of Aix-en-Provence according to Maurus mirrors the monastic developments of the period. There she was miraculously provided for by angels lifting her to the heavens each day, nourishing her with the Eucharist.

Meanwhile, miracles associated with her relics multiplied in Marseille. Her relics, and her legacy with them, were formally transferred to Vézelay Abbey in Burgundy. The apostolic claims of France were deepened by this move. By the eleventh century, the church of Vézelay came under the reforming wing of Cluny, and the church's patronage shifted from the Virgin Mary to Mary Magdalene, with papal approval following.[11] A Cistercian version of Mary Magdalene treated her as a model for the life of contemplation and reform, elevated in station by Jesus himself from reformed sinner to apostle (specifically as the apostle to the apostles).[12] Historian Margaret Arnold describes the "multiplicity of Magdalenes" that developed from medieval legend and liturgical remembrance as evidence of a rich popularity and accessibility in contrast with the almost ethereal Virgin Mary: "Mary Magdalene, on the other hand, offered the hopeful example of an ordinary woman, even one with a sinful past, who had renounced the flesh for contemplation and pious attachment to Christ."[13] The Mendicant version of Mary Magdalene particularly stressed her preaching, which suited a movement of preaching orders.[14] In striking ways, her story came to mirror the arc of the church's story, points out Arnold: "Her progress from sinner to penitent, from prodigal to ascetic, from witness to missionary, describes the arc of the church's founding narrative."[15] Through the eyes of France, Mary Magdalene came to be without question the most significant female preacher and evangelist in Western Christian memory.

By the thirteenth century, Mary Magdalene's story and her relics were repositioned to Aix-en-Provence. *The Golden Legend* reflects that shift in a number of ways, including by recounting how Peter left Mary Magdalene in the care of Maximin, described as one of the seventy-two disciples sent by Jesus.[16] Under threat of persecution, she was herded onto a rudderless boat along with Maximin, her brother Lazarus, her sister Martha, and Martha's maid Martilla, and guided by God's will alone to land at Marseille. To be sure, considerable variation on this story exists, which is cause for confusion.

My family and I visited the church at Les-Saintes-Maries-de-la-Mer, which dates back to the ninth century and is purported to mark where she disembarked on the southern coast of Gaul near Arles. She is described there as among "Three Marys" along with Mary of Jacob, Salome, or Cleopas (the trio varies but also echoes the names of some of the seven Eastern Orthodox myrrhophores). Interestingly, a maid named Sarah is included, which connects with an early Ethiopic version of the *Epistula* that names a mysterious Sarah as the first alongside Mary Magdalene and Martha at the resurrection tomb.[17] The list of names truly varies depending on the site and source. There is agreement, however, that she set out to evangelize the towns of Marseille and Aix, preaching Christ all the way to the governor of the province.[18] The destruction of temples and idols was followed by the building of churches in Marseille. Lazarus was elected bishop of Marseille, and the same evangelism came to Aix where Maximin was elected bishop. Mary Magdalene then withdrew to a cave in the wilderness for thirty years to live as a hermit.[19]

And so, France came to claim Mary Magdalene by remembering her as more than a witness to the resurrection but also a missionary, preacher, and evangelist to France as well as a model of the contemplative, severely ascetic, and hermitic pious life.[20] To this day, her story is linked to the area known as Saint-Maximin-la-Sainte-Baume.

Bienvenue to La Sainte-Baume

Curious to learn more about her remembrance in France, our family visited the town of Saint-Maximin-la-Sainte-Baume (near Aix-en-Provence) to see the immense Basilique Sainte Marie Madeleine, where her relics are housed. Upon entry, we headed to a side chapel and stumbled upon an altar with an inconspicuous bas-relief on gilt wood dating to 1536. The artist John Beguin took four panels to capture the life of Mary Magdalene. By his handiwork, she is depicted first as a disciple and follower, hearing and receiving the teaching of Jesus in Jerusalem. In the next scene, she offers her devotion to Jesus by washing his feet during a meal (a nod to her association with Mary of Bethany). She then encounters the risen Lord in the garden as the first witness to the resurrection. In the final panel, she leaves the Holy Land for the shores of France as a Roman soldier nearly overtakes her boat as it is casting off. When grouped together, the touchstones reflect the fullness of her discipleship as student, follower, witness, and preacher. This is France's apostle.

From there we headed ten miles outside the town of Saint-Maximin-la-Sainte-Baume on the winding, bumpy, and narrow roads in the forest of Sainte-Baume. My heart was set on visiting the mountain cave church called Grotto de Sainte Marie-Madeleine that overlooks the valley and is considered one of the most important churches to remember Mary Magdalene. What would we encounter?

We climbed up the mountain by way of the steep terrain called Chemin des Rois.[21] Five hundred years before us, the court of King Francis I had taken an official pilgrimage there. We were literally walking in the way of the kings. But it was hot—dripping-down-your-back hot. The sun was beating down. The air was thick. When our five-year-old got too tired, my husband hitched him onto his back. No one would have mistaken our family of five for seasoned hikers or even typical pilgrims. Of course, we laughed and groaned along the way. "How much longer?" might have been asked once or twice. "It's going to be worth it," I kept saying. We were about to discover if I was right.

The site is considered holy because Mary Magdalene is believed to have lived out the remainder of her life in the cave of Sainte-Baume after evangelizing the region (though this account conflicts with the Eastern Orthodox tradition). In the ninth century, the mountain cave became more central in the Western church's account of Mary Magdalene after two popes visited. Their visits occurred in the years immediately after the crowning of Charlemagne as Holy Roman Emperor in 800. The Western church was reclaiming its identity following the fall of the Western Roman Empire and the apostolic heritage that came with that.[22] The Holy Roman Empire was looking to Mary Magdalene to root its Christian lineage to the apostolic tradition reaching directly back to Jesus Christ.

As we crested part of the mountain and walked out onto the esplanade of the Grotto to overlook the breathtaking view, our eyes immediately fell upon the magnificent, life-size, bronze Pietà statue by Marthe Spitzer.[23] A classic Pietà captures the particular grief that Mary, as the mother of Jesus, experienced after Christ's dead body was taken down from the cross (called the Deposition of Christ). In a Pietà arrangement, she holds his body in her arms with a profound sorrow. The viewer is invited to observe her grief and to empathize with the motherly pain of losing her son. The Pietà reminds Christians that Jesus actually died.

But Spitzer's version of the Pietà offers a different glimpse of the moment.[24] This version includes Mary Magdalene, who is kneeling and weeping at the foot of Christ as Mother Mary holds his limp body. Art historian Vassiliki Foskolou explains how Mary Magdalene's veneration of the crucified Christ is not a feature of Byzantine iconography but one that enters art history with the mendicant orders.[25] In this way, the image is right at home. The expression of Mary Magdalene's love for Christ is evident in the positioning of her body kneeling before mother and son as she buries her face into his garments. To look at Mary Magdalene in her devastation is to recognize a grief that is more accessible since it comes from one of his followers. Her presence makes it clear that she has not deserted him, even in the most hopeless moment after his death. All that is left is burial, and yet she grasps hold of her faith in Christ as she grasps hold of his dead body. She touches him, as 1 John 1 reminds us.

The statue also underscores the beautifully intertwined stories of Mother Mary and Mary Magdalene. To consider the two together moves our hearts and minds from the cradle to the tomb, where both women tended to the physical body of Jesus in its most vulnerable moments at the beginning and end of life. One can imagine how they held, touched, cleaned, and cared for Jesus Christ's actual body. Seventeenth-century German writer Catharina Regina von Greiffenberg reflects on this pairing, concluding, "The salvific seed of woman did not reject women, refusing to be served by them. Since he dignified them by his own being made flesh of a woman, he therefore also found them worthy to witness his death. He wanted to begin his life emerging from this sex and to end it in their company."[26] God willingly gave himself over to these women, who saw firsthand the surprising and breathtaking expression of God's power incarnate in those helpless moments of human life: birth and death. To include both biblical women in the Pietà was a way to represent the fullness of the gospel that is too easily missed when Marys are conflated, isolated, or treated as rivals. So much good theology is possible when the Marys are paired.

And with that, we stepped inside.

The mountain cave church remembers Mary Magdalene with seven stunning stained-glass windows completed in the 1970s and '80s. The biblical texts and theological themes depicted in the windows reflect an ongoing association of Mary of Bethany with Mary Magdalene, which means that Sainte-Baume follows the medieval Western account that Mary Magdalene was the sister of Lazarus and Martha. Her identification with the sinful woman of Luke 7 also persists.

Among the biblical accounts that are rendered, the second window highlights John 20:14–18, which suggests Mary Magdalene is the first disciple to encounter the risen Lord. The French church favors this passage no doubt because it underscores that Mary is not only the first witness but also the first to touch the risen Lord (often translated, "Do not touch me," but better understood as clinging). Her touch is among the reasons for her status as an apostle (1 John 1).[27]

Each stained-glass window celebrates Mary Magdalene as an exemplar of Christian discipleship. The third window invites us to see how Jesus's words from John 7:37–38 apply to her story: "Let anyone who is thirsty come to me, and let the one who believes in me drink." She drank of the living water that Christ offered. She longed to be filled and believed, and Christ welcomed her into his ministry.

Three of the windows appear to attribute the stories of Mary of Bethany to Mary Magdalene: the anointing of Jesus at Bethany, the resurrection of Lazarus, and the meal at Bethany. In John's Gospel the meal foreshadows Jesus's death on the cross. Judas and Lazarus are depicted as onlookers with two very different responses: disapproving and approving. The careful reader of Scripture will nonetheless recognize some confusion here that goes beyond artistic license. The John 12 account, for example, teaches that Mary of Bethany anointed Jesus's feet with perfume, though the window presents a priestly anointing as on his head. Again, her touch and care for Jesus's body underscores her apostolicity.

Meanwhile, the identification of Mary Magdalene with the meal at Bethany signifies her commitment to grow in knowledge of Christ's teachings. She is the one who sits at Jesus's feet, choosing "the better part" (Luke 10:42). We should again read this interpretation through the lens of her apostolic status: in that moment we see her receive the teachings of Christ directly, and what is received is passed down. We can trust her witness because she has learned from Christ himself.

When treated as the sister of Lazarus, she also becomes the witness to Lazarus's resurrection before she witnesses Christ's resurrection. The church reads her in the place of Mary of Bethany and from this story confirms her affectionate disposition. She kneels before Jesus and declares her faith in him. "Lord, if you had been here, my brother would not have died," she says while weeping. Jesus was greatly moved by her devotion and disturbed in his spirit to the point that he began to weep (John 11:32–35). The weeping Mary Magdalene is well remembered in the history of Christianity, and not only with Lazarus's death but also with Christ's. The final homage to Mary Magdalene connects her story to the anointing of Jesus's feet as the anonymous sinner woman of Luke 7. In these ways, the mountain cave church maintains the Western medieval reading of her life for the contemporary church.

Mary Magdalene's importance for the church in France persists.[28] Interestingly, both the Western and Eastern churches' accounts of Mary Magdalene's last days reflect how the monastic life had come to be seen as the ultimate expression of Christian devotion. Through medieval eyes, Mary Magdalene is transformed into the exemplary hermit who withdraws from the world and lives only on the sustenance provided by God's intervention. Medieval stories about her life in the cave of Sainte-Baume resonate closely with prophets such as Elijah in 1 Kings 17:6 and the supernatural provision of food and shelter. In France, the historic remembrance of her moves from identifying her as a disciple of Jesus and apostle, then as a preacher and evangelist, and finally as an ascetic hermit.

Our family took seriously our time in the cave. To be in that place was to be drawn to remember Mary Magdalene, to consider her story more carefully according to the biblical accounts, to ponder her role in the history of the church, particularly in France. Although we could not be certain that Mary Magdalene lived out the remainder of her life at Sainte-Baume, as claimed, we certainly worshiped the Lord there with our minds and our hearts. The experience pushed us to probe further: What is happening when we go to holy places connected to Christian history? How can a trip like this encourage our faith in Christ, even with the uncertainty of the facts?

Fostering Spiritual Remembrance

After our arduous hike up to the cave, we were approached by a volunteer providing hospitality on behalf of the Dominicans. As he handed out water, we shared pleasantries in French. When I mentioned that we were coming from Chicago, he looked at me with astonishment. "How did you know about this place?" He apparently never expected to see American tourists taking time to explore this obscure religious site. We were well off the beaten path. All the informational signs were in French, I noticed. I just smiled and answered matter-of-factly, "Nous sommes Chrétiennes" (We are Christians), but I meant so much more than that.

For me to say "We are Christians" was a kind of declaration that we are spiritually joined together in Christ. Ephesians 2 gets at this marvelous connection by declaring that through the blood of Christ Jesus we are reborn so that we are no longer strangers or aliens to one another but members of the household of God. The passage is illuminating when we consider that place in France and the very next verse: "built upon the foundation of the apostles and prophets, with Christ Jesus himself as the cornerstone" (Eph. 2:20). We are being "joined together" (v. 21) as a holy temple where God's presence dwells. Through Christ drawing near and drawing us near (we "who once were far off," v. 13), we have come near to one another.

The memory of a family is greater than one individual, and so too our individual memories are made greater than ourselves by receiving God's story and the story of God's "family of faith" (Gal. 6:10). Just as the story of a family household expands with each new member, so too our stories become intertwined with the communion of saints, including the apostle Mary Magdalene, in such a way that our stories cannot be untangled. This can be difficult to comprehend and to live out daily, but it starts with cultivating spiritual remembrance.

The act and necessity of spiritual remembrance ties us together even as we recognize that different Christian traditions practice remembrance in different ways. Some readers may be all too familiar with pilgrimage and everything that is included with it: shrines, relics, and the iconography of saints. Pilgrimage values the sacredness of places and the role of the senses in forming one's faith. For others, remembrance may be exclusively or primarily cultivated through reading and reflecting on Scripture as the first and final authority for forming our minds (Col. 3:2). Wherever your convictions may fall in this regard, remembrance is not something that Christians should take lightly, especially when we recognize the integral role that remembrance plays in our covenantal relationship with God.

Scripture declares over and over that God remembers us. The Creator of time and all things in heaven and on earth remembers each of us. Jesus declares in Matthew that God cares for us so much that he even knows how many hairs we have on our head (Matt. 10:30). Psalm 8 grapples with the imbalance of this undeserved love: Who are we that you would remember us, O God? Just as God's words brought this world into being, so God's remembrance of us sustains our very lives. In fact, to be forgotten by God is equated with death in Psalm 88:5: "like those whom you remember no more."

In Scripture, God's mindfulness of his people is a mark of his blessing (Ps. 115:12). To be remembered by God is to receive his lovingkindness and faithfulness (Pss. 98:3; 136:23). The psalms testify to a God who does not forget those who suffer (Ps. 9:12, 18). God's remembrance of us began before we knew ourselves, when we were knit together in our mother's womb (Ps. 139:13–16), and it extends even beyond the time when our memory fails us in our final years. With the psalmist, we may ask, "Where can I go from your spirit? Or where can I flee from your presence? If I ascend to heaven, you are there; if I make my bed in Sheol, you are there" (Ps. 139:7–8). In Genesis, when God remembered Noah and the animals, the water receded (Gen. 8:1). God remembered Rachel at her most desperate point (Gen. 30:22). In Isaiah, God's remembrance is even greater than that of a pregnant woman to the child in her womb or a nursing mother to the child at her breast: "Even these might forget, yet I will not forget you" (Isa. 49:15). We follow a God who is quick to remember to save and slow to remember our sins against us (Isa. 43:25; Heb. 8:12; 10:17). That remembrance continues in the New Testament with Jesus, who remembers us in prayer (John 17:20; Heb. 7:25). Did you know Jesus prays for you? There is simply no height or depth that can obstruct God's love from reaching us (Rom. 8:39). God's faithful remembrance is the stuff that preserves our lives; it is covenantal (Gen. 9:15–16; Exod. 2:24; 6:5; Lev. 26).

Cultivating spiritual remembrance in the Christian life can powerfully shape our understanding of both ourselves and God (Ps. 63:6). A quick look at Deuteronomy reveals an overabundance of reminders to remember God's covenant with his people. But to see this as punitive or nagging is to miss the true intention. To reflect on God's covenant is to remember that God is relentlessly faithful and gracious. Our God is a just God who saves his people from bondage. Our God is unchanging in benevolence toward each generation. Our God is the God of Abraham, Isaac, and Jacob. How he has been, so he will be.

The most breathtaking expression of this benevolence is revealed at the cross and the empty tomb. Our new covenant is sealed by the blood of Jesus Christ, shed for the remission of our sins. Our faith is rooted in the one who is fully God and fully human, Jesus Christ, who is the same yesterday, today, and forever (Heb. 13:8), and he commands us to remember him when we accept the bread and the cup in communion with one another. Though disagreement reigns over what exactly happens in that moment, even so, all Christians can lean into Jesus's own instructions to "do this in remembrance of me" (Luke 22:19). The promise proclaimed and the promise represented in that communion moment are markers that invite our bodies to feel and experience in a tangible way the nourishing promises that Christ truly offers to us. Remembrance here is the maturation of our faith from milk to solid food (1 Cor. 3:2). With open hands and hearts, we receive the bread and the cup as an act (at least!) of spiritual remembrance that Christ died for us, lives for us, and reigns in power for us until he comes again. We do this in fellowship with one another and in response to the teaching of God's Word. Remembrance is a key part of our worship together as Christians.

Remembrance is also eschatological. When we remember God, we also look to the eternal promise that we have been given through Christ's bodily resurrection (Rom. 8:10–11). It is like turning your head both ways before crossing the street. We look to the past and to the future because of the promise of fellowship with one another as brothers and sisters in Christ. This is how I understand Jesus's own words, commending us to remember "her" (Matt. 26:13; Mark 14:9). Three Gospel women go unnamed as they anoint Jesus's head or feet with perfume. In Mark, the act angers the disciples, but Jesus comes to her defense, saying, "Let her alone!" (Mark 14:6). It would be nice to know for sure who she was, but it may also be a blessing that she is not named here so that remembering her is an invitation (even permission!) to remember women who have shown their devotion to Christ no matter who they are. Jesus honors her act by investing it with a meaning that went beyond her own understanding. She was devoutly preparing his body for burial, and this was a prophetic act. The Son of God gives over his body to the preparations of womanly hands in a way that is integral to the good news of Christ's birth, death, and resurrection: "Wherever this good news is proclaimed in the whole world, what she has done will be told in remembrance of her" (Matt. 26:13). Our remembrance of her has become tied to our remembrance of Jesus Christ by Christ's own prediction.

But our remembrance can also be imperfect. To remember rightly is complex. After all, we see through a glass dimly in the here and now (1 Cor. 13:12). Some things are forgotten that should not be forgotten or distorted that should not be distorted. We can also misremember in such a way that diminishes or exaggerates. There can be a blurred line between mementos, historical artifacts, and relics, which can too easily become focal points that distract from the true power at work in our lives.

I experienced this hesitation when we entered the crypt that held Mary Magdalene's relics in Sainte-Baume near the mountain cave church. It was dark, cool, and cramped as our family descended into the crypt. The kids immediately quieted down, sensing something serious afoot. We peered through the glass and the ornate golden reliquary. It took a second, and then we all realized that we were looking at a skull. We had been discovering Mary Magdalene together as a family, and she was so humanized to us by this experience that coming face-to-face with the skull was a jolt. We exited the crypt, feeling as though we had seen something very private. Setting aside the question of its authenticity, what did it mean to see her skull?[29] I paused to ruminate over my mix of emotions and thoughts.

Colloquially, the word "relic" has a complex connotation today. It typically signifies something that is past due, aged, void of value and impact. But that is the exact opposite of its original meaning. In Western medieval Christianity, relics gained prominence as objects invested with the holiness of a saint by association. They became treated as vehicles for transferring holiness first by touch and then by sight, and there is scriptural precedent for that. Jesus's healing of the bleeding woman (Matt. 9:20–22; Mark 5:25–34; Luke 8:43–48) is one reason the practice developed as it did, but we can also see this dynamic at work in Acts 19:12, which recounts the healing power of even handkerchiefs touched by Paul.

During the Protestant Reformation, the Reformers were critical of relics. By that time, it was well known that a relics industry and black market were thriving in the shadows of the church. In Calvin's *Treatise on Relics*, he wrote the following about the skull of Mary Magdalene: "The same thing may be said of the head of Mary Magdalene, which is shown near Marseilles, with eyes of paste or wax. It is valued as much as if it were God himself who had descended from heaven; but if it were examined, the imposition would be clearly detected."[30] Calvin's comment reflects the concern of the Reformers with an industry abusing popular piety and encouraging faith practices that had come to invest too much power in material objects to the point of displacing the true mediatory power of Jesus Christ. Passive vehicles of God's power were becoming identified as agents of God's power, and this was shunned as idolatry. He continues with skepticism by pointing out the conflicting claims of holding the authentic bodies of Mary Magdalene and Lazarus, saying, "Of their numerous relics scattered over the world I shall not speak. I would merely inquire whether Lazarus and his sisters ever went to preach in France; for those who have read the accounts given by ancient historians of those times cannot fail to be convinced of the folly of this fable."[31]

We've come a long way since the Reformation, but the temptation of idols remains. What relics get right is the importance of the act of remembrance as members of the body of Christ, but faithful remembrance only bears fruit when it strengthens our union with Christ and points us back to the revelation of God's Word.

Through remembrance (in Scripture and in a visit to France), we can take seriously our bond with Mary Magdalene among the communion of saints, along with everything that she has meant for the Christian faith—but ultimately our goal is not just to look *at* her but to look *with* her at the risen Lord Jesus Christ and to run with her to share the good news of Christ's resurrection.

See. Touch. Hear. Run!

Think again on the words of 1 John 1. Jesus's followers saw Christ with their very own eyes, touched him with their very own hands, heard his voice with their very own ears. This matches Mary Magdalene's experience. The apostolic witness to the incarnate and resurrected Lord has been faithfully handed down and written down for us by the inspiration of the Holy Spirit that we too might see, touch, hear, and run with the revelation of God's beloved Son. For when we receive Christ, we also enter into fellowship with all those who proclaim him, including the apostle Mary Magdalene: "What we have seen and heard we also declare to you so that you also may have fellowship with us, and truly our fellowship is with the Father and with his Son Jesus Christ" (1 John 1:3). Then we are called to "remember the words previously spoken by the apostles of our Lord Jesus Christ" (Jude 1:17). When we accept Christ, we are counted among those who have not seen him but love him and believe in him (1 Pet. 1:8), so that the communion we share with the saints is more than just our church or even our branch of the church. Our communion with one another in Christ is timeless and invisible just as it is local, contextual, and tangible.

I experienced this in a powerful way during a visit to the National Library of France in Paris. The archive in the city is massive, spanning areas both above and below ground. It is also notoriously bureaucratic, and securing access is elaborate and expensive. There are multiple security measures in place. You walk down numerous staircases and are screened from head to toe. After interviewing for access, you take an elevator down to an escalator. You traverse long and longer hallways. Another staircase awaits, leading to another elevator that takes you up until you have no idea how you got where you are.

Assigned seating is the custom, and there are forms to sign for photo permissions. Then you wait for the books to be brought to you. For some time, the same archivist brought me one French Bible after another. She was from French-speaking Africa. One day, she shyly whispered to me in French, pointing to herself and saying "Evangelique," which means "French Protestant." She looked quizzically at me, pausing, cautious, wondering. I knew exactly what she meant and I knew what courage it took for her to dare to ask me that. She was saying, "I follow Jesus Christ. Do you?" I instantly and exuberantly responded, "Moi aussi!," meaning "Me too!" To my utter amazement, with scholars and archivists around us in this dead-quiet room, she hugged me.

We were two followers of Christ, strangers to each other, yet gripping each other's hands and smiling at one another like long-lost friends. I asked her how she knew to approach me. She said, "No one looks at these Bibles." Scripture had led us to recognize each other, and it felt as though we already knew each other because we knew Christ as Lord.

The communion we share with others who confess Christ is a global communion extending into every direction and reaching into every age. This communion (even if we don't acknowledge or recognize it!) exists not by our own power or effort but through the One who entered time and space for us and gathered us to himself and each other by the power of the Holy Spirit despite our differences (Gal. 3:28; 1 Cor. 12).

If remembrance is key, it's important that we remember rightly insofar as it is possible. The certainty that we long for cannot always be settled by the claims of historical sites. We must turn to God's revelation in Scripture to look more closely for Mary Magdalene in the Gospels.

FIVE

A Woman Possessed— and Healed

A Real Dilemma

"Was Mary Magdalene a prostitute?" I was dropping off my daughter at ballet, and without context, point-blank and out of the blue, another mom asked me this question in the hallway (because they know me there). I responded quickly, "Not according to how the Gospels introduce her." She seemed relieved.

Then I added, "Actually, she was demon possessed!" (Luke 8:2). Her face fell, and I nodded sympathetically. It was as if we were both asking, Well, what do we do with *that*?

It's a dilemma for our churches: if we strip Mary Magdalene of her association with prostitution, we still have to address her demon possession. It's a barrier in the pulpit, it's a barrier to the Bible commentaries (I can't tell you how many avoid explaining what that means!), it's a barrier at Bible study, it's a barrier at Vacation Bible School, and it's a barrier in our own devotional reading. The truth is that when we retrieve Mary Magdalene's story from the biblical text and away from the tropes that confuse and mislead, some questions are answered but others are raised. Scripture is clear that she was possessed by demons and that she was healed by Jesus. It's part of her story. So, what do we make of Mary Magdalene's demon possession?

Today, Christians in the modern West are alienated from biblical accounts of demons and spiritual warfare. We are more likely to be informed by popular depictions of demonic activity from shows such as *Stranger Things* or, for an earlier generation, *Buffy the Vampire Slayer*. I was a child when the book *This Present Darkness* swept across the evangelical world, shaping imaginations about spiritual warfare. Readers of that time were fascinated with angel stories, which gave way to a slew of controversial books about heaven.[1] It can be hard to know how to evaluate claims of supernatural encounters or experiences, even when reading them in the Bible.

While Americans today remain fascinated with spiritual beings such as angels and demons, we are inherently skeptical about the elements of Scripture that don't fit easily into a scientific or medical framework. We are far more likely to accept events in both Scripture and contemporary life that can be explained by medicine, psychology, or sociology. At the same time, though, as followers of Christ, we believe in both the visible realm and the invisible realm, and we confess that the triune God is the Creator of both. The Nicene Creed declares it this way:

"We believe in one God, the Father Almighty, Maker of heaven and earth, and of all things visible and invisible."[2] We also cannot ignore the places where Paul urges the church to put on the armor of God against the schemes of the devil, since "our struggle is not against blood and flesh but against the rulers, against the authorities, against the cosmic powers of this present darkness, against the spiritual forces of evil in the heavenly places" (Eph. 6:12). Paul's perspective both confronts and clashes with the Western, post-Enlightenment mindset.

When we broach the delicate subject of demon possession, we begin from the standpoint that God is almighty and that goodness and redemption is assured through the atoning work of his Son. We may not always feel assured of this when we experience suffering or when evil seems to assail us, yet that is our promise and therefore our hope. God's purposes will not be, cannot be, thwarted, though they can be difficult to grasp. Pastor-author Tish Harrison Warren describes the dilemma well: "I have come to see theodicy as an existential knife-fight between the reality of our own quaking vulnerability and our hope for a God who can be trusted."[3] And yet, God is greater than the evil of this world, overcoming evil with good (Rom. 8:28; 12:21).[4] Paul's words in Romans 8 especially have been a source of great comfort for Christians throughout history who have faced trials: "For I am convinced that neither death, nor life, nor angels, nor rulers, nor things present, nor things to come, nor powers, nor height, nor depth, nor anything else in all creation will be able to separate us from the love of God in Christ Jesus our Lord" (8:38–39). Remembering this promise is the best place to start as we probe this difficult dimension of Mary Magdalene's life. We take it as an opportunity not to belabor a challenging feature of the text but to recognize the victorious healing and restoration possible through the power of Jesus Christ. This is, in fact, one thing Scripture wants us to remember about her: Mary Magdalene was healed by Jesus.

By recognizing her suffering through demon possession, we draw attention to a dimension of Jesus's ministry that we might easily pass over out of discomfort. Yet we turn to this topic to grasp more fully what the coming of God's kingdom means for us and our world. For, you might ask, when we cast aside or look askance at the supernatural elements of Scripture—healings, changing water to wine, the feeding of the five thousand, a God who condescends to take on flesh, and even Christ's bodily resurrection—what are we left with? When we take seriously Scripture's teachings on the invisible realm, we will find that we are not only attending better to the text but also connecting better to our global brothers and sisters who say they experience spiritual warfare as a daily reality. Historian Philip Jenkins stresses a similar point: "On occasion, the social background of the Global South allows readers to see dimensions of the [biblical] text that have been largely lost in a postindustrial world."[5] Mary Magdalene's story reminds us that Christ alone can pierce the darkness that assails our lives. At the end of the day, her healing is good news for us all.

Her Present Darkness

Mary Magdalene's backstory comes to us briefly in Luke 8:2, where she is mentioned as one "from whom seven demons had gone out."[6] We are told that she and other women were "cured of evil spirits and infirmities."

The brevity of the account indicates that it's a key aspect of her story but does not define her life. We walk a delicate line here in recognizing its importance *but* not dwelling on it more than necessary. Oxford scholar and apologist C. S. Lewis tackled the topic of demons in his compelling work *The Screwtape Letters*. In the preface, Lewis writes, "There are two equal and opposite errors into which our race can fall about the devils. One is to disbelieve in their existence. The other is to believe, and to feel an excessive and unhealthy interest in them. They themselves are equally pleased by both errors and hail a materialist or a magician with the same delight."[7] We shall take heed of his advice to the best of our abilities.

Mary Magdalene's experience of torment is not detailed. Nonetheless, numerous incidents recorded in Scripture provide a window into what her experience of such evil might have been. The Gospels and Acts attest that demon possession could cause extreme physical, emotional, and spiritual suffering.[8] For example, in the same chapter of Luke that references the women that Jesus heals, we learn of the man from the region of the Gerasenes (8:26–39). He was living in burial caves, without clothing, cutting himself with sharp stones. He would wander the caves day and night howling like an animal.[9] Chains could not subdue him. When Jesus meets the man, who responds to the name Legion, he commands the demons to leave the man, and he casts them into a herd of pigs that immediately rush into the nearby lake and drown. Only after Jesus healed the man was he able to sit, fully clothed and in his right mind. His healing included being restored to the community. Although he begged to join Jesus, Jesus sent him home to proclaim what God had done for him. By contrast, Jesus welcomed Mary Magdalene and the other women healed of demon possession to join his traveling ministry.

Details here shed light on historical understandings of demonic activity. Jewish understandings of demonology located unclean spirits in tombs and bodies of water, both of which feature in Luke's account.[10] Ancient magic also claimed that knowing the name of the demon(s) could ensure control over them. Exorcists, meanwhile, commonly used fumigation or magical incantations to remove demons. There is some debate as to how Jesus's practices compare with that of exorcists of the time.[11]

By all accounts, Jesus was a very effective exorcist, so much so that it raised questions: Who is this, that even the demons obey him?[12] Jesus's startling authority over demons distinguished his exorcisms from other exorcisms both Jewish and pagan. While others would commonly call on a powerful name or declare "I adjure you" to the demon, Jesus simply said, "I command you" (Mark 9:25). He alone has the power necessary for casting out evil.[13]

Like the Gerasene man, Mary Magdalene is said to have had numerous demons, seven to be exact. That number is meaningful in Scripture and most likely highlights the severity of her struggle. Jesus specifically talks about a heightened evil presence with reference to seven demons in Luke 11. In that exchange, Jesus criticizes exorcists for leaving the victims even more susceptible to evil spirits instead of healing them definitively:

> When the unclean spirit has gone out of a person, it wanders through waterless regions looking for a resting place, but not finding any it says, "I will return to my house from which I came." When it returns, it finds it swept and put in order. Then it goes and brings seven other spirits more evil than itself, and they enter and live there, and the last state of that person is worse than the first. (Luke 11:24–26)

Applying this explanation to Mary Magdalene, it is plausible that she too experienced failed exorcisms that exacerbated her situation.

At the time, it was believed that killing a demon was possible only if the host died, though trapping or binding demons in water or the atmosphere was thought to disable their power.[14] Jesus is, therefore, revealed as both gracious and powerful in preserving the life of the Gerasene man while also casting out the demons once and for all. The same is true for Mary Magdalene. The true evil is defeated not at her expense but to her deliverance and restoration to the community.

Even sources outside the Gospels speak of Jesus as a successful exorcist and healer.[15] Scholarship also widely supports the historicity of exorcisms.[16] The power of Jesus's name over the invisible realm served as a prominent evangelistic tool in the earliest centuries of Christianity.[17] In that sense, Mary Magdalene's initial encounter with Christ is emblematic of a core aspect of his ministry.

Blaming the Victim

After reading about Mary Magdalene's healing, we might wonder *how* she came to be possessed by demons. This could quickly degenerate into, What did she do to deserve it?

During the Middle Ages, demons were thought to be attracted to someone who cavorted with evil. The more sinful a person, the more susceptible they were to evil. Demon possession signaled someone's depravity. For this reason, some accounts of Mary Magdalene in church history have linked her demon possession to her alleged prostitution. She is treated as though she deserved demon possession. Didn't she bring this on herself by her promiscuity?

In the history of the Western church, an allegorical reading of the seven demons supposedly served as a biblical foundation for the seven deadly sins, as suggested by Pope Gregory the Great (though it was never official church teaching): "What is designated by the seven demons except the universal sins? . . . Mary had seven demons because she was filled with the totality of vices."[18] Although Scripture does not equate demon possession with sexual immorality, the interconnection of these separate issues resulted in essentially blaming Mary Magdalene for her own demon possession. The penitent Mary Magdalene thereby served as an example not of typical human sinfulness but of the *ultimate* human sinfulness.[19]

Yet Jesus himself consistently rejected the practice of blaming the victim for their own suffering. In his encounter with a man born blind, the disciples asked him, "'Rabbi, who sinned, this man or his parents, that he was born blind?' Jesus answered, 'Neither this man nor his parents sinned; he was born blind so that God's works might be revealed in him'" (John 9:2–3). This perhaps opens a door for us to think anew about Mary Magdalene's circumstances. As in other healing accounts, we are directed to dwell not on the sin but on the *sign* of God's work revealed. This approach better aligns with the New Testament understanding that, as biblical scholar Craig Keener observes, "exorcism is connected closely with the gospel of the kingdom, as a concrete manifestation of the deliverance it brings."[20]

No doubt, these matters are complex and sensitive. But rather than regard Mary Magdalene as the epitome of sin due to false claims of prostitution and allegorical readings of the number seven, we would do better to understand her story as one in which evil had accosted her. To be sure, we must account for our own wrong actions. But sometimes things happen to us not by our own hand but by the hand of another. Sometimes we can be forced or overpowered by sin and evil not by our own choice but by the actions of another. In such cases, the afflictions of evil are not something that we invited or even anticipated.

During the Protestant Reformation, Martin Luther turned medieval teachings about the devil on their head. He claimed that the most faithful, rather than the most sinful, attracted the interest of demons, and he would sing hymns in defiance of their power.[21] His most famous hymn, "A Mighty Fortress Is Our God," speaks to this outlook:

> And though this world with devils filled should
>   threaten to undo us,
> we will not fear, for God hath willed His truth to
>   triumph through us.
> The prince of darkness grim, we tremble not for him;
> his rage we can endure, for lo his doom is sure;
> one little word shall fell him.

If Luther is right, it's possible that Mary Magdalene was targeted for such extreme demon possession not because she was so sinful but because she was going to be *so* important. She was, after all, the one who would come to the tomb only to find it empty. She was the one who would meet the resurrected Christ in the garden. She was the one called and sent by Jesus and who ran to the disciples, declaring, "I have seen the Lord" (John 20:18). Could there be a more significant role for her to play? From this standpoint, her story becomes something else entirely from what we might have assumed.

At the end of the day, this brief mention in Luke highlights the transformative power of Jesus to heal those he encountered as well as the compassion that he tirelessly showed, notably toward suffering women. His inclination to heal their suffering is a truly stunning thing to behold. He did not flinch at their touch, though it should have rendered him unclean by Jewish standards. As we witness in the case of the bleeding woman and the raising of Jairus's daughter (also found in Luke 8 along with Mary Magdalene), he has compassion on women who suffer. We also see him skirting Sabbath restrictions to heal a woman whose back was so bent over she could not stand straight (Luke 13:10–17). In response to criticism, Jesus reclaims the Sabbath as a day for healing and freedom from bondage. A similar healing story involving a man with a withered hand appears in Matthew, where Jesus claims that "it is lawful to do good on the sabbath" (Matt. 12:12).[22] In the Lukan example, although the woman had already suffered for eighteen years, Jesus makes it clear that he does not require one more day of suffering from her, as the religious leaders do. We should count it a comfort that when a leper asked Jesus, "Lord, if you are willing, you can make me clean" (Luke 5:12), Jesus did not withhold healing or ignore him. Instead, he responded, "I am willing."

When Jesus encountered Mary Magdalene, he did not blame her for her suffering. He healed her. He was willing.

But we shouldn't stop there! Jesus models, just by the fact of Mary Magdalene's deliverance, an everyday ministry of care and compassion for the whole person—body, mind, and soul: "When he saw the crowds, he had compassion for them" (Matt. 9:36). "When he went ashore, he saw a great crowd, and he had compassion for them" (14:14). "I have compassion for the crowd" (15:32). Mark's and Luke's Gospels stress this point as well.[23] Compassion characterized the way he looked on the needs of those around him. He looked on them and saw them to their bones, the hurt and suffering, and he lamented (as when he wept with Mary of Bethany at the death of her brother Lazarus) before transforming it. Jesus did not turn a blind eye to the real suffering that comes from living in our fallen world.

Care of Bodies, Minds, and Souls

In January 1540, Martin Luther's family experienced a crisis common to many families and yet too rarely acknowledged publicly or by the pastoral care of the church.[24] His wife, Katharina von Bora, had a miscarriage that left her gravely ill, to the point that she was unable to walk for months. Like most parents of their time, Luther and Katharina were no strangers to the untimely death of a child, having lost their daughter Elisabeth in 1528 after just one year of her life. The heartbreaking loss in 1540 was followed by the death of their second daughter, Magdalena (b. 1529), who passed away in 1542 at age thirteen after enduring sickness. Luther experienced a profound grief that led him to Scripture with sensitive eyes. Out of his own experience and with sympathy for the many parents (particularly mothers) facing the tragic loss of a child, Luther poured himself into writing an afterword for Wittenberg Reformer Johannes Bugenhagen's piece on Psalm 29. Luther's "Consolation for Women Whose Pregnancies Have Not Gone Well" was published in 1542 and outlived the original book to which it was attached.

There he strongly defended mothers of goodwill against the culture's tendency to lay the tragedy at their feet. There is no guilt to carry, Luther declared to those blamed or quick to blame themselves. No doubt with Katharina in mind, Luther affirmed the anguished prayers of mothers struggling to articulate their grief to God in the face of prenatal and postnatal loss, though one question remained for his audience: Is there a place in God's presence for the unbaptized, stillborn child? This pastoral care situation had never been handled easily for a church that maintained that infant baptism washed away original sin. Yet, with theological reform came new opportunities for the consolation of female bodies in particular, and Luther took time to assure grieving mothers that God's promises were not rooted in the administration of baptism alone but in the covenantal promise that God made to the families of believers: "Who can doubt that those Israelite children who died before they could be circumcised on the eighth day were yet saved by the prayers of their parents, in view of the promise that God willed to be their God? God has not limited God's power to sacraments but has made a covenant with us through God's own word."[25] Luther reassured grieving parents that God's power and fatherly care was not bound to a water ritual no matter how important baptism was to the life of the church.

Would Luther have written this piece if he had not been a husband and a father as well as a pastor and theologian? It seems unlikely. The work, the struggles, and the spiritual lives of women had become accessible in ways that had not been possible when clergy were not permitted to marry.

The pastoral care of women—body, mind, and soul—may be something that our churches struggle to provide, but it is not something that Jesus overlooked in his own ministry. Jesus did not refuse to talk to women, touch them, or be around them for fear of how it might look. He did not block them from his ministry because they were women. He invited them and welcomed them to join him. In fact, when Jesus called the disciples "friend," it included the group of women. He was friends with women. With that proximity, perhaps he could see and know more of what women face, just as Luther was able to do having married Katharina.

Jesus never turned a blind eye to the suffering of those around him, including the women, and we too might adopt that approach here. Before we close the file on Mary Magdalene's suffering, we might practice compassion toward what she faced. In doing so, we too will love our neighbor, even a neighbor we count among the communion of saints.

A New Kingdom Come

Even though Scripture declares the power of God and
Jesus Christ to overcome the evil of our world, it does not
downplay or underestimate his enemy. If a tree is known
by its fruit, this certainly applies to the devil's work of
wielding the manipulative power of temptation and de-
ception. In the Gospel of John, Jesus describes the devil
as wholly corrupt and therefore as one who acts in full
concert with his fallen nature. Jesus rebukes the devil as a
liar and a murderer, calling him the "father of lies" (John
8:44).[26] In describing himself as the Good Shepherd, Jesus
warns that the devil is a "thief" who "comes only to steal
and kill and destroy" (John 10:10). The devil and his fallen
angels seek to obstruct God's will at every turn. In the parable of the weeds, Jesus describes the devil as the enemy
who sows weeds amid the good harvest (Matt. 13:24–30,
36–43). John's Gospel claims that Judas was influenced by
the devil when he betrayed Jesus (13:2). Peter writes, "Like
a roaring lion your adversary the devil prowls around,
looking for someone to devour" (1 Pet. 5:8). The imagery
of a lion was a potent reference at a time when the Roman
Empire was known to throw Christians into the arena
with hungry lions. In denouncing this enemy who sows
death, Jesus proclaimed, "I came that they may have life
and have it abundantly" (John 10:10).[27]

Christ's power to deliver from demons and to heal is
a signal of the arrival of his restorative kingdom. For example, when Jesus experienced pushback over his power
to cast out demons, he retorted, "But if it is by the finger
of God that I cast out the demons, then the kingdom of

God has come upon you" (Luke 11:20). If we identify Mary Magdalene with prostitution, we might inadvertently think that her story is drawing us to focus on moral failure. But this is no ethical lesson. To forget her deliverance from seven demons is to miss the whole point of what she represents in Jesus's ministry. She is a herald, a sign of God's kingdom that is both *here* and *yet to come* under the reign of Jesus Christ. She became a herald by way of her healing, and she was called to be a herald for Christ by Christ himself at their encounter in the garden. Mary Magdalene's true story is not a lesson in ethics but an all too easily forgotten lesson in the power and authority of Jesus Christ.

The Gospels and Acts consistently indicate that Jesus's name alone is powerful enough to cast out demons and heal. The twelve disciples are sent out by Jesus with this authority and the charge to proclaim the kingdom (Matt. 10:1; Mark 6:7; Luke 9:1–2). And yet the disciples also struggle with the idea that those outside of their inner circle would receive the ability to cast out demons: "Master, we saw someone casting out demons in your name, and we tried to stop him because he does not follow with us" (Luke 9:49). Jesus not only allows it; he continues to expand the numbers of those to whom he gives authority. This was never going to be a power maintained merely by the twelve. Soon seventy are sent in pairs proclaiming the arrival of the kingdom of God and healing (Luke 10:1–20).[28] Given that Luke has stressed that Mary Magdalene and the women were with Jesus, biblical scholar Richard Bauckham includes them among the seventy.[29] That could mean that Mary Magdalene, who had been cured of seven

demons, was already proclaiming God's kingdom even
before the resurrection and perhaps casting out demons
herself. Mary Magdalene's story reminds us that our hope
rests in Jesus Christ, all that he has done and all that he
has promised to do, even when faced with demons.

An Anchor of Hope, Not Despair

The French words for "hope" (*espere*) and "despair" (*de-
sepoir*) come from the same root. They are two sides of
the same coin. Sometimes it is easy to toggle between
the two.

After a car accident that left me with a severe concus-
sion and two years of daily, debilitating migraines, I was
visited by despair. It happened in a time before concus-
sions were really taken seriously, and it was hard to know
what was happening. Without sufficient sick leave and no
other way to financially support our family, I went back to
work much too soon. I struggled to teach in class. Thank
God for a husband who could easily step in on my behalf
in those moments. Each day began with searing pain, and
I feared that I would never have another day without debilitating pain. Fear and despair were my companions
that long season. Playing with our young daughter was a
physical struggle, and I fretted over whether I would be
able to have another child. I had just launched into my
work and ordained ministry after years of preparation,
sacrifice, and study. The worry that it might all be coming
to an end just as it was beginning disturbed me. I felt that
I was sinking under the weight of it all with no recourse,
no relief. My prayers and ability to hope were strained

apart from the care of loved ones and the church around me. By God's grace alone is that season behind me.

To be sure, we all have our own stories of being tossed about by the waves. We all need an anchor for the storms of life.

Jerusalem University College has a tradition of taking students on a boat to the middle of the Sea of Galilee and dropping anchor for lecture, prayer, and devotional reflection. I experienced it as a student in the 1990s and years later as a professor during a summer session. To be in the same place where Jesus calmed the storm (Matt. 8:23–27; Mark 4:35–41; Luke 8:22–24) has been one of the most meaningful moments of my life.

I can vividly recall the waves lapping against the side of the boat. The slow rocking back and forth. The rapid movement of the clouds, which one moment invited the beaming sun and the next provided needed shade during what was becoming a hot day. I can still imagine, just as I could then, Jesus sleeping in the boat, surely exhausted from teaching and managing the demands of those who followed and surrounded him. But to sleep soundly through a storm? That's where my experience falls short. My favorite plastic cups declare "There are no bad lake days," but of course there are. What we need—on both good days and bad days—is a good anchor.

Before the cross was used as a regular devotional symbol for the Christian faith, early Christians fixed their eyes on the symbol of the anchor. The anchor of hope (or *anchora spei*) offered profound comfort for those facing persecution in the Roman Empire. To look to the anchor was to remember the promise of resurrection and eternal life given to believers in Christ suffering in the storm. To look to the anchor was to see the surety of hope rooted in a person, though not just any person. Scripture declares, "We have this hope, a sure and steadfast anchor of the soul, a hope that enters the inner shrine behind the curtain, where Jesus, a forerunner on our behalf, has entered" (Heb. 6:19–20).[30] He alone is our anchor.

From the fifth century on, the symbol of the anchor all but disappeared from Christian usage until the Protestant Reformation. Thomas Vautrollier, a French Protestant refugee and printer, escaped to England during the reign of Queen Elizabeth and established a printing press there. The first works he published were sermons by Martin Luther and eventually the English edition of John Calvin's *Institutes of the Christian Religion*. He adopted the anchor as his printer's symbol, and it adorned every title page of his Protestant printings even after he passed away. As Calvin declared in his *Institutes*, "For our assurance, our glory, and the sole anchor of our salvation are that Christ the Son of God is ours, and we in turn are in him sons of God and heirs of the Kingdom of Heaven, called to the hope of eternal blessedness by God's grace, not by our worth."[31]

Mary Magdalene was in the midst of a storm when she crossed paths with Jesus. She was struggling under the weight of seven demons and found that only Jesus Christ could anchor her life. If we continue to view her as a prostitute and thereby blame her for her own demons, we will miss how Scripture magnifies through her story the healing power of Jesus Christ to overcome even the greatest of evils that assail our lives. To cast out demons is a sign of the arrival of God's kingdom. By tracking Mary Magdalene's story of healing,[32] we are reminded that Jesus offers redemption for our lives on earth now and for what is to come. He is more powerful than the devil. He is our anchor, who loves to heal, call, and send surprising, unexpected people to glorify his name.

Healing, it turns out, is not the end of Mary Magdalene's story. It was just the beginning of her faithful following.

SIX

The "Certain Women" in Jesus's Inner Circle

Unexpected Company

Oberammergau is a quaint town in Bavaria, Germany, known internationally for its woodcarving and its world-famous passion play. Every ten years, its five thousand residents reenact the story of Jesus's suffering, death, and resurrection. They've been performing the play regularly since the early seventeenth century, when the town prayed that God would spare them from a plague and promised to present the story of Christ's life. The popularity of the play has not diminished with time, though the play itself can last for five hours or more. It continues to be well attended by visitors from around the world.

But over time, audiences have grown less familiar with the story of Jesus. How do you introduce Jesus to an increasingly biblically illiterate audience?

In 2010, important changes were introduced to update the play for a modern audience.[1] Before then, Jesus had been introduced to audiences in the first act as he cleansed the temple of the money changers. It's a hard opening that featured an angry Jesus with little context as he overturns tables and causes a ruckus. In the updated version, Jesus enters the stage riding a donkey surrounded by joyful children and mothers waving palms. Chitter-chatter fills the stage as Jesus interacts with people, picking up children and mingling. Rather than the angry table-turner, Jesus is presented as a joyful, gentle Savior. The triumphal entry of Jesus into Jerusalem[2] is combined with his care for children. It is a compelling and disarming way to introduce someone whose name may be well known across the world but whose story is often not as familiar.

Oberammergau's opening act mirrors the Gospels' claim that Jesus cared for little children (Matt. 19:13–15; Mark 10:13–16; Luke 18:15–17). We are reminded that Jesus was born and came near to us as Emmanuel, "God is with us" (Matt. 1:23), in the flesh of a child, and he never scorned the company of children. Yes, many demanded his time. Yes, he bore on his shoulders the mission of the salvation of all. But he was not too busy for children. Children were not interruptions, even though the disciples could not see it at the time. In trying to protect Jesus from being overwhelmed by the masses of people and the many needs placed on him, the disciples acted like bouncers at times rather than ushers in the scriptural accounts. Jesus corrected them, saying, "Let the children come to me, and do not stop them, for it is to such as these that the kingdom of God belongs" (Luke 18:16).[3]

As it turns out, the Gospels are replete with this pattern in which Jesus withdraws, the crowds follow, and he shows compassion on them (Matt. 15:32). For those easily hassled or frustrated by the demands of others (you know who you are), it's surely a mark of Jesus's divine love that he responds with compassion rather than annoyance in these situations. We are more like the disciples, saying, "Send the crowds away," while Jesus benevolently responds, "They need not go away" (Matt. 14:13–16; see also Mark 6:36–37; Luke 9:10–17). He had taught for three days and was worried that the crowds would faint on the journey home without food, so Jesus fed them (Matt. 15:32; Mark 8:3). It's a reminder to us that his ministry was no scam; this was no Fyre Festival, the fraudulent luxury music gathering that was held in the Bahamas in 2017. For that event, people paid thousands of dollars to attend only to be left with shoddy, even dangerous, accommodations, food, and sanitary conditions. In contrast, Jesus delivered more than what was promised; he fed their minds, hearts, bodies, and souls.

Jesus also made room for the least of these, including women in need.

You would think that the disciples had learned their lesson. But they make the same mistake in the next chapter of Matthew's Gospel. "Send her away!" they say about the Canaanite woman who was begging Jesus to save her daughter from demonic possession (Matt. 15:22–28). They could not recognize or value the great faith that Jesus saw in her. Time and again, we see Jesus providing people with what they need: from blessing to food to healing.

At some point, a similar exchange took place for Mary Magdalene. As we learned in the previous chapter, one of the few details that Scripture includes about her life is that she was healed of seven demons (Mark 16:9; Luke 8:2). Jesus saw that she was in need and took compassion on her. Presumably she too showed great faith in that moment. The Gospels do not reveal the details, but from that healing came new life and inclusion in the ministry of Jesus. It's striking that when Mary Magdalene crossed paths with Jesus, she followed him. Even more than that, he welcomed her.

Crossing Paths with Royalty

Jesus healed numerous people in the Gospels, but their stories are shared selectively. Sometimes we learn their names, sometimes we don't. More often than not, we never hear about them after their healing. No doubt, Jesus's numerous healings, including the healing of the bleeding woman (Matt. 9:20–22; Mark 5:24–34; Luke 8:42–48), the resurrection of Jairus's daughter (Matt. 9:23–26; Mark 5:35–43; Luke 8:49–56), and his healing of the paralytic man (Matt. 9:1–8; Mark 2:1–12; Luke 5:17–26), were all transformative and memorable encounters. Otherwise, the Gospel writers would not have recorded them. They reveal Jesus as the Son of God and show how his forgiveness restores our souls and our bodies. The kingdom of God brings salvation to the whole person! Yet we rarely have the privilege of seeing what happened to such people after their healing. Mary Magdalene's story, however, reveals more.

In truth, not everyone who wanted to join Jesus's traveling ministry was invited, even those who asked to follow. Lest we take Mary Magdalene's inclusion among the disciples for granted, consider the demon-possessed man of Mark 5:1–20. He pleaded with Jesus after he was freed from Legion to allow him to join Jesus's ministry. The text states that Jesus instead sent him to bear witness in the Decapolis to what the Lord had done for him, and those who heard were amazed. In other cases, circumstances and obligations proved insurmountable for those who expressed initial interest in following Christ (Luke 9:57–62). But not so for Mary Magdalene, who was not only healed but also invited to join and follow Jesus on the way. It was not only that she was willing but that she was invited.

Years ago, Queen Elizabeth II waved at me. My husband and I were living in Scotland at the time during our first years of marriage while pursuing graduate school education. We subsisted primarily on eggs and tea, but we had some wonderful adventures. One summer, we made a point to visit Balmoral Castle, the royal residence in Scotland, and to see the Highland games held there. Unexpectedly (to us), the Queen and Prince William showed up to greet those gathered. Excitement rippled through the crowds. We enjoyed the event, which included bagpiping, Scottish dancing, and lots of heavy objects being thrown, but we ended up leaving early. It was just the two of us walking along a quiet, country road when I heard a car coming. I looked back to see the queen's car approaching, and I stopped in my tracks. I started to wave, totally fixated on her car. For a split second, we locked eyes and exchanged a brief wave. I can still remember her face in that moment.

We were no more than a few feet away; my smile, however, was a mile wide. I enjoy recounting my brush with royalty.

But the truth is, there's only so much to the story. Queen Elizabeth II did not stop the car to greet me. She did not invite me to join her and Prince William. Of course not! And my life was not at all changed by that moment, though it makes for a great story.

When Mary Magdalene crossed paths with royalty, when she met the King of kings, her life was completely transformed. In a sense, Jesus *did* stop the car for her, greet her, and invite her along. She was welcomed on the journey. In that regard, her story distinguishes itself from many other biblical figures. But she was not the only woman included alongside the twelve.

Certain Women Welcomed

With Mary Magdalene's introduction in Luke 8:1–3, we discover that she is the first of "certain women." They are not just any women but particular women traveling with Jesus alongside the twelve through cities and villages, spreading the good news of God's kingdom.[4] We know them as "Mary, called Magdalene, . . . Joanna, the wife of Herod's steward Chuza, and Susanna, and many others" (vv. 2–3). Yes, many others! Luke describes them as women who had been cured of evil spirits and infirmities. We are not privy to their healings, but as with Mary Magdalene, they too become witnesses to his healing power and participants in the journey. This is surely one of the most surprising aspects of Jesus's ministry: he welcomed women rather than sending them away.

To many in the church, this portion of Luke's Gospel is virtually unknown. Very rarely are we taught to understand that Jesus traveled with the twelve *and* with "certain women," a distinct group featured at the most critical moments of the story. To accommodate this in our thinking might require us to dramatically alter our assumed dynamics of Jesus's inner circle.

McSweeney's, a satirical website, features an article that imagines Jesus receiving student evaluations as if he were teaching a college course today. One student comments, "Definitely plays favorites. Calls on the same twelve guys over and over. I even heard he took them out to dinner."[5] Another pretend student writes, "Plays favorites. (Sorry, we can't all be John 'The Beloved')." It speaks to the perception but not the reality presented in the Gospels. The fact is that the twelve disciples were not the only group traveling with Jesus.

Easter Sunday is the high point of the Christian year. Of course, every Sunday is a "resurrection day," but Easter is special. On that morning, having made it through the forty-day season of Lent, we celebrate the event that gives us hope and grounds our trust in God's eternal promises: the resurrection of Jesus from the dead. "He is not here but has risen" (Luke 24:5). But, unless you've been paying attention, the empty tomb might not be the only surprise on that morning. Suddenly, as if out of nowhere, at the center of the most pivotal event in human history, these women appear front and center. We might wonder where they came from, but the truth is that they had been there all along. The Gospels tell us that they were followers or disciples of Christ with him on the journey. Biblical scholar Nijay Gupta makes sense of it this way: "We might do better to think about Jesus' followers and disciples in tiered categories or concentric circles."[6] Meaning that Jesus lives out his mission of proclaiming the good news with the twelve disciples that he chose, as we expect. *And* women are included among his followers, whom Jesus also regularly taught. They are all disciples—insofar as the word itself means "learner" or "student," and they address Jesus as "teacher" (which Mary does)—though they are not among the twelve.[7] How would the women be received?

The women's presence with Jesus could have served as fodder for his Jewish detractors at a time when co-education was unusual.[8] Their presence thus indicates yet another way in which Jesus surprises with the company he keeps. Biblical scholar Lynn Cohick cautions against extremes, though, and notes that it was "acceptable behavior" for women to follow a religious figure at this time, especially given that some of the women had male relations (sons and husbands) within the group already.[9] In some cases, these would have been mothers or wives. Mary Magdalene's case differs insofar as she does not appear to be either.

Our reaction to the inclusion of women in Jesus's ministry journey has a lot to do with our own expectations.[10] Recently, our family has enjoyed watching *The Chosen*, the television miniseries that recounts the life of Christ. There are many things that I appreciate about this particular production (and I have my quibbles too!), but one thing that has stood out to me is a sensitivity to presenting both male and female followers traveling with Christ.[11]

Too often that is a surprise even to churchgoers from traditions that elevate the Bible above all.

Perhaps this is an opportunity to take another look at the "certain" women with Jesus. They've been there all along. But the presence of these women involved more than just traveling with Jesus.

Jesus's Patronesses

The church has on many occasions received the patronage of women who have used their power and wealth to impact the faith in some way. Helena (ca. 255–330) was a Greek woman of low rank who became the wife of Constantius I, a Roman emperor, and later the mother of Emperor Constantine. She came to prominence when her son became emperor, which afforded her room to advocate for Christianity. She traveled to the Holy Land late in life and was instrumental in founding churches, including the Church of the Nativity in Bethlehem and the Church of the Holy Sepulchre in Jerusalem. According to tradition, Helena discovered pieces of the true cross of Christ during her visit, which she brought back to Rome. Her impact on Western Christianity, particularly Roman Catholicism, is still evident today.

Three of the Gospels indicate that the "certain women" traveling with Jesus used their economic[12] means to support Jesus from Galilee all the way to Jerusalem (Matt. 27:55–61; Mark 15:40–41; Luke 8:3).[13] Essentially, they were benefactors or patrons of Jesus's ministry,[14] and Mary Magdalene was the first named among them. How could this be that these women supported his ministry?

Women had more financial recourse during the New Testament era than is typically assumed. They made up a tenth of patrons of religious leaders in the Mediterranean at the time.[15] A woman's financial well-being was often connected (though not limited) to her dowry, which the husband held as a trust that she might support herself and her children after his death or divorce.[16] That money belonged to her and her family, but she could also own property or earn money from working. Meanwhile, according to Roman law, partial inheritance was passed down to a Roman woman through her father rather than from her husband.[17] Jewish women received gifts from their parents in lieu of that law applying to them.[18] In fact, women owned one-third of all property across the Roman Mediterranean territories,[19] dowries were returned at divorce, and wealthy widows might choose not to remarry due to lack of necessity. If the marriage was considered *sine manu*, that meant that fathers maintained legal authority over a daughter, not a husband over a wife.[20] As Cohick explains, "In the Roman Empire, married women could hold property and wealth apart from their husbands."[21]

Patronage and social status went hand in hand, and these "certain women" held high social standing.[22] Luke in particular highlights elite female converts (Acts 17:1–34).[23] In his Gospel, he includes Joanna's connections to power and wealth through her marriage to Chuza, financial administrator of Herod's court. Since most people married within their own class and financial status, this indicates Joanna's wealth and social standing as well as her access to education and to important political and religious figures. Some scholars have considered whether Chuza is the rich royal officer in John 4:46–54. Others suggest that Joanna is perhaps the same woman as Junia, the only woman to be greeted by Paul as an "apostle" (Rom. 16:7),[24] a title she would have earned by being present at the empty tomb (Luke 24:10).[25]

Luke invites us to see Mary Magdalene in connection with Joanna. Since Joanna is the only one named in Luke 8 as being married, it's possible that Mary Magdalene was a wealthy widow. Or perhaps she never married because of the demon possession from which she suffered or which resulted in a divorce.[26] She might have earned her wealth in the marketplace, where women could run businesses as men did.[27] There are possible explanations, but as biblical scholar Susan Hylen writes, "A woman's property ownership isn't what the gospel authors were usually interested in. They were focused on telling the story of Jesus, not the financial state of his followers."[28] In any case, Mary Magdalene had independence and resources to serve Christ and his ministry this way, and she was not the only woman to hold this role.

In his classic allegory, *The Pilgrim's Progress*, John Bunyan, the seventeenth-century Puritan preacher, took time to praise the women disciples who supported Jesus. He writes a beautiful monologue for the innkeeper Gaius, who speaks on behalf of women to remove the reproach that follows them. Yes, he observes, death and the curse entered the world because of a woman (a reference to Eve). And yet, he adds a reference to Jesus's mother Mary: "So also did Life and Health; *God sent forth his Son, made of a Woman.*"[29] This juxtaposition of Eve and Mary reflects the church's long-standing tendency to place the blame of humanity's fall at Eve's feet, even though both she and Adam sinned. Jesus's female disciples fare much better: "I read not that ever any man did give unto Christ so much as one Groat; but the Women followed him, and ministered to him of their Substance."[30] Consider what Bunyan highlights here: yes, Jesus ministered to the women, but the women also ministered to Jesus! This is a wonderful example of how freedom in Christ frees us to glorify God with who we are and all that we have. Certain women lived out that generosity in ways that furthered Jesus's reach and impact. Like the anointing women, he accepted their expression of devotion.

The women's financial contributions to Christ's ministry have often been overlooked by the church in an effort to stress the poverty of Christ and his countercultural teachings on wealth. Within the church's history, monasticism recommitted to vows of poverty among the clergy. Similarly, modern theology has often drawn parallels between Jesus's incarnation as taking on a kind of poverty through being born human (2 Cor. 8:9; see also Phil. 2:7, where the incarnate Christ "emptied himself" by taking on human flesh). Some traditions emphasize his material poverty in order to demonstrate his solidarity with the poor.

The New Testament does not shy away from presenting Jesus loving the poor and criticizing the rich. And yet Scripture depicts Jesus living among those who had resources and means to freely give in response to the ways that he freely gave to them. Interestingly, both his male and female followers made economic sacrifices. By following Jesus, the male disciples left their families and therefore forewent some of the potential economic earnings that they would normally have provided.[31] Certain women, meanwhile, contributed from the provision that was theirs to keep or distribute. Both sacrificed financially, which is an important corrective to how the narrative of Jesus's life and ministry has been told and understood in our churches. Jesus was not in want because of the community of followers around him. In this case, the women provided for him and his ministry (including the twelve) out of their resources.

Following, Not Followers

Often we can compare portions of Scripture that are placed side by side in order to find unexpected significance. Their intentional placement in relation to each other might illuminate the author's intended meaning. In Luke 8:3, the account of the women who "ministered to them out of their own resources" is placed immediately before Jesus's well-known parable of the sower (Luke 8:4–8). What might this mean?

In the parable of the sower, seed is spread over untilled soil as was the custom of the day. Many dangers threatened the flourishing of the seed, from being trampled underfoot to being devoured by hungry animals to lacking fruitful conditions for growth (hard and dry conditions) or lacking hospitable conditions for longevity. In line with Jesus's own explanation of the parable (Luke 8:11–15), we might apply it to his followers. In Judas's case, the seed falls on the rock and neither takes root nor flourishes in his life, which leads to disastrous decisions and a disastrous end.[32] In Peter's case, the seed thrives in his life but is threatened by the thorns that choke and over-whelm the soil and the growth of the seed. His example is nevertheless encouraging: though he falters in his time of trial, Jesus offers him forgiveness and a new opportunity to follow (John 21:17). Luke reveals that Jesus had prayed for Peter's deliverance (Luke 22:32–33), and so we see the will of Christ at work in Peter's life despite his failure. What about Mary Magdalene and the "certain women"?

By Scripture's account, Mary Magdalene has been ren-dered, by Christ's healing hand, the good soil in which the seed can grow and produce a hundredfold. This is how we are instructed to remember her, though not because she is the only example of good soil in the Gospels. Mary Magdalene followed Jesus all the way through his minis-try to his death on the cross and the empty tomb. It is a journey that we are also called to take as faithful followers of Christ. To follow Christ means directing our lives so that they pivot around him, his calling, his mission. At the center of that concentric circle is Christ, which puts us all in the same position as the disciples. According to the Gospels, Mary Magdalene did this. In response to her healing, she redirected her finances, her time, and her pres-ence courageously and without fail to Christ's ministry. Jesus welcomed her devotion that endured to the end.

In a culture dominated by social media, we can eas-ily dwell more on followers than following. Author and journalist Katelyn Beaty stresses that this focus threatens the authentic mission of some of our most well-known churches as well as many churches longing to make a no-table impact.[33] This fixation on generating followers and building platform is a tempting and insidious motivation that can shift our focus away from following Jesus and finding our identity in Christ. Suddenly our own self-constructed identity becomes the priority.

I entered the workforce just as the idea of one's brand and branding became common corporate speak. Authors, academics, and even clergy are often expected to think carefully about one's brand. But to follow Jesus is to join a revolution in the best sense of the term: a reorienting of *who* we are and *whose* we are so that we revolve not around ourselves but around Christ our Lord and Savior.

Jesus Revolution

Chuck Smith (1927–2013) was a straitlaced pastor of a dying church in the 1960s when his life, faith, and ministry were transformed by an encounter with the hippie evangelist Lonnie Frisbee. He took a risk and opened his church doors to hippies, and as it happened, Jesus walked in with them. The Calvary Chapel movement helped transform the expectations of an era turned anti-religious. In a time of deep distrust of religious and other traditional institutions, the so-called Jesus movement took the communal impulses of the hippie era and created a distinctly evangelical counterculture, featured in the 1971 *Time* cover story "Jesus Revolution."

The 2023 movie of the same name about Smith's ministry portrays a generation willing to jump on any bus, take a ride in any car. They are desperate and seeking truth. The movie resonates today because we too are a desperate generation. Grasping to understand what it means to be human, both male and female, and made in the image of God.[34] Searching for dignity and peace to calm the inner restlessness and malaise. Today, we scroll and scroll in search of prophets and truth that is both hidden and revealed by unseen algorithms. We willingly listen to any interesting (or outrageous) voice on social media for a second or two, and so we are formed by the random, disconnected voices of our time in ways that we do not recognize. G. K. Chesterton is attributed with the compelling observation that to stop believing in God doesn't lead to belief in nothing but to belief in anything.[35] Who will feed the sheep of our generation? God loves to send unexpected people to direct us to the true bread that alone can fill our bottomless hunger in the midst of such abundance.

Scripture's reference to the women who followed Jesus and ministered to him out of their own resources is like the little boy's lunch in the feeding of the five thousand. It may not seem like much, but by God's power to magnify, it has the potential to inspire and invite us all to join the journey and to give what we are and what we have to the Lord.

Luke 8 is a reminder that Jesus's inner circles included women alongside men. In fact, these were women who witnessed and experienced firsthand the power of Jesus to heal supernaturally. Biblical scholar Richard Bauckham directs us to consider their likely participation among the seventy (or seventy-two) who were sent by Jesus to declare the kingdom of God (Luke 10:1–22).[36] We know that these women provided financially for his ministry and followed him to cross, tomb, and even Pentecost. Luke names "certain women" again in the upper room prior to Pentecost along with Jesus's mother Mary (Acts 1:14). Their place there, together with the twelve, began with Jesus welcoming their following, faithfulness, and devotion.

Those who traveled with Jesus were immensely blessed by the privilege and the responsibility of following him. Jesus declared to them, "But blessed are your eyes, for they see, and your ears, for they hear. Truly I tell you, many prophets and righteous people longed to see what you see but did not see it and to hear what you hear but did not hear it" (Matt. 13:16–17). You and I, we were not chosen to be direct witnesses, but Mary Magdalene was. And yet there is a moment for us all when we are invited to be healed like her, to leave the water jar behind like the Samaritan woman, or to drop our nets like Peter. We too are challenged to step out of the boat in faith and join Jesus on the water. We too are challenged to drink from the cup that he offers.

Like Mary Magdalene, we have been invited to journey with Jesus. Not on our terms but his. Not according to our vision but his. Not by our power but his. And with following comes the act of witness and proclamation to everything that Jesus Christ means for this world.

SEVEN

Go and Tell
like Mary Magdalene

Meet Me at the Tomb

Our children enjoy hearing my husband and me recount their birth stories. They smile and laugh as we go through what has become a familiar litany of highlights. The oldest was born while we lived abroad, and because they had no room in the hospital at our arrival, she was almost born in the taxi. Our middle child was nearly full term but growing so big that we had to schedule an induction. We arrived at the hospital bright, early, and fully prepared only to discover that I was already in labor. She laughs when we describe her as being considerate for being on time. Finally, our youngest shocked us all by arriving weeks early. A snowy day in December nearly derailed our trip to the hospital, but with his sisters waiting in the room next door, he came into the world. In telling these stories again and again, we joyfully recount the details of their entrances into life and into our family. Every twist and turn is a small joy that seems to gather us closer to one another.

In a similar way, we are invited to delight in telling and retelling the profound story of Jesus Christ's resurrection from the dead. This is not the story of his birth but his rebirth. He who was dead is alive again! That miraculous event leads to our rebirth and our gathering together as the family of God, both here and now and into eternity. When we tell this story and marvel at these details, we cannot ignore the presence of Mary Magdalene and her prominence. No matter how much or how little we understand of her, we cannot overlook her part in that moment, which is the basis of the Christian faith. This woman who experienced the healing of Jesus, faithfully followed him, provided for his ministry, and did not desert him at the cross is given the great honor, privilege, and responsibility of serving as the first witness to Christ's resurrection. She gets to tell the story.

Mary Magdalene faithfully followed Jesus from his ministry in Galilee to the cross in Jerusalem. As biblical scholar Nijay Gupta puts it, "The Gospels call her Mary of Magdala to identify her with a place. We might also call her Mary of Golgotha, because she was there; she showed up for Jesus when almost no one else did."[1] Scripture is painstakingly clear that Mary Magdalene and others were present when Jesus was nailed to the cross. She is directly named in Matthew, Mark, and John as a witness to Jesus's death along with "many women," some of whom are also named (see table 7.1). And though Luke doesn't specifically name her, she was certainly among those whom he records as being at the cross (23:55; 24:10): "All his acquaintances, including the women who had followed him from Galilee, stood at a distance watching these things" (23:49).

In John's Gospel, Mary Magdalene attends faithfully at the foot of the cross, along with Jesus's mother, Jesus's aunt, the disciple John, and Mary the wife of Clopas. They watch and weep as Jesus suffers a criminal's sentencing and dies a criminal's death (John 19:25). Their mournful devotion and resilient presence are recounted by John, "the disciple whom Jesus loved," who is the only male disciple recorded there with them.[2] Despite the agony of crucifixion, Jesus took time to ensure the care of his mother Mary to John's household. And so she remained

TABLE 7.1

Women at the Cross

Matthew 27:55–56, 61	"Many women . . . looking on from a distance" Mary Magdalene Mary the mother of James and Joseph The mother of the sons of Zebedee
Mark 15:40–41	Women "looking on from a distance" Mary Magdalene Mary the mother of James the younger and of Joses Salome "Many other women who had come up with him to Jerusalem"
Luke 23:49	Women "who had followed him from Galilee, stood at a distance watching these things"
John 19:25	"Standing near the cross" Jesus's mother, Mary His mother's sister Mary the wife of Clopas* Mary Magdalene

*It is unclear if Mary's sister and the wife of Clopas are two different women. Marianne Meye Thompson, *John: A Commentary*, New Testament Library (Louisville: Westminster John Knox, 2015), 399.

with the disciples. Following Jesus's resurrection and ascension, she was there on the day known to the church as Pentecost, when the Holy Spirit was poured out on the disciples (Acts 1:14). This is the first time since Luke 2 that she has been named. Biblical scholar Beverly Gaventa points out that this mention of her name links Luke's Gospel and Acts while also revealing her commitment to the ministry of her son.[3]

It is significant that Mary Magdalene kept vigil alongside Jesus's mother Mary and the disciple John at the cross. Their presence was not necessarily without risk.[4] Though other Gospels indicate that the women were witnessing these events from afar (Mark 15:40), at some point Mary Magdalene drew near. These three (John, Mary the mother of Jesus, and Mary Magdalene) each represent primary groups that had supported Jesus from the annunciation of his birth to the moment he willingly spread out his arms to die. If his mother Mary and her sister represent the ongoing devotion of Jesus's family, then Mary Magdalene represents the commitment of the "certain women" from Galilee to Jerusalem, while John reflects the ongoing commitment of a remnant of the twelve, though scattered in that moment. They are all among his disciples.

The Gospels stress that Mary Magdalene not only witnessed Jesus's death but was present for his interment in the tomb. Mark notes that she "saw where the body was laid" (Mark 15:47). Matthew describes her as witnessing Joseph of Arimathea lay Jesus's body in his new tomb, and she is present when the stone is rolled shut while "sitting opposite the tomb" (Matt. 27:61). Luke notes, "The women who had come with him from Galilee followed, and they saw the tomb and how his body was laid" (Luke 23:55). They see the body in the tomb. They see the tomb closed. Importantly, Mary Magdalene literally knows where the body is buried.

The Sabbath creates a kind of pause, and a waiting period sets in. God is at work in the quiet, though they do not yet understand.

Acclaimed American filmmaker Terrence Malick exquisitely captures, in the quickest of flashes, those tender, everyday moments that happen within a family. Simple, quiet vignettes of everyday life gain profound presence and significance under his masterful lens. Lying on the grass, hearing the crickets, laughing, embracing, eating, dancing, holding a baby, and working the fields are all featured in his movies with notable profundity. The title for his film *A Hidden Life* (2019) is said to have been chosen from George Eliot's classic novel, *Middlemarch*: "For the growing good of the world is partly dependent on unhistoric acts; and that things are not so ill with you and me as they might have been, is half owing to the number who lived faithfully a hidden life, and rest in unvisited tombs."[5] Eliot's account is drawn from Colossians 3:3: "For you have died, and your life is hidden with Christ in God."

On that Sabbath day, Jesus's tomb went unvisited, but the hidden work of God continued in anticipation of the glory that would come the next morning.

Early on that resurrection morning, the women arrived at the tomb after observing the Jewish Sabbath. Mark's Gospel notes that they worried about how they would move the stone at the entrance of the tomb, a detail that invites us to consider their alarm when they see it rolled away and an angel inside (16:3–5). They had come to anoint the dead body in keeping with Jewish custom (Mark 16:1; Luke 23:56). We noted earlier that, to remember Mary Magdalene correctly, we must not conflate her story with the story of others, including the many women who anointed Jesus. She was not the "sinner" woman who anointed his feet (Luke 7:36–50), nor was she the woman who anointed Jesus at Bethany (Matt. 26:6–13; Mark 14:3–9), and she is not to be confused with Mary, the sister of Lazarus, who anointed Jesus (John 12:1–8). But Mary Magdalene does have an anointing story. Her anointing story comes when she expects to anoint a dead body that she witnessed being entombed days before. Instead, she discovers an empty tomb.

In every case, angels or descriptions of angels greet the women. Mary Magdalene, the one who was once possessed by seven demons, now encounters God's messengers. As Mary the mother of Jesus once received the good news of Christ's coming from the angel Gabriel (Luke 1:26–38), so now Mary Magdalene receives the good news from angels that "he has been raised" (Matt. 28:6). She who was healed and restored for new life is given a new calling. In Matthew, both the angels and the risen Lord commission the women to "go and tell" (28:7, 10). The echo of their commands offers confirmation of God's will that they should carry this news.

Although the specific group of women and the number of women differ somewhat depending on the Gospel account (see table 7.2), every account mentions Mary Magdalene's presence at the empty tomb. In John's Gospel, she is initially the only follower to discover the empty tomb and the first to encounter the risen Lord. That fact alone

TABLE 7.2

Women at the Empty Tomb

Scripture	Women	Angels	Encounter with Jesus and Telling Others
Matthew 28:1–10	Mary Magdalene The "other Mary" (mother of James and Joseph; see Matt. 27:56, 61)	"An angel of the Lord" rolled back the stone and sat on it (v. 2) "Come, see the place where he lay. Then go quickly and tell his disciples" (v. 6)	"Suddenly Jesus met them" (v. 9) "Go and tell my brothers" (v. 10)
Mark 16:1–10	Mary Magdalene Mary the mother of James Salome	"Young man dressed in a white robe" (v. 5) "Look, there is the place they laid him. But go, tell his disciples and Peter" (vv. 6–7)*	"They said nothing to anyone, for they were afraid" (v. 8) "She went out and told those who had been with him" (v. 10)
Luke 24:1–12	Mary Magdalene Joanna Mary the mother of James "And the other women with them"	"Two men in dazzling clothes" (v. 4) "Remember how he told you, while he was still in Galilee" (v. 6)	"They told all this to the eleven and to all the rest" (v. 8) Two disciples on the way to Emmaus encounter the risen Christ and mention the women, who "came back and told us" (Luke 24:22–24)
John 20:1–18	Mary Magdalene	"Two angels in white sitting" (v. 11)	"Jesus said to her, 'Woman, why are you weeping?'" (v. 15) "But go to my brothers and say to them . . .'" (v. 17) "She told them . . ." (v. 18)

*Mark 16:8 has led to much consideration in biblical studies: "So they went out and fled from the tomb, for terror and amazement had seized them, and they said nothing to anyone, for they were afraid." The longer ending of Mark, likely a later addition, claims that Mary Magdalene shared the news. Most scholars agree that they certainly ended up telling the disciples, even if they were at first afraid.

is remarkable and should lead the church to pause and reflect: What could Mary Magdalene's presence at the empty tomb mean for the church today?

Weeping Woman

When I was in kindergarten, a sweet boy, a classmate of mine, doted on me. I still recall moments of playing on the playground with him. We laughed and chased each other. His face is a fog in my memory, but I remember him. He gave me little gifts and told his family about me. His sister and my oldest brother were in high school together, and she was kind to me. She would pick him up after school, and he would wave to me.

One day, after I had gotten home from school, I was sitting on the floor in the family room watching cartoons. The phone rang and my brother answered it. I did not overhear what was said, but a moment later, he came into the living room with news that I could not get my head around: the boy had died in a tragic accident. I could not understand what my brother was saying because it did not seem real to me. When I went back to school, the boy wasn't there anymore. His sister no longer came around. It was terribly sudden. One minute he was there, and then he was gone. At that young age, I felt a grief that I could not articulate.

Mary Magdalene's grief over Jesus must have been tremendous. Scripture highlights her tears, and they have been remembered outside of Scripture as well. She wept and wept at the shock of it all. To any who have lost a loved one, you will know that three days is not long enough to grasp that loss, if you ever do. It is still fresh. Things are not as they should be. In Jewish practice, the first *seven* days of mourning excluded washing, working, intercourse, or study.[6]

John's Gospel stresses Mary Magdalene's grief. She becomes distressed upon discovering the empty tomb and runs to get Peter and John (John 20:2), who are stunned by what they see. Though they return to their homes, she remains at the tomb, distraught and weeping. She lingers as if there is nowhere else she could possibly be in that moment. Where is Jesus's body? She stands outside the tomb weeping. Her every action is paired with weeping, and so she weeps as she bends down to look into the tomb (John 20:11–15). "Woman, why are you weeping?" the angels who are sitting where Jesus's body had been ask her (20:13). Little did she know how quickly her lamenting would turn to rejoicing.

Mary Magdalene's tears have been recognized outside the sphere of the biblical text. Diane Apostolos-Cappadona sees in Pablo Picasso's *Weeping Woman* a tribute to the holy tears of Mary Magdalene.[7] But Mary Magdalene has also been ridiculed for her tears. As the Roman Empire persecuted Christians, the second-century Greek philosopher Celsus scorned the Christian faith for placing the burden of proof of Christ's resurrection on the testimony of a woman. The Christian theologian Origen reports that the philosopher Celsus undermined the credibility of Mary Magdalene's witness by characterizing her as the hysterical woman:

> Speaking next of the statements in the Gospels, that after His resurrection He showed the marks of His punishment, and how His hands had been pierced, he [Celsus]

asks, "Who beheld this?" And discrediting the narrative of Mary Magdalene, who is related to have seen Him, he replies, "A half-frantic woman, as ye state."[8]

Celsus also claimed that Mary Magdalene was the only witness to Jesus's resurrection, which Origen stringently contested by citing Matthew's version, which includes a second Mary.[9] The conflict is a testament to the prominence of Mary Magdalene's widely known role in the events from early on.[10] Because female emotionality was used to limit their witness in both Roman and Jewish legal settings, Mary Magdalene's weeping was both a sign of her heartfelt devotion to Jesus and something that, by the standards of her day, disqualified her from serving as a good witness. And yet Jesus's treatment of a weeping woman stands in stark contrast to the customs of his context.

The resurrection of Lazarus is probably one of the most well-known stories pointing to the divine power of Jesus. But this story also contains an important marker of his humanity and tenderness. When Lazarus's sister, Mary of Bethany, drops to her knees before him and weeps over the death of her brother, crying out, "Lord, if you had been here, my brother would not have died," Jesus is disturbed and moved by her emotion (John 11:32–33). Even though he knows that he is about to undo the death of Lazarus, he still weeps with her (11:35). Then he turns her lamenting into rejoicing.

Jesus does not avoid, overlook, or belittle a weeping woman.

Mary Magdalene's weeping has been regarded in a variety of ways in the history of scriptural interpretation.

It has sometimes been removed from its context in the biblical narrative to point to her as an example of true repentance. All too often and too easily, the tears of the "sinner" woman in Luke 7 are linked to Mary Magdalene's tears at the empty tomb. By that conflation, she becomes the troubled sinner crying in grief. And even when her connection to the woman in Luke 7 is rejected, her tears have been treated as a signal of disbelief.[11] Why have the tears of Mary Magdalene been treated this way? Though Peter "wept bitterly" after his threefold denial of Christ, he is not defined by or belittled for this moment in the way that Mary Magdalene has been for her tears (Matt. 26:75; Mark 14:72; Luke 22:62).

In the history of the church, Mary Magdalene's weeping has sometimes required defending and nuancing. Christine de Pizan (1364–ca. 1430), for example, was born in Venice and educated by her father. Upon the deaths of her father and her husband, she turned to writing to support herself in 1393 and is regarded as "the first professional woman writer in Europe."[12] In her *Book of the City of Ladies* (1405), she strives to recover the good examples of women in the Bible, including Mary Magdalene, who serves as a counter to the negative readings of women in Scripture. Pizan critiques the common trope about women in her day that "God made women to weep, talk, and weave."[13] She stresses that women are made in the image of God and are good creations just like men (Gen. 1:26–27), and they played a significant role in salvation history.[14] In response to those who attack women for weeping, she responds, "If our Lord Jesus Christ, from whom no thought is hidden and who knows and sees into every heart, had thought that women's tears spring only from weakness and simple-mindedness, His sublime dignity would never have allowed His own esteemed and glorious body to weep tears from compassion."[15] Essentially, yes, women do weep—but, as Pizan points out, so did Jesus.

Pizan's defense of Mary Magdalene as a good and true representative of female devotion to Christ, even while in tears, gives us insight into how the image of the weeping Mary Magdalene has complicated her remembrance. Though her weeping has at times been interpreted as an expression of repentance for sin, or a sign of her lack of faith, or a weakness of her womanhood, today we might see her tears through a different lens.

Mary Magdalene grieved in that garden as a disciple, as a patron of Jesus's ministry, as a sister, and as one wholly devoted to God by every indication of Scripture. What a shock it must have been to have seen Jesus suffer and die in such a shameful and heart-wrenching way on the cross. What courage it took to watch his agonizing death and the entombment of his body and to neither look away nor run away. What a heart she must have had to stand in the quiet of the garden, faced with the prospect of his absence from this world, and to still seek his presence. After all, she had been his primary patron since Galilee to the end.

Do we see her there in that garden standing at that juncture between night and new dawn?

Renewing Eden

The sculpture department of the Louvre houses a wooden statue of Mary Magdalene by Gregor Erhart from about

1515–20 that alone is worth the price of admission.[16] To the casual observer, she could easily be mistaken for Eve. She is depicted as naked with long, flowing hair but with a nakedness that could signal either a sinful past or one restored in Christ. The long hair links her to the anointing passages and to the ascetic Mary Magdalene of *The Golden Legend* (the medieval collection of stories about saints). A bevy of historical reasons led to her being fashioned this way. Would we recognize her without the nameplate?

Perhaps we notice her standing in the garden. She turns around when Jesus speaks to her, but she does not recognize his face yet. Jesus calls her "Woman" (John 20:15). In our culture, the word is tinged with a derogatory tone. But here Jesus is inquisitive, concerned, and caring as he asks, "Woman, why are you crying?" The moment echoes another encounter in a different garden: Adam and Eve had eaten of the forbidden fruit and clothed themselves out of shame and recognition of their nakedness. When they heard God walking in the garden, they "hid themselves from the presence of the Lord God" out of fear (Gen. 3:8). God calls out, "Where are you?" (v. 9).

It takes her a second to see him. Like the disciples on the way to Emmaus who speak with Jesus and eat with him yet do not know him until he breaks the bread (Luke 24:13–35), she doesn't recognize him at first. She assumes that she is speaking to the gardener, and the history of Christian interpretation has not always been kind to her for that mistake. Biblical scholar Holly Carey explains, "It is important to recognize that no one in the story assumes that an empty tomb indicates that Jesus's prophecies have come true—that he has, in fact, been raised from the dead."[17] But in a way, she was speaking to *the* Gardener, through whom "all things came into being" (John 1:3). Then Jesus calls her by name, "Mary!" And she knows him instantly.

In John 10, Jesus describes himself as the Good Shepherd of the sheep (v. 11). He loves his sheep. He cares for his sheep. He will lay down his life for his sheep. And the sheep of his flock know his voice: "He calls his own sheep by name and leads them out" to good pasture, and "the sheep follow him because they know his voice" (vv. 3–4).

For a season, my husband David and I lived in Scotland where he worked for the Church of Scotland. His ministry actually spanned two churches (or kirks, as they are called): one in the city and one in the country. One Sunday, he was tasked by the lead pastor to preach on John 10. The challenge was that there were actual shepherds in the kirk. How could he, a native of Los Angeles, speak to this congregation about sheep? We laughed and fretted over the irony of the situation. Then, with all due diligence, he reached out to one of the shepherd boys in the congregation to see if he might shadow him one day in the field. David headed to the fields and the flock, and everything outlined in John 10 happened right before his eyes. The sheep came running when they heard their shepherd boy's voice. They flocked to him and followed where he walked. And they scattered when they heard my husband's voice.

Mary Magdalene knows the voice of the Lord.[18] She answers when he calls her name. She is a true follower. There is no hiding in shame here. When the women encounter the risen Jesus, they throw themselves at his feet, gripping him and worshiping him (Matt. 28:9). Since worship is due only to God, they are proclaiming with that action that Jesus is the Son of God, the Messiah, the Anointed One. It is an act of belief.

In John's Gospel, Mary's grief shifts so suddenly from weeping to rejoicing that she grabs hold of Jesus, not wanting to let go. Translations and interpretations have struggled to understand this moment and exchange. The KJV's translation—"Touch me not"—has tended to dominate modern readings. As previously noted, early Christian understanding of this passage shifted from seeing Jesus as protecting Mary Magdalene from his touch in the midst of ascension to him protecting himself from her touch. But Jesus did not avoid the touch of women. In fact, Mary Magdalene's affection and devotion was met by Jesus with a commission. "Stop clinging to me, because you have a message to bring!" was the idea (John 20:17).[19] Jesus was sending Mary Magdalene, and in no way was this expected.

At the garden tomb, Mary Magdalene becomes a type of new Eve paired with the Virgin Mary in bringing a message of new life. The three serve as touchstones in God's unfolding saga of redemption from creation to the incarnation to the cross and resurrection, though many more women contribute to this arc as well. By reading the story of Mary Magdalene through the lens of other figures, including women in the Bible, we draw on the practice known as typology. A person or an event in the Old Testament finds its fulfillment in another person or event in the New Testament. This approach is not tantamount to conflating the two things, for a type of something is not the same as the thing itself. Instead, typology can offer a sound theological reading of the text as it looks to comparisons, similarities, and prefigurations between God's people as they interact with God and his plan for salvation. For Mary Magdalene to be a type of Eve at the garden tomb conveys the way God's revelation unfolds with coherence. It is an affirmation of the consistency of God and the restorative arc that God has directed from Hebrew Scripture to the New Testament. It is also reminiscent of the earliest understandings of Mary Magdalene, as we've already seen, though not in a way that furthers the blame often laid solely at Eve's feet without recognition of Adam's part.[20]

Mary Magdalene quickly adjusts from her grief-tinged surprise and receives her commission. *Apostle*, or *apostolos*, means "one who is sent,"[21] and when Mary Magdalene was sent, she ran (Matt. 28:8).

Beautiful Feet

During my first year in college, I was asked to write a statement of faith for one of my classes. I was a religious studies major, so I labored over every point. I included the affirmation that the women discovered the empty tomb and encountered the risen Jesus. At the time, I felt that I was carrying a heavy burden to rightly articulate how women contributed to the salvation story. The red-pen response that I received from my professor was thought-provoking: "Why does this matter?" I could not quite articulate an answer at the time. Nonetheless, it has proven to be a helpful question that has stayed with me: What does it matter that Mary Magdalene found the tomb empty, encountered the resurrected Lord, and was then sent to bear witness?

Why does it matter? Well, for one, we do not *expect* Jesus's women followers to play this role. Mary Magdalene's part in the drama of salvation is surprising. After all, Peter and John do return to see the empty tomb according to two accounts, and yet they do not encounter Christ there (Luke 24:12, 24; John 20:3). They run just as Mary Magdalene did, and yet Christ does not appear to them in that moment. The fact that Jesus appears to Mary Magdalene (and the women) instead of Peter and John is almost incomprehensible.

Biblical scholar N. T. Wright stresses that the recounting of the story of the women discovering the empty tomb in the Gospels would have served no helpful apologetic purpose for Christianity as it sought to establish itself. In fact, the story of the women invites ridicule.[22] Because women were not regarded as credible legal witnesses, it must be "that everyone in the early church knew that the women, led by Mary Magdalene, were in fact the first on the scene, or that the early church was not so inventive as critics have routinely imagined, or both."[23] Essentially, there is no good reason for the Gospels to repeat this story over and over unless it were true, because it only serves to undercut the claims of Christianity from its inception. That is a persuasive reason to believe it! The very presence of this surprise in the context of the text speaks to its authenticity. Richard Bauckham explains, "Since these narratives do not seem well designed to carry conviction at the time, they are likely to be historical. . . . If even the evangelists who record these stories were not entirely comfortable with them and sought to reduce their implications, then it is all the more striking that they record them at all. The role of the women must have already been so well established in the tradition that no Gospel writer could simply suppress it."[24]

The surprise continues when, according to two of the Gospel accounts, Jesus himself sends Mary Magdalene to proclaim his resurrection. In Matthew, Jesus commissions Mary Magdalene and "the other Mary" to "go and tell" the disciples (28:10). In Mark, they are instructed by the angel to "go, tell his disciples and Peter" (16:7). In Luke, the women share the news of the empty tomb with the disciples, though we hear about it through the account of the two disciples going to Emmaus (24:22–23). In John, Mary Magdalene is alone commissioned by Jesus to bear witness to his resurrection. He instructs her, "Go to my brothers and say to them, 'I am ascending to my Father and your Father, to my God and your God'" (20:17).[25] Out of her mouth comes the very promise of God offering kinship, adoption, and eternal belonging. This is the moment toward which everything has been building for the women who followed Jesus from Galilee to Jerusalem.

Scripture tells us that Mary Magdalene's authority as a credible witness comes from Christ himself. No doubt basing the truth of the resurrection on the testimony of a woman once possessed by demons was risky. Yet the patterns of Scripture remind us that time and again God does the unexpected: choosing an elderly couple to have a child, choosing a man who struggles to speak to lead his people to freedom, choosing a boy to defeat a giant, choosing a young virgin to bear the Savior, choosing a formerly demon-possessed woman to bear witness to the defeat of death.

In one sense, Mary Magdalene was just the right witness. She had experienced Jesus's power to heal and save, she had participated in Jesus's ministry from Galilee, and she had witnessed his death on the cross. From a faith perspective, Mary Magdalene's proclamation holds credibility because she was instructed and commanded by Jesus himself to go and tell. The words of the angel about Jesus's death and resurrection ring true: "Remember how he told you. . . . Then they remembered his words" (Luke 24:6, 8). Mary Magdalene is not only a credible witness; she is called by the risen Lord himself.

Adding to the veracity of the account, the Gospel writers record the male disciples' doubt upon hearing the news: "But these words seemed to them an idle tale, and they did not believe them" (Luke 24:11). Though a culturally appropriate response at the time, it required correction.[26] Peter and John seemed more willing to entertain the possibility that the women's testimony might be true (Luke 24:12; John 20:3). The fact that the women's testimony was eventually accepted is readily apparent by its recording in the Gospels. The witness of the women in Luke is also confirmed in the account of the disciples on the road to Emmaus, which reports that some "found it just as the women had said" (24:24). Jesus's subsequent appearance to the eleven further confirmed that what the women had said was true. They are his witnesses.

In fact, in Luke 24, the eleven and their companions are gathered together (v. 33), which would include Mary Magdalene and the other women who have returned to tell the eleven and the others the good news of his resurrection.[27] While they are gathering, then, Jesus appears to them and says to them all: "You are witnesses of these things" (Luke 24:48). Later, Paul relays these events in his sermon at Antioch, saying, "For many days he appeared to those who came up with him from Galilee to Jerusalem, and they are now his witnesses to the people" (Acts 13:31).

There is simply no story of the New Testament church without Mary Magdalene and the other women, who are among the last at the cross and the first at the empty tomb. As Paul declares in Romans 10:14–15, "And how are they to hear without someone to proclaim him? And how are they to proclaim him unless they are sent? As it is written, 'How beautiful are the feet of those who bring good news!'" These were unexpected, beautiful feet that ran to proclaim the resurrection of Christ.

I Have Seen the Lord!

The Song of Simeon is the name given to the words of Simeon, a devout Jew, upon witnessing the fulfilled promise by the Holy Spirit that he would not die until he had seen the Messiah. When Jesus was presented at the temple by his parents, Simeon took the child in his arms and declared:

> Master, now you are dismissing your servant in
> peace,
> according to your word,
> for my eyes have seen your salvation,
> which you have prepared in the presence of all
> peoples,
> a light for revelation to the Gentiles
> and for glory to your people Israel. (Luke 2:29–32)

His words have been remembered and put to music as a hymn, titled the *Nunc dimittis*, which is still sung in some churches during evening worship.

But there was someone else in the temple that day: Anna, the daughter of Phanuel, of the tribe of Asher. Her encounter with the baby Jesus on that day is mentioned in just three verses immediately following the prophet Simeon's prophecy (Luke 2:36–38). Anna had been a widow for most of her life and never remarried. She remained at the temple for fasting and prayer. When she saw Jesus, she rejoiced and prophesied that he was God's answer to the redemption of Jerusalem.

As a woman proclaiming the good news of the risen Christ, Mary Magdalene reflects the ministry of Anna. Like Anna waiting at the temple faithfully, Mary Magdalene returns and lingers at the tomb. Like Anna recognizing Jesus as a baby, Mary Magdalene recognizes Jesus when he calls her name. Like Anna prophesying that Jesus the Redeemer has come, Mary Magdalene is called to proclaim that Christ is risen. Like bookends in Luke's Gospel, Anna and Mary Magdalene point us to Jesus Christ, the Son of God, the Messiah, our Redeemer. In the words of Mary Magdalene, "I have seen the Lord!" (John 20:18).

In truth, women have always born witness to the identity of Jesus Christ from his first moments in the womb. Luke describes when the pregnant Virgin Mary visited her cousin Elizabeth, who was pregnant with John the Baptist. When Elizabeth heard Mary's greeting upon arrival, John the Baptist heard it too and leaped in Elizabeth's womb. Filled with the Holy Spirit, Elizabeth cried out, "Blessed are you among women, and blessed is the fruit of your womb" (Luke 1:42).[28] Later, in Jesus's ministry, Peter confesses Christ as the Messiah (Matt. 16:13–20), and Jesus's exchange with Lazarus's sister, Martha of Bethany, leads to her declaration of faith: "Yes, Lord, I believe that you are the Messiah, the Son of God, the one coming into the world" (John 11:27). Both his male and female followers have opportunity to confess Jesus as the Christ.

Women were such an important part of Christ's ministry that Scripture notes when they converted alongside men (Acts 5:14; 8:12), particularly noting the conversion of leading women such as the businesswoman and first convert of Europe, Lydia (16:14). We see this in the account of Saul (Paul), who is recounted "dragging off both men and women" (8:3; 22:4) and was zealous in hunting down men and women (9:2). Women have never been inconsequential followers of Christ. As German theologian Jürgen Moltmann declared in a quote that launched a thousand memes: "If the women were all the time silent, then we would have no knowledge of the resurrection of Christ."[29]

In the end, Mary Magdalene is like all those who, having encountered Christ, want others to meet him as well. She is like both Simeon and Anna. She is like John the Baptist, who declared, "Here is the Lamb of God who takes away the sin of the world!" (John 1:29). Mary Magdalene points us to the cross and, ultimately, to the empty tomb and to the risen Lord. We turn our attention to her not only to know her rightly as a remembered sister of Christ but also for the sake of following Christ. To reflect on her story is to take seriously what Scripture says about Jesus. To recognize her apostolicity with the long tradition of the church both East and West is to realize that God calls and sends the unexpected. To recapture her example for the church today is to remind ourselves that we too are invited to be healed by Christ's power, to follow him alone, and to "go and tell" others that he has conquered death on our behalf. We too are called to point and declare, "I have seen the Lord!" We too are called to run "in preparation for the gospel of peace" (Eph. 6:15) according to his purposes, his will, and for his glory alone.

"He is not here. He is risen!"

EIGHT

The First Apostle
Chosen by Christ

Opening Walls, Tearing Curtains

On November 9, 1989, around 11:30 p.m., the Berlin Wall opened.[1] It was wholly unanticipated. I was in elementary school at the time and can still recall seeing the headlines and watching the footage of that momentous evening. The Cold War was thawing before our very eyes under the leadership of Mikhail Gorbachev, though we still worried about nuclear war. Remarkably, when the Berlin Wall opened, not a single person lost their life and not a single shot was fired. The tides had turned, washing away the Soviet Union.

Soon after came the tearing of the Iron Curtain. Though President Ronald Reagan's historic words at Brandenburg Gate may still ring in our ears—"Tear down this wall!"— this part of the story is not his or even Gorbachev's. Scholar

Mary Elise Sarotte describes the wall's demise as accidental; it was the result of a botched press conference that seemed to permit a temporary travel policy between the East and West. Gorbachev's celebrated "openness" to reform did not actually include a plan to open the wall. And no one could have anticipated Harald Jäger.

Jäger was a second-tier passport-control officer who happened to be the night watchman at a key checkpoint the evening the press conference took place. When crowds on the Eastern side began to swell, demanding passage into the West, Jäger received only belittling responses from his supervisor as he inquired over and over about what to do. The policy in place dictated that once a person left East for West, they were not allowed to return. But when faced with a young couple pleading to return home to their sleeping children, Jäger relented.

Jäger's decision to disobey the directive and let them travel back and forth proved monumental. Before midnight, tens of thousands of people had amassed at the wall demanding to cross. Jäger concluded that his officers would need to either start shooting people or open the wall. Grappling with his own recent cancer prognosis (later discovering it was a false alarm), Jäger ordered his company to open the wall. As Gorbachev slept, the Berlin Wall was opened, checkpoint by checkpoint, to the utter astonishment of the waking world. The European landscape was transformed in that moment, as it turned out, by the decision of one night watchman.

Scripture offers us the good news of a different kind of wall opened and a different kind of curtain torn, both of which impacted not only Mary Magdalene but all of us. Like the young German couple longing to be reunited with their children, God the Father desires to be reunited with his children (Gal. 1). God's Son was sent to break down the wall of human sin and death to make a way for us to receive abundant life, including everlasting life with him. This work of the triune God is revealed and accomplished through Christ in the womb, at the cross, and at the tomb.[2]

But what do we make of Mary Magdalene's presence at this remarkable turning point in salvation history, standing at the opening of the empty tomb and witness to the resurrection? If God could have orchestrated it however he chose, what could it mean that *she* was the night watchman there?

Each night, our family undertakes the extended ritual of putting little ones to bed. No child of ours is prepared to sleep, we have discovered, without going through the whole routine: snack, reading, brushing teeth, prayers, and song. Bedtime reading includes children's Bible stories, but my husband and I can rarely hold our tongue when parts of the story are missing or theological layers are left out. I suppose that's what you get when your parents are theologians in ministry. There's also an energy and an excitement to those exchanges as we teach our children to grapple with the challenge and opportunity of embracing the good news revealed in Scripture.

One night, I was reading a short children's book tracing Jesus's whole life and ministry in broad strokes; not an easy task for a children's book, to be sure. I can't recall if I had read it before, but it dawned on me as I turned the pages that not a single woman disciple was depicted as being called by Jesus, discovering the empty tomb, or encountering the resurrected Lord. Instead, Jesus's "friends" discover that he has been raised from the dead, and a group of male disciples are portrayed as hoisting Jesus on their shoulders in celebration. The female followers of Christ are nowhere to be seen, as though their part in the story is inconsequential.

And yet, Mary Magdalene's presence at the empty tomb is not at all debated in the Christian tradition. Every Gospel testifies to her being there (and, in all but one case, with other named women who also ministered to Jesus). Like a night watchman standing at the wall, she was attentive when others were not. We know that she as well as other named women (see table 7.2 in chap. 7) promptly arrived as soon as the Sabbath observance lifted "very early on the first day of the week" (Mark 16:2) or "while it was still dark" (John 20:1).[3] There is risk here for them.[4] Two of the Gospels explain that Mary Magdalene drew near to the tomb to anoint Christ's body, which we explored in chapter 2 as a kind of priestly act. But instead of offering a priestly anointing upon her arrival, Mary Magdalene departs with a priestly commission to proclaim Christ's resurrection. How do we make sense of such a monumental turn of events?

The New Testament invites us to consider how Jesus's death and resurrection transformed the priesthood. Three of the Gospels report that, in the moment Jesus took his final breath with a loud cry from the cross, the temple curtain tore "in two" / "from top to bottom" (Matt. 27:50–51; Mark 15:38; Luke 23:45). Different interpretations of this event circulate among scholars.[5] If referring to the inner curtain, it would have served as the barrier to the Holy of Holies. By its tearing, Jesus's death opened up a door in the wall, so to speak, to God's holiest dwelling, a space restricted exclusively to the high priest who entered once a year on Yom Kippur, the Day of Atonement (Lev. 16). By that restriction, no woman had ever entered God's holiest dwelling place. Theologically speaking, the torn curtain entwines Mary Magdalene's role in the unfolding story in a way that may help us make sense of this unexpected turn of events.

The account of the torn curtain resonates with other parts of the New Testament. The book of Hebrews, for example, describes Jesus as high priest and worthy sacrifice, who has enabled us to approach the throne of grace (4:16). Christ lifted barriers and extended our access both to the triune God and to one another. Peter describes in his first epistle a new priesthood as inaugurated through Christ: "You are a chosen people, a royal priesthood, a holy nation, God's own people" (1 Pet. 2:9). Paul, meanwhile, teaches that faith in Christ has rendered us children of God, baptized in his name, and belonging one to another so that former divisions such as Jew or Greek, slave or free, male or female, are also transformed (Gal. 3:28). A new creation was dawning.

The Gospels show us that Jesus Christ's shift from death to life has a profound impact on those who witness Christ's resurrection. Mary Magdalene is the first to glimpse the transformation, and her place there at that moment is not an inconsequential detail that we can leave off or include as we like. To make sense of her presence there at that monumental juncture in human history, we must see that this moment is also her apostolic calling, marked by the rending of the curtain. As Craig Keener writes, "Perhaps the old veil was 'rent' because the new order would not fit it."[6] In a sense, she figuratively takes the first steps through the opening that Christ's death on the cross and resurrection alone has made possible.

The Threshold

I am especially struck by the detail that Mary Magdalene stands grieving at the opening of the tomb wall (John 20:11). We can picture her in that space, at that extraordinary turning point, her feet planted on a kind of threshold between bodily death and new life. N. T. Wright points out that John's prologue finds its telos in chapter 20: "John declares from the start, with the obvious allusion to Genesis 1:1, that his book is about the new creation in Jesus. . . . Easter is the start of the new creation."[7] John recounts that she bent down to look inside the tomb, leaning, as it turns out, into new purpose. From that point forward, several pieces of her calling to Christ's ministry unfold from the text.

It's interesting that the Gospel writers do not give us insight into the initial invitation or welcome that Jesus extended or that Mary Magdalene sought when she joined his ministry in Galilee as a patron. Her story of calling is not given to us to remember save this one. Not only does Jesus call her by name, she was also the first person called by him after the opening of the tomb. Her calling was followed by a commissioning, which she received directly from Christ himself so that she became the first person (or among the first group of people) to be sent by Jesus to share the good news: "Go and tell" (Matt. 28:10; John 20:17).

Too often we make this choice, this calling, happenstance, coincidence, or exception. How else can we explain this surprising turn of events that Mary Magdalene of all people is the first apostle after the resurrection chosen by Christ? It defies easy explanation to be sure, and yet we see her there as the firstfruits of a new priesthood at the very dawning of the new creation forged in Christ that is no longer exclusively Levitical and no longer exclusively male. The qualifications for the priesthood are shifting before our eyes, no longer rooted in a person's traits but in a person's union with the Son of God. When the genealogy of the priesthood shifted through Christ, this created space—inexplicable space by way of a torn curtain and an open wall—for Mary Magdalene.

To claim the title of "apostle" for Mary Magdalene is not merely a retrieval of a shared, global church tradition, whether lost, obscure, or unknown. We can appeal to the highest biblical definitions given in Scripture for apostolicity as it applies to Mary Magdalene's Gospel story:[8] (1) she accompanied the twelve in Christ's ministry, (2) witnessed his death and resurrection, and (3) was "sent" on a divine mission (Luke 10:3; Acts 1:21; 1 Cor. 9:1–2; 15).[9] The New Testament's use of the term aligns with the meaning of "witness" and "messenger," which reflects her journey with Christ from Galilee to Jerusalem and the commissioning she received from him. In Ephesians 4:11, Paul declares that Jesus "himself granted that some are apostles, prophets, evangelists, pastors and teachers," situating himself in the former category. In fact, Paul's claim to apostolicity as divine command rather than human authority further confirms Mary Magdalene's apostolicity: "Paul an apostle—sent neither by human commission nor from human authorities but through Jesus Christ and God the Father, who raised him from the dead" (Gal. 1:1, 11–12). Because Mary Magdalene too was directly sent by the risen Christ, and there is no higher authority, these two callings complement each other in an illuminating way. For the church to accept Paul's claim to apostolicity—though he considered himself the "least of the apostles" and "unfit" because he persecuted the church (1 Cor. 15:9)[10]—also places Mary Magdalene among that select group according to Scripture's own criteria.

Think again about Mary Magdalene on the threshold of the open tomb. A new priesthood was being inaugurated by Christ involving some of the most surprising, unexpected people, including women, fishermen, and tax collectors. Another layer of God's abundance comes into focus when we retrieve and remind the church of Mary's importance today. As Jesus declares, "Very truly, I tell you, whoever receives one whom I send receives me, and whoever receives me receives him who sent me" (John 13:20). What could it mean for Christians to receive Mary Magdalene, the first apostle sent by Jesus Christ?

The "Earthquake Readiness" Badge

I was born on a fault. The San Fernando fault line, to be exact, located in Southern California. As a child, we were constantly preparing ourselves for the "big one"—the earthquake that would be bigger than anything we had ever experienced. The San Francisco earthquake of 1906 still loomed large in the California mind. We had not only fire drills but earthquake drills. For Brownies (the first stage of Girl Scouts), I received badges for crafts, for friendship, and for white gloves and party manners. And then I had the "earthquake readiness" badge. I was ready.

One sunny morning in 1987, my mom was braiding my hair before school when an earthquake hit. The whole house started shaking and rumbling. We watched the books fly off the shelves. Pillows toppled off chairs. A glass fell and broke. But we were prepared.

The bed was already latched to the wall. The bookcases bolted. As soon as the shaking started, my mom and I looked at each other in the mirror and said together in that split second (almost like a script), "It's here!"

We rushed to the doorframe. We knew exactly how to position our bodies after plenty of practice. We braced ourselves. The Whittier Earthquake of 1987 was thirty seconds long. In those few seconds, like a flash, our whole world began to shake around us. There was very little to do. There was no stopping it. Even though we were prepared, and even though it stopped after thirty seconds, we were shaken. Even when the world stopped trembling, we continued trembling at the power that we had witnessed and felt that was so much greater than ourselves.

Similarly, the in-breaking of the kingdom of God that was ushered in with Christ was no passive event. The incarnation of Christ was an earthquake-like disruption reaching from heavenly to earthly orders all the way into human hearts. With Jesus's death on the cross, Matthew records an earthquake in addition to the torn curtain later followed by a second earthquake caused, it seems, by the rolling away of the tomb's stone.[11] As biblical scholar Robert H. Gundry explains, in Matthew, "the earthquake is a prelude to the opening of tombs."[12] Are we ready for resurrection?

Renewed readings require renewed practice as we seek to remember Mary Magdalene rightly. When we draw all the biblical and historical pieces together, a mosaic forms that is multifaceted but still coherent. Mary Magdalene emerges as a model of *readiness* for the church, both men and women, for the fullness of discipleship.[13] She proclaims Christ in word *and* deed. She was ready to be sent because she was ready to follow.

Ready to Follow

Mary Magdalene models a readiness to follow Christ that, if remembered and shared, could certainly inspire our churches today. Her life, according to the Gospel writers, testifies to how Jesus can bring healing, wholeness, and transformation to those who suffer. Jesus Christ alone is able to drive out the demons that bind us. Scripture invites us to remember her as healed and free, and what a transformation that must have been!

Her response to Christ's healing is equally powerful. She seems to embody Paul's teaching in 1 Corinthians 9 that our freedom in Christ is the freedom to serve. She redirects her life to follow Jesus. The good news here for all of us is that our life before Christ does not disqualify us from the healing that Jesus offers, nor does it disqualify us from following him and joining his ministry. Her healing confirmed Jesus's identity as Savior and the coming of his kingdom, and it brought credibility to her testimony when she declared to the disciples, "I have seen the Lord" (John 20:18). She enriched the testimony of Jesus's ministry, just as our testimonies of Christ's transformative power can enrich the ministry of our churches. As he ministers to her, she ministers to him however she is able.

She was ready to follow, and her life reflects a persevering faith in Christ from Galilee to the cross to the closing of the tomb. She never turns her back on Christ after being healed, according to what we know from Scripture. Her sins, whatever they might have been, are not mentioned by the Gospel writers, though she is certainly a redeemed sinner like all who believe in Jesus Christ. Yet, we are directed to remember her as a faithful follower to Jesus. Even amid the twelve being scattered by the crisis of Jesus's arrest, and Judas's betrayal, and Peter's fear, she perseveres in faith.[14] Even when filled with grief, she perseveres in faith.

In an era of dechurching and faith deconstruction, Mary Magdalene can serve as a model of steady faith in Christ, even when our churches fail us and hurt us. By focusing on following Christ, she was able to invest in the community of believers *during* times of crisis and hardship. She was a tower of strength after all, which signals her importance in the group.[15] Her strong faith is a central part of her legacy and, if remembered rightly, could be an inspiration for our churches today as a model of faithful discipleship.[16]

Ready to Give

When I was in fourth grade, in the middle of the school year, my family moved from Los Angeles to West Texas—from the world of Hollywood to the home of Buddy Holly. It was a culture shock. On the drive, we noticed that the ground got flatter, the sky larger, the accents thicker, and the people friendlier. As we drove into our new neighborhood, people on the sidewalks waved as we drove by. My brother and I laughed in disbelief. "Do you know them?" we asked our parents warily. We had left a beautiful home near Studio City for a humble pastor's manse in the panhandle. We walked into the house for a short tour and came to the kitchen. Every single cupboard had been packed full to the brim with food. Our entire refrigerator was jammed with meals in a practice known in West Texas as a "pounding." Even as a child, I was stunned. I had never experienced such hospitality, let alone from a community that did not even know us. I remember seeing the joy and disbelief on my parents' faces as I felt what it was like to receive abundance from the church family.

Mary Magdalene's readiness to follow was coupled with a readiness to give. She provided financial support for Jesus's ministry as a benefactor, but she also reprioritized her life to offer her time and presence to Christ's ministry. She made herself "ready for every good work," as we are reminded to do (Titus 3:1; 2 Tim. 2:21). The ministry of giving is truly powerful. Mary Magdalene gave of her time but also her talent and treasure. She gave of her focus, learning from Jesus as his disciple. Karla Zazueta describes her as the first "female seminarian."[17] She gave freely to Jesus even when she thought he was dead, even when her association with him put her at risk. Her ordinary example is truly extraordinary.

In her readiness to give to God, she reminds churches that every good and perfect gift comes from God (James 1:17), who is the giver of all good things. We hold our gifts, therefore, loosely that we might be ready to give back to God's glory alone. We give not as those under duress or compulsion but out of a cheerful, willing, and ready heart (Matt. 6:3; 2 Cor. 9:7). As our lives move through different seasons, we must resolve to give and then give again of who we are and what we have because of *whose* we are. It will not always look the same in every season of life. Knowing Mary Magdalene's story can inspire the discipleship of giving in our churches today, no matter our season of life.

Ready to Run

Because she was ready to follow and ready to give, Mary Magdalene was ready to run when Jesus called her to proclaim the core truth of the Christian faith: that he is alive! Paul describes this news as being of "first importance" (1 Cor. 15:3). Christ's followers are called to receive and to hand on what was handed to us: namely, that Christ died for our sins, that he was buried, that he rose again, and that he appeared to his disciples, both men and women (1 Cor. 15:3–6). Our testimony is built on the foundation of the apostles (Eph. 2:20).

Our churches could do more to recognize the importance of the particular way that God arranged this critical turning point. Jesus set a new precedent by calling Mary Magdalene to the task and sending her as the first apostle. Her place at the threshold of the tomb is not a fringe story but a central component of the intentional unfolding of God's plan for salvation. Called to tell the disciples of the fulfillment of what Jesus had foretold (Luke 24:6), she was obedient. Despite their initial disbelief (Mark 16:14; Luke 24:11), nevertheless she persisted. Her priestly task of proclamation set in motion a sequence of events that led Christ's followers, both men and women, to go to the place where they would receive the Great Commission and to await in the upper room the coming of the Holy Spirit with Pentecost. As Bauckham writes, "The experience of the women is not only chronologically prior but also indispensable for the men's experience. Only because the men believe and obey the revelation brought them by the women can they themselves see the Lord."[18] Mary Magdalene's presence in that moment is not inconsequential or accidental. She was chosen as the first apostle by the resurrected Lord, and it matters because God could have done it another way.

By her story the church is challenged to recognize its own walls that prevent female believers in Christ from proclaiming the good news and from being ready to be called and sent. For where would the church be today if the male disciples had not listened to Mary Magdalene? If they hadn't let her speak when she found them that morning? If they had ignored her completely? And what are we missing today if we don't allow those women who are gifted, called, and sent to preach the good news of Jesus Christ with which they too have been entrusted? If we take Mary Magdalene's calling and sending seriously, how would it change our churches today?

Just imagine how the church's ministry could be enriched if the biblical account of Mary Magdalene was known in our churches today as a model of Christian discipleship. After all, Scripture commands us to be ready, not only to follow Christ daily now but in anticipation of the age to come. In Matthew 24:44 the followers of Christ are urged to "be ready" for the unexpected hour of Christ's return, the next big earthquake to disrupt.

Remembering the Forgotten Women

When it comes to women in history, including women in the Bible, we are often left excavating things unknown, forgotten, distorted, or overlooked.

Plautilla Nelli (1524–88), a nun during the Italian Renaissance, was also a painter. She became well known in her time for her artwork. She created a studio of artist nuns, and her paintings, bought and sold by the elite of Florence, became a source of important financial income for her convent. Though it was not customary at the time, she signed her name to her artwork along with the invocation "Orate pro pictora" or "Pray for the woman painter." But her life and contribution to Christian art were nearly forgotten entirely. Her work, including her *Last Supper* measuring more than 22 feet wide and nearly 6 feet high, had been lost and unknown. It is only recently that her work and the work of other female artists have been discovered buried and forgotten in cellars and attics.[19]

Similarly, Mary Magdalene's place in the biblical story has been buried in the cellars and attics of our churches. We forget her when we overlook the many times that each Gospel names her and where Jesus himself calls her by name. We forget her when we associate her with prostitution rather than remembering her as the one released from seven demons. In forgetting that pivotal piece to her story, we remove a crucial witness and testimony to Christ's power to overcome the evil one. But there's more. By forgetting Mary Magdalene's place in the Gospels, we miss how she and certain women traveled with Jesus and that Mary Magdalene was the first among them. In forgetting this aspect of Jesus's ministry, we overlook the financial support that he received from women, such as Mary Magdalene, to undertake his ministry. When we forget her among his traveling followers, we miss seeing how Jesus discipled and taught both men and women in his inner circles.

Most grievously, forgetting Mary Magdalene requires us to forget her witness at the cross and the closing of the tomb. We forget her encounter with the risen Christ at the empty tomb and her early morning run. We miss how she was the first to witness the risen Lord and the first apostle called and sent by Jesus to proclaim his resurrection. If the testimony of Christ's resurrection rests on the first witnesses, then to forget Mary Magdalene at the empty tomb and before the risen Lord is a disastrous case of the church's collective memory loss. Her readiness to run is the outworking of her readiness to follow and give of herself and her resources to Christ's ministry.

Most importantly, we miss seeing her preach the good news by the authority of Christ's command. Interestingly, church history claims that her sending was not merely to relay a message but to proclaim the gospel. On this point, Bauckham writes, "It is clear that Mary's own commission to 'go and tell' (20:17) is not exhausted in the delivering of her message to the disciples: she is certainly more than an 'apostle to the apostles.'"[20]

She is also apostle *among* the apostles.

When we look closely at her place in the redemption story, we begin to see a pattern in Scripture of a God who surprises us by whom he calls and sends, both women and men. By attuning ourselves to her story, we learn to read Scripture more closely for the unexpected, that we might grow in our understanding of the triune God and as disciples of Christ in the church today. We begin to see a God who calls women to preach.

To remember Mary Magdalene as well as the certain women of Galilee who traveled with Jesus is to remember that Jesus called both men and women to work together for his kingdom. By refusing to forget Mary Magdalene, we are reminded that *both* "men and women moved by the Holy Spirit spoke from God" (2 Pet. 1:21).

Ultimately, we turn our eyes to Mary Magdalene because Scripture directs us to her. To what end? When we receive Mary Magdalene, we receive the one who called and sent her. When we finally see her, we can see *with* her, to the one she sees and knows. When we see with her, we can run *with* her to share the good news of Jesus's rising.

She has handed it on to them, and they to us.

Now, it's our turn.

Are we ready for the earthquake that opens tombs?

Epilogue

Mary Magdalene for the Church Today

The Church Is a Garden

The scene is a garden, again. A different garden, this one in Milan and centuries later in 386. Augustine, originally from North Africa, had spent years wandering, seeking truth through different philosophies. He now found himself in Italy, increasingly distressed over the state of his life, and he had withdrawn with a troubled and restless heart.[1] He would later describe his state of turmoil as "hanging back from dying to death and living for life."[2] With tears streaming down his face, he pulled at his hair and flung himself in anguish under a fig tree, the psalmist's words in his thoughts and on his tongue: How long, O Lord? (Ps. 79:5).[3] Then the singular sound of a child's song broke through, catching his ear: "Take up and read! Take up and read!"[4] He picked up the Bible and flipped to Romans 13, where he found this text: "Let us then throw off the works of darkness and put on the armor of light. . . . Put on the Lord Jesus Christ, and make no provision for the flesh, to gratify its desires." It was the most fitting message at the most fitting moment. The last vestiges of his hesitation passed away, and he turned his life over to Christ.

Augustine's experience of the revelation of God through Scripture as an in-breaking into his life—speaking, teaching, and redirecting while also fostering a deep conviction and confirmation of God's truth in his heart—was a turning point not only for him personally but for the faith of the wider church as well. In retelling that moment in his spiritual autobiography *Confessions*, he planted an expectation that God speaks to us through the written Word,[5] that the reality of our sin and the truth of Christ's saving work can be revealed through an encounter with the text, that our lives can be transformed by Scripture, and that we can receive the good news of the gospel in the garden.

Gardens punctuate the story of Christianity, from Eden to Gethsemane to Augustine's garden in Milan. In a way, the church *is* a garden.[6] It is where our faith takes hold, where we can be fed and nurtured, where we harvest the fruit of our faith. The church becomes a garden when the seed of the gospel is sown and takes root (such as in the parable of the sower in Matt. 13). The church is a garden when, like Mary Magdalene before us, we encounter the presence of the gardener there ("I am the true vine, and my Father is the gardener," John 15:1 NIV), who cultivates the soil in such a way that new life is possible. Augustine reflected after his conversion, "This gardener was sowing in her [Mary Magdalene's] heart, as in His own garden, the grain of mustard seed."[7] Like Augustine, we encounter in the garden the seed of the gospel that breaks new ground in our life, bringing to light something we did not see, correcting something we did not understand, making us new. When the church is the church, it acts as a garden where hard tasks—the tilling of the soil, the removal of rocks, the irrigation of the land—lead to true flourishing.[8]

Today, we are being invited to *take up and read* from Scripture about the forgotten Mary. Here is our chance to see her not only as an important part of the biblical text but, above all, to encounter Christ, who revealed himself to her and who called and sent her to serve as the first apostle. Perhaps you, like me, did not really see her before. Perhaps you did not fully understand her part in Christ's ministry. So many of us are in that position because of the confusion and scandal that is so often associated with her name. But what would it mean for the church today to remember Mary Magdalene rightly, to take her biblical calling and sending seriously? How would it transform our churches?

Sowing: Are We Reading and Hearing the Stories of Women in Scripture?

In his famously winsome way, Eugene Peterson (translator of The Message) identifies the obstacle that seems to befall every well-meaning New Year's resolution to read the Bible in a year: Leviticus. He writes, "Leviticus, I am sure, is responsible for more people giving up on a systematic, page-after-page reading of the Bible than anything else."[9] But what happens if we skip Leviticus, particularly Leviticus 19:18? We would miss the command found there to love our neighbor.[10] We would miss the call to *love*, in Leviticus of all places!

Perhaps we assume that only certain parts of the Bible can speak to us. Or maybe we are simply avoiding grappling with the hard places in Scripture that are difficult to understand or accept. As biblical scholar Esau McCaulley has so profoundly taught and modeled, these are the moments to wrestle like Jacob until the text delivers its blessing.[11]

In every generation of Christians there are difficult parts of Scripture, though not every generation of Christians has found the same parts of Scripture difficult. One of the first heresies of the church came from Marcion, who tried to remove all the Jewish connections to Christianity. Marcion tried to forge a faith apart from Hebrew prophecy and fulfillment in Christ, and the church's leadership put its foot down.

One way to value Mary Magdalene's calling and sending is to take stock of which parts of Scripture are informing our church communities, including our own reading of Scripture and which parts we seem to be missing. Are we sowing seeds in the garden that include the women of the Bible? Do we engage with, as historian Beth Allison Barr describes it, "the great cloud of female witnesses"?[12] Do they have a place in the liturgical cycles of our worship and in the sermons preached from our pulpits? In some churches, the pastor's sermon series may guide the selection of Scripture passages. That can be helpful insofar as a pastor may know exactly which text a congregation needs to hear, but it might also mean that pastors choose well-known or favorite passages over more difficult or challenging texts. In some churches, the lectionary may shape the selection of the texts. This cycle of readings is meant to draw the church's attention to the main narrative of Scripture, typically over a three-year period, but there are still portions of the Bible left out.[13] Which texts we choose and which ones we overlook shape our perspective on God while also perhaps revealing our blind spots, our go-to biblical favorites, and a tendency of cultural presentism.

During the Protestant Reformation of the sixteenth century, reforming efforts sought to root its practices in *lectio continua*, the continuous reading of Scripture in sequence over a period of time. This kind of practice can ensure that difficult topics or issues are not easily overlooked. Complex figures are not necessarily ignored. *Lectio continua* can help fix our attention on the whole biblical canon, while ensuring that preaching on the women of the Bible takes place from the pulpit. This approach finds its grounding not in a principle of diversity but in the understanding that to interpret the parts of Scripture faithfully, we must know the whole of Scripture.

One dynamic we might find at work in our churches is that the stories of women in the Bible are reserved for women's ministry or women's retreats. To be sure, we should bring the stories of women in the Bible (and from church history) to the women of the church today, but we have to be careful that those stories are not partitioned off from the rest of the church gathered on Sunday. When the stories of women are excluded from the pulpit, a kind of hermeneutical segregation sets in. We begin to read the Bible in a way that was not intended. The story of God's redemptive work through believing men and women is an interwoven, fully integrated, and shared story. The calling and sending of women in the Bible matters for women *and* men.[14] We are, after all, colaborers made in the image of God. Carolyn Custis James describes this as the "blessed alliance," according to the Genesis account.[15] In that case, Mary Magdalene's example and her proclamation is meant for the whole church, including men, just as Peter's example is meant for the whole church, including women.

The question is simple: Are our churches willing and able to grapple with these texts with care and insight so that the congregation can see God's work through women in the Bible, as well as God's work through men?[16]

The seeds of Scripture that are sown in the garden should not exclude the valuable contributions of women in God's redemptive story and the way in which the mission of the church has been pursued by men and women together. Mary Magdalene was in the garden with Jesus. Have our congregations grappled with what that means?

Cultivating: Are We Cultivating the Gifts of Women?

A significant number of young, single women and professional women are leaving the church.[17] This demographic shift upends long-standing trends and assumptions regarding the presence of women in the church. These developments challenge the church to reexamine not only our pastoral care and inclusion of women but the way we cultivate the gifts of women. Jesus was attentive to such things.

Public theologian Rebecca McLaughlin points out that each of the Gospels "bears female fingerprints."[18] The way that Jesus is seen by women is not missing from the Christian story, though we are often slow to recognize it. What women saw is actually essential to our faith.[19] We should not cut short the implications. When we take Mary Magdalene's example of calling and sending seriously, we are invited not only to look at Jesus through her eyes ("I have seen the Lord!" John 20:18) but to glimpse how Jesus in turn saw Mary Magdalene.

Her story is a prominent reminder (though not the only one!) that Jesus did not turn a blind eye to women in his pastoral care and among his ministry leadership. Even while hanging on the cross, he looked out for his mother Mary (John 19:26–27). Even when jostled by the crowds, he healed the hurting, bent, and broken bodies of women (Luke 8:43–48; 13:10–17). He neither ignored nor overlooked the widows (Mark 12:41–44; Luke 7:11–17). He brought women back to life from death (Mark 5:21–43). In Mary Magdalene's case, he pulled women out of the depths of a demonic grip.

But for all that he did for women, he never built his power on their backs. Instead, he willingly healed them and incorporated them into his ministry by calling, teaching, and sending them. He received financial support from them, and he invited them into the inner circles of his traveling ministry (Luke 8:2–3). He received their acts of pious devotion willingly and instructed us to see and remember them (Luke 7:36–50).

Drawing together all these parts of Scripture, we are able to go beyond glimpsing how women saw Jesus to *how Jesus saw women*. Though the world elevates sons, Jesus sees the most marginalized woman and calls her a "daughter of Abraham" (Luke 13:16). Even when the world is uncomfortable with the devotion of a sinful woman, Jesus makes sure we see her and remember her. "Do you see this woman?" he asks (Luke 7:44).[20] Do we?

Perhaps Jesus recognized the value of women in God's kingdom not only because "all things have been created through him" (Col. 1:17) but because he did not segregate himself from women during his ministry on earth. He never claimed that, because he was a man, he couldn't minister to a hurting woman or teach her or send her or look at her or talk with her. No, he spoke to them, broke bread with them, equipped them for the work of his ministry. He was a brother to the twelve and to the women followers and disciples, including Mary Magdalene. And when the time came, the risen Jesus declared to all of them the coming of the Holy Spirit: "You are witnesses of these things. And see, I am sending upon you what my Father promised" (Luke 24:48–49).

When the church takes the calling and sending of Mary Magdalene seriously, the gifts of women for faith and ministry are cultivated for growth. Are the women of our church encouraged to grow in their faith, discern their gifts, and follow God's calling on their lives? Are the women of the church equipped to both serve and lead? Are the women of the church, both gifted and equipped, given opportunities to lead prayer, read Scripture, and preach from the pulpit? Are the women of the church involved in the leadership decisions of the church? When the church sees women *as Jesus saw women*, it will begin to embrace the colaboring of women in the church.

Blossoming: Are We Encouraging Women in the Church to Blossom for the Glory of the Gardener?

When the fullness of the seed is sown and proper cultivation follows, the subsequent blossoming brings glory to the Gardener: "Consider the lilies, how they grow . . . even Solomon in all his glory was not clothed like one of these" (Luke 12:27).

Under the care of Jesus, Mary Magdalene blossomed. Drawn out from dark places, she was brought into the light. She was taught and equipped to participate in Jesus's ministry. Jesus received financial support from her. When Jesus called and sent her, she was ready to run and proclaim the good news of the resurrection. If there is one reason to support women who have been equipped and called to preach, it's that Jesus did so.[21]

Mary Magdalene was sent to proclaim the crux of the Christian faith (1 Cor. 15:14), and she was commissioned by Jesus Christ himself to the task. When women are barred from preaching the good news simply because they are women, the church is missing what Jesus did when he called and sent Mary Magdalene. We know that it was hard for the male disciples to accept: "But these words seemed to them an idle tale, and they did not believe them" (Luke 24:11). Yet, just as Jesus did not scorn being born of a woman, he also did not scorn sending one.

If the church is to emulate the New Testament church in the mission of Christ, it must grapple more earnestly with the implications of the witness of Mary Magdalene. Are restrictions on women in our churches creating more or less gospel proclamation? Would our churches

215

listen to Mary Magdalene if she came to bear witness in our assemblies or would we dismiss her because she is a woman? To those who might say that Mary Magdalene is the exception to the rule, Matthew's Gospel notes that she is joined by a second Mary, and they are both directly instructed by Jesus to "go and tell" the brothers (Matt. 28:10). Herein lies one of the values of the diverse resurrection accounts: the one where Mary Magdalene is alone denotes her particular significance, while the ones where she bears witness among a group of Jesus's female disciples deny that she is an exception. The faithful "certain women" who traveled with Jesus and witnessed from the cross to the tomb represent a new era of ministry, which became fully inaugurated at the coming of the Holy Spirit at Pentecost (Acts 2).

All these things have been seen in the text and declared by women for centuries across the generations, though not always with awareness of one another. It has not escaped women's attention that Mary Magdalene's calling and sending by Jesus himself opens the door for their own calling and sending. During the medieval period, Christine de Pizan noted, "If woman's speech had really been so disgraceful and unreliable as some would have it, then our Lord Jesus Christ would have never seen fit to decree that so glorious a mystery as His most glorious resurrection would first be announced by a woman."[22] Pizan concludes that the speech of women is God-given so that women might better serve him.

Before I left for seminary, my mother gave me a book signed by Fleming Rutledge with a message of encouragement written inside. Years later, we all three had the privilege of sharing a meal together. We represented different generations of women, all called to preach, all called to ordination in the church. It was a reminder that the blossoming of the garden is to the glory of God alone. As Paul writes, "I planted, Apollos watered, but God gave the growth. So neither the one who plants nor the one who waters is anything, but only God who gives the growth. . . . For we are God's coworkers, working together; you are God's field" (1 Cor. 3:6–9). What we do, we do to the glory of the one true Gardener.

We Have Roots

Twentieth-century French philosopher Simone Weil writes, "To be rooted is perhaps the most important and least recognized need of the human soul."[23] She goes on to consider the living roots of human life from work to community. But what about our spiritual roots?

Too often, the Protestant tradition has tried to function apart from roots. But these roots are part of our story whether we recognize them or not. When we confess Jesus Christ as Lord and Savior, we are automatically drawn into a communion that is far greater than just ourselves, far greater than just our local church. The first words of Paul's influential letter to the church in Corinth may seem geared only to those in Corinth. But in the very next line Paul addresses the Corinthian Christians "together with all those who in every place call on the name of our Lord Jesus Christ."[24] That's us, friends! Those words challenge us to take off our church blinders and begin to see how Christ draws his believers to himself (John 12:32). We who confess Christ are linked to one another, and it connects us across time, place, and space. We are linked to Jew and Gentile, male and female, slave and free (Gal. 3:28). We are linked to our sister, Mary Magdalene.

In Christ alone we are part of an intricate root system that connects us to the visible and the invisible by the power of the Holy Spirit. There is no age, no generation that is not touched by the work that God is doing. Nothing can hinder or diminish the glory that God is working across generations. By faith in the Son, a new family is being formed that binds us to life eternal through union with Christ. Galatians 6:10 describes it as a "family of faith." We have been drawn into the story of God's great undoing of death, as Rutledge explains.[25] A new structure is being built and joined together spiritually (Eph. 2:21–22) by the one who entered time and space for us and is also beyond time and space. No human hand is capable of building such a wonder. We are being joined and built to grow together with the apostles Peter and Paul, and we are also being joined and built to grow together with the apostle Mary Magdalene.

Do we see her now, traveling with Jesus, standing at the cross, grieving at the tomb, encountering the risen Lord in the garden, being sent by Jesus to proclaim the good news? She may not be who we thought she was or who we expected, but when we remember her rightly she becomes a faithful example who can surprise us and spur us on to proclaim "I have seen the Lord" (John 20:18). Are we ready to receive the one who was sent by Christ? Are we ready to run with her?

Acknowledgments

The wonderfully challenging task of uncovering the forgotten Mary Magdalene has proven to be deeply enriching and rewarding work. Discerning her expansive story has required and challenged me to weave together many different threads across disciplines. In this book, I am drawing from marvelous minds in biblical studies, sifting through the density of church history, offering theological reflection, and always seeking to work from a pastor's heart and mission for the church. I have learned so much through the process, and there are many to whom I am indebted.

I am immensely grateful to gifted (and giving) professors who have invested in me over the course of my educational journey from a liberal arts education to seminary training to the university, which has made this cross-disciplinary project possible. Given the focus of this book, I want to mention the several scholar-mentor-professors at Westmont College in Santa Barbara, California, who have been instrumental in my life, faith, and education in biblical studies. Thank you to Dr. Robert H. Gundry for first opening my eyes to the historical background of the New Testament and the intricacies of New Testament Greek. His mentoring of me over the years has been one of the greatest blessings of my life. I am also appreciative of Dr. Tremper Longman for providing me with a foundation in hermeneutics and biblical theology that has been so instrumental. There are hardly words to express how much Dr. Karen Jobes means to me. She was first a beloved professor of mine in advanced Greek and later became a colleague and friend (and always an inspiration!).

Since I began teaching at Wheaton College, I have been thankful for so many encouraging colleagues, some of whom have also become creative collaborators and close friends. In that regard, I am particularly thankful for New Testament scholar Amy Peeler. There is such joy in the meeting of minds for the glory of God and the care of the church. The pieces that we have written together for *Christianity Today* (*CT*) magazine on Jesus's mother Mary and Phoebe were some of the first seeds of my thinking that led me to write this book on Mary Magdalene. Thanks also to our former editor at *CT* (now cherished friend!), Andrea Palpant Dilley, for seeing the potential of this work and making a way for its inclusion, development, and promotion. In 2024, that *CT* baton was passed on to the gifted Kara Bettis Carvalho with our appreciation.

The desire to better understand Mary Magdalene in both Scripture and church history was first fostered by a sermon that I preached in 2018 on Luke 8 at my church, First Presbyterian Church of Glen Ellyn, where I serve as a parish associate. When Kristen Padilla, director of the

220

Women in Ministry Center at Beeson Divinity School at the time, called to invite me to deliver the plenary talks at Beeson's first Women in Ministry conference, Mary Magdalene was my first thought. Speaking at that gathering in 2021 was a milestone moment in my life, and I am richly blessed by Kristen's friendship and her ongoing encouragement of this project.

I want to also thank the Center for Pastor Theologians (CPT), which has been an important community for clerical fellowship as both a scholar and an ordained minister. My Augustinian Fellowship within the CPT provided helpful feedback at an early stage in my project for which I am appreciative, and a plenary talk at the 2023 CPT conference gave me an added opportunity to share more of my work. Thank you to Joel Lawrence and Rae Paul, as well as Todd Wilson and Gerald Hiestand.

The content of this book was further enriched by a visiting research fellowship received from the American College of the Mediterranean in Aix-en-Provence, where our family spent the summer. During our time in Provence, we visited the places where Mary Magdalene was remembered as an evangelist of France, and those excursions made their way into the book. I am grateful for the support of the former dean Laura Montgomery and the Global and Experiential Learning office at Wheaton College as well as provost Karen Lee, who made this onsite experience possible through faculty research grant support. Time in France has always been enriched by our longtime, precious friendship with the Worré family, whose home in Paris has been a second home to us over the years as a base for further research and community.

We are grateful for all that we share together, especially our faith in Christ.

Special thanks are owed to my editor at Brazos Press, Katelyn Beaty, who saw the potential of my work to reach a broader audience. She is well known for her keen eye and insightful perspective, and those traits have undoubtedly improved this project. She has my gratitude and appreciation for the time that she gave to my project! Thanks also to Erin Smith and Shelly MacNaughton for their help in getting me ready for this process and work in the promotion and marketing of the book. I'm grateful to Eric Salo, my copy editor, for his good eye and improvements to the manuscript. Anna Gissing's assistance at various points with research and discussion of the material was appreciated. It has been a pleasure to work with the team at Brazos/Baker.

Several of my own stories and faith experiences are woven into this book along with those I have cultivated as sermon illustrations in the pulpit for congregants and devotionals in the classroom for students. In the book, I mention my growing up in Lubbock, Texas, as the place where my faith in Christ took deep root. I want to thank the ministry of Westminster Presbyterian Church, where my father, Rev. Dr. John Powell, served as lead pastor and where my middle brother, Rev. Elliott Powell, now serves. Many families there, including my own, contributed to my understanding of Scripture and the formation of my heart, mind, and life for God, including the Gillans, Joneses, Shanklins, Keelings, and Sanders families as well as a vibrant youth group. Christ-centered friendships from Lubbock have brought so much joy to my life, and we continue to be prayer partners with one another into our forties. I am immensely grateful for Shannon Aycock Powell, who has been my closest lifelong sister of the heart turned sister-in-law, for her unfailing encouragement and love. She never fails to cheer me on and inspire me, including in this project, for which I am grateful.

This book would not have been possible if it weren't for the love and support of my husband, the Rev. Dr. David McNutt, who is my partner in life and ministry as well as my best friend. Not every author is so blessed to be married to a senior editor at a major Christian publishing house, so I am immensely grateful for the insight that he gives me in my work and calling. Our three beloved children—Priscilla, Geneva, and Finnegan—bring immeasurable joy to our lives and now know Mary Magdalene's name and story better than many adults. I am grateful to them for faithfully trekking to each and every Mary Magdalene site we could visit in southern France with interest and cheerful anticipation. I pray that she will continue to be an inspiration to their faith and model for discipleship as they grow in the Lord.

I have dedicated this book to my loving mother, the Rev. Dr. Pamela Powell, and to my aunt of the heart, Rev. Karen Berns, who first pointed me to the women of the Bible and have modeled for me what it means to serve in the ministry of the church. They were among the pioneering women of the 1970s entering seminary and ordained ministry out of a sense of calling and dedication to serve Christ. I am grateful for their example, love, and mentoring. I stand on their shoulders not only as a woman in ministry but as a woman also colaboring for Christ alongside my husband, as they did before me.

At the core of this book is the simple truth that Jesus calls both women and men to be part of his ministry together, and he sends them to serve and declare his good news. The Gospels point us to Jesus, at key moments through the eyes and actions of Mary Magdalene, and my hope is that this book can, in whatever way God chooses, give Christians in the church new insight into her story and confirmation that her example *can* serve as a model of discipleship for women and men with renewed purpose and clarity today.

Notes

Introduction

1. For more on the term "God-man," see Anselm, "Why God Became Man," in *A Scholastic Miscellany: Anselm to Ockham*, ed. and trans. Eugene Fairweather, Library of Christian Classics (Philadelphia: Westminster, 1956), 100–183.

2. Jesus is described as a "brother" in Heb. 2:10–12.

3. Unknown artist (Sienese School), *Crucifixion*, ca. 1285, egg tempera with gold on panel, 94.0 cm × 134.9 cm, Fitzwilliam Museum, Cambridge, #564, https://data .fitzmuseum.cam.ac.uk/id/object/629. Thanks to the Fitzwilliam Museum for their correspondence and to Dr. Fred Sanders at Biola University for directing me to this painting.

4. John 19:25 indicates there was another Mary present (Mary, believed to have been the wife of Clopas), who is frequently forgotten from the scene as well. Moreover, the sister of Jesus's mother is also named. Scholars debate whether she too is named Mary or if Mary of Clopas is the sister of Jesus's mother. See Richard Bauckham's chapter on Mary of Clopas in *Gospel Women: Studies of the Named Women in the Gospels* (Grand Rapids: Eerdmans, 2002), 203–23. He concludes, "Both Clopas and his wife Mary were disciples of Jesus who traveled with him from Galilee on his final journey to Jerusalem" (212).

5. None of these passages reference Mary Magdalene by name except for the resurrection passages.

6. The museum reports that Mary Magdalene was likely a later addition to the painting, added in the fourteenth century, which became vulnerable to abrasion and flaking. As Daniela Bohde points out, depictions of Mary Magdalene at the foot of the cross did not become a practice until 1300. Bohde, "Mary Magdalene at the Foot of the Cross: Iconography and the Semantics of Place," *Mitteilungen Des Kunsthistorischen Institutes in Florenz* 61, no. 1 (2019): 3–44, https://www.jstor.org/stable/26817868.

7. For example, Katherine Ludwig Jansen, *The Making of the Magdalen: Preaching and Popular Devotion in the Later Middle Ages* (Princeton: Princeton University Press,

2000); Diane Apostolos-Cappadona, *Mary Magdalene: A Visual History* (New York: T&T Clark, 2023); Margaret Arnold, *The Magdalene in the Reformation* (Cambridge, MA: Belknap, 2018); and Joan Taylor and Helen Bond, *Women Remembered: Jesus' Female Disciples* (London: Hodder & Stoughton, 2022).

8. A good model for embracing the difficult stories of the Bible is John L. Thompson's *Reading the Bible with the Dead: What You Can Learn from the History of Exegesis That You Can't Learn from Exegesis Alone* (Grand Rapids: Eerdmans, 2007). He writes, "By learning to attend to marginalized characters in Bible stories, we just might learn to see our neighbors with new and compassionate eyes" (5).

9. John Calvin, *Institutes of the Christian Religion* 1.6.1., ed. John T. McNeill, trans. Ford Lewis Battles, Library of Christian Classics (Philadelphia: Westminster, 1960), 1:70.

Chapter 1 The Women of Scripture and a Hermeneutic of Surprise

1. Terran Williams, *How God Sees Women: The End of Patriarchy* (Cape Town, South Africa: Spiritual Bakery, 2022), 15.

2. *Saturday Night Live*, season 49, episode 15, aired March 30, 2024, on NBC, available at "Easter Cold Open—SNL," YouTube video, 5:57, posted by Saturday Night Live on March 31, 2024, https://youtu.be/RxhwjPgJGbU.

3. Keeping the Marys straight is tricky. In the biblical text, there is Mary the mother of Jesus (or Mary of Nazareth), Mary of Bethany (sister of Lazarus and Martha), Mary the mother of James and Joseph/Joses, and Mary of Clopas. Some treat these names as referring to separate women, while others speculate as to whether they function in a couple of cases as different references to the same person.

4. The Greek indicates different versions of her name: "Mary the Magdalene" (Matt. 27:56; Mark 15:40, 47; 16:1, 9; John 19:25; 20:1, 18), "Mirim the Magdalene" (Matt. 27:61; 28:1), "Mary who was called Magdalene" (Luke 8:2), or "the Magdalene Mary" (Luke 24:10).

5. These details are drawn from Richard Bauckham, ed., *Magdala of Galilee: A Jewish City in the Hellenistic and Roman Period* (Waco: Baylor University Press, 2018). He explains that her epithet "most certainly means that she came from a place called Magdala" (59). In church history, Magdala was identified with Mary Magdalene's birthplace and became a destination for Christian pilgrimage during the Byzantine period (21).

6. Bauckham, *Magdala of Galilee*, 59, 349.

7. The site was abandoned for nearly a century after an earthquake in 363 before being adopted as a small Arab village that survived until Jewish settlers arrived in 1948. Bauckham, *Magdala of Galilee*, 21.

8. Bauckham, *Magdala of Galilee*, 59–60.

9. Bauckham, *Magdala of Galilee*, 6. Greek and Latin writers called the place "Taricheae."

10. Diana Butler Bass's viral sermon delivered at the Wild Goose Festival deserves recognition for its contribution to transforming and enlivening thinking around Mary Magdalene. Diana Butler Bass, "All the Marys," sermon, Wild Goose Festival, Union, North Carolina, July 17, 2022, available at https://dianabutlerbass.substack.com/p/all -the-marys.

11. See Joan E. Taylor, "Missing Magdala and the Name of Mary 'Magdalene,'" *Palestine Exploration Quarterly* 146, no. 3 (September 2014): 205–23; and Elizabeth Schrader and Joan E. Taylor, "The Meaning of 'Magdalene': A Review of Literary Evidence," *Journal of Biblical Literature* 140, no. 4 (2021): 751–73.

12. Hugh of St. Victor's *On Sacred Scripture and Its Authors* is key to this interpretive tradition. See Ian Christopher Levy, *Introducing Medieval Biblical Interpretation: The Senses of Scripture in Premodern Exegesis* (Grand Rapids: Baker Academic, 2018).

13. James F. McGrath, *The A to Z of the New Testament: Things Experts Know That Everyone Else Should Too* (Grand Rapids: Eerdmans, 2023), 107; see also 46, 106–8. Jesus used figurative language or imagery of the gate (John 10:7) and the vine (John 15:1) to communicate his person and work more effectively.

14. For an evaluation of Taylor's view (that Magdalene is an honorific title) from a philological perspective, see Bauckham, *Magdala of Galilee*, 360–61.

15. For an insightful and accessible guide to reading Scripture well, see Andrew Abernethy, *Savoring Scripture: A Six-Step Guide to Studying the Bible* (Downers Grove, IL: IVP Academic, 2022). For a work that draws from the tradition of biblical hermeneutics for the church today, see Brandon D. Smith, *Taught by God: Ancient Hermeneutics for the Modern Church* (Brentwood, TN: B&H Academic, 2024).

16. Martin Luther, "Sermons from the Year 1529" (Weimarer Ausgabe 29:272–73), in Susan C. Karant-Nunn and Merry E. Wiesner-Hanks, eds., *Luther and Women: A Sourcebook* (Cambridge: Cambridge University Press, 2003), 82–83.

17. Jerome, Epistle 127, *To Principia*, 22, col. 1090, in *Jerome: Select Letters*, ed. Jeffrey Henderson, trans. F. A. Wright, Loeb Classical Library 262 (Cambridge, MA: Harvard University Press, 1933), 450–51.

18. Augustine, "Homilies on the Gospel of John," Tractate 121.3, 5, in *A Select Library of Nicene and Post-Nicene Fathers of the Christian Church*, 1st series, ed. Philip Schaff, 14 vols. (New York: Christian Literature, 1886–1889; repr., Peabody, MA: Hendrickson, 1994), 7:438.

19. The importance of this reading is explained in Nijay K. Gupta, *Tell Her Story: How Women Led, Taught, and Ministered in the Early Church* (Downers Grove, IL: IVP Academic, 2023), 24–25. Carolyn Custis James explores the significance of the term in *Malestrom: Manhood Swept into the Currents of a Changing World* (Grand Rapids: Zondervan, 2015), 49–58.

20. See E. Anne Clements, *Mothers on the Margins? The Significance of the Women in Matthew's Genealogy* (Eugene, OR: Pickwick, 2014). Matthew signals here the inclusion of the Gentiles in Jesus's mission. See Samuel B. Hakh, "Women in the Genealogy of Matthew," *Exchange: Journal of Contemporary Christianities in Context* 43, no. 2 (2014): 109–18; Craig Keener, *The Gospel of Matthew: A Socio-Rhetorical Commentary* (Grand Rapids: Eerdmans, 2009), 79–80; and Richard Bauckham, *Gospel Women: Studies of the Named Women in the Gospels* (Grand Rapids: Eerdmans, 2002), 27.

21. Jeannine K. Brown, "Interpreting Gentile Women in Matthew: Misrepresentation, Misappropriation, and a Missed Chance," *Journal of Gospels and Acts Research* 6 (September 2022), 21.

22. Brown, "Interpreting Gentile Women in Matthew," 21.

23. Recognizing names in the Bible as women's names has not always been clear. Lucy Peppiatt offers a helpful summary on how this has affected recognition of women

as apostles, as in the case of Junia. Peppiatt, *Rediscovering Scripture's Vision for Women: Fresh Perspectives on Disputed Texts* (Downers Grove, IL: InterVarsity, 2019), 120–22.

24. See Kirsteen Kim and Hoon Ko, "Who Brought the Gospel to Korea? Koreans Did," *Christianity Today*, February 9, 2018, https://www.christianitytoday.com/history/2018/february/korean-christianity.html.

25. For more on Bible women in China and Korea and the Nevius Plan that prioritized self-supporting Indigenous churches and the Bible class movement in Korea, see Alice T. Ott, *Turning Points in the Expansion of Christianity: From Pentecost to the Present* (Grand Rapids: Baker Academic, 2021), chap. 9.

26. See Kenneth E. Bailey, "Women in the New Testament: A Middle Eastern Cultural View," *Theology Matters* 6, no. 1 (2000), 1–2.

27. These details from the life of Kim Gang come from Kim and Ko, "Who Brought the Gospel to Korea?"

28. Jesus also uses the word "woman" on many occasions in the Gospels (Matt. 15:28; 26:10; Luke 13:12; John 2:4; 4:21; 19:26; 20:13, 15).

29. For a full and accessible overview of biblical hermeneutics, see Stanley E. Porter and Beth M. Stovell, eds., *Biblical Hermeneutics: Five Views* (Downers Grove, IL: IVP Academic, 2012), esp. chap. 8.

30. I recommend Craig Keener's immensely helpful resource *The IVP Bible Background Commentary: New Testament*, 2nd ed. (Downers Grove, IL: InterVarsity, 2014).

31. Colleen Walsh, "Twins in Space," *Harvard Gazette*, February 6, 2019, https://news.harvard.edu/gazette/story/2019/02/at-harvard-a-discussion-of-twins-in-space.

32. Vicky Stein, "If This Space Study Is Right, Humans Have Never Left Earth's Atmosphere," PBS News Hour, February 28, 2019, https://www.pbs.org/newshour/science/if-this-space-study-is-right-humans-have-never-left-earths-atmosphere.

33. Peppiatt includes a list of the women referenced in the book of Acts that reflect this distinction. Peppiatt, *Rediscovering Scripture's Vision for Women*, 118–19, citing Carolyn Osiek, Margaret Y. MacDonald, and Janet H. Tulloch, *A Woman's Place: House Churches in Earliest Christianity* (Minneapolis: Fortress, 2006), 88–95.

34. The prophets may be the exception. John L. Thompson writes, "It seems that the prophets never mention women, whether real or metaphorical, except to serve as villains and bad examples." Thompson, *Reading the Bible with the Dead: What You Can Learn from the History of Exegesis That You Can't Learn from Exegesis Alone* (Grand Rapids: Eerdmans, 2007), 93.

35. Willie James Jennings, *Acts*, Belief: A Theological Commentary on the Bible (Louisville: Westminster John Knox, 2017), 49.

36. Jennings, *Acts*, 47.

37. Emphasis mine. Gamaliel's words are an echo of Jesus himself who instructed Judas to "leave her alone" when a different Mary (Mary of Bethany) used costly perfume of pure nard to anoint Jesus's feet and wiped them with her hair (John 12:7).

38. This idea of Mary Magdalene as a model disciple echoes Karen Jo Torjesen, *When Women Were Priests: Women's Leadership in the Early Church and the Scandal of Their Subordination in the Rise of Christianity* (San Francisco: HarperSanFrancisco, 1993), 33–34.

39. Craig S. Keener, *The Gospel of John: A Commentary* (Grand Rapids: Baker Academic, 2003), 2:1141.

40. Keener, *Gospel of John*, 2:1140.

41. Daniel Nayeri, *Everything Sad Is Untrue (A True Story)* (Montclair, NJ: Levine Querido, 2020), 124, 153.

42. Christopher Watkin's work considers the Bible's perception of the world as akin to social critical theories that bring "the world into focus, to draw some aspects of the world into the foreground, and to leave others in the background or make them altogether unnoticed." Watkin, *Biblical Critical Theory: How the Bible's Unfolding Story Makes Sense of Modern Life and Culture* (Grand Rapids: Zondervan Academic, 2022), xviii.

43. See also Matt. 12:23 and Mark 5:20.

44. Keener, *Gospel of Matthew*, 265.

45. A portion of this section was first published in Jennifer Powell McNutt, "Glad Tidings Come in Times of Terror," *Christianity Today*, December 21, 2021, https://www.christianitytoday.com/ct/2021/december-web-only/advent-nativity-terrorism-glad-tidings.html.

46. "Lisa Beamer | 'Lord, Our Lord, How Majestic Is Your Name' | Psalm 8 (09/10/2021)," YouTube video, 22:36, posted by wheatoncollege on September 7, 2022, https://youtu.be/prFzDowxZWg.

47. This is the subtitle of her book. Lisa Beamer, *Let's Roll! Ordinary People, Extraordinary Courage*, with Ken Abraham (Wheaton: Tyndale, 2002).

48. See A. B. Curtiss, *The Little Chapel That Stood* (Escondido, CA: Oldcastle, 2003).

Chapter 2 Will the Real Mary Magdalene Please Stand Up?

1. Dominic Green, "Charles III, the Priest-King," *Wall Street Journal*, May 11, 2023, https://www.wsj.com/articles/charles-iii-the-priest-king-anointing-abbey-britain-faith-anglican-church-b8cbc599.

2. The image is referenced in Margaret Arnold, *The Magdalene in the Reformation* (Cambridge, MA: Harvard University Press, 2018), 38. Thanks to Steven Tyra for drawing this image to my attention.

3. Amanda Kunder, "The Patristic Magdalene: Symbol for the Church and Witness to the Resurrection," in *Mary Magdalene from the New Testament to the New Age and Beyond*, ed. Edmondo F. Lupieri (Leiden: Brill, 2020), 119.

4. Historian Marina Warner offers a summary of recent literature on Mary Magdalene in "Multiplying Marys," *London Review of Books* 46, no. 4 (February 22, 2024), https://www.lrb.co.uk/the-paper/v46/n04/marina-warner/multiplying-marys.

5. The topic is much more expansive and complex than can be covered here. For a detailed overview, see Kunder, "Patristic Magdalene," 105–27. Kunder does not track the matter chronologically but thematically.

6. Irenaeus of Lyon, *Against Heresies* 5.31.1. He likely intended Mary Magdalene, given reference to John's Gospel. Irenaeus makes no connection between Mary Magdalene and the sinner woman of Luke 7, who anoints Jesus's feet. *Against Heresies* 3.14.3.

7. Tertullian, *Five Books against Marcion* 4:18 (ANF 3:376).

8. Tertullian, *Five Books against Marcion* 4.18: "The behaviour of 'the woman which was a sinner,' when she covered the Lord's feet with her kisses, bathed them with her tears, wiped them with the hairs of her head, anointed them with ointment, produced an evidence that what she handled was not an empty phantom, but a really solid body, and that her repentance as a sinner deserved forgiveness according to the mind of the Creator, who is accustomed to prefer mercy to sacrifice. But even if the stimulus of her repentance proceeded from her faith, she heard her justification by faith through her repentance" (*ANF* 3:376).

9. Tertullian, *On Modesty* 11 (*ANF* 4:85).

10. Tertullian explains that the Luke 7 woman was "inaugurating His sepulture with ointment," though that is the purpose of Mary of Bethany's anointing in John 12. *On Modesty* 11 (*ANF* 4:85).

11. Tertullian, *Against Praxeas* 23 (*ANF* 3:618).

12. See András Handl, "Tertullian on the Pericope Adulterae (John 7,53–8,11)," *Revue d'Histoire Ecclésiastique* 112 (2017): 5–34.

13. Tertullian, *Against Praxeas* 25 (*ANF* 3:621).

14. Reference to her touching Jesus "out of love" has been interpreted as a confla-tion with the phrasing found in Luke 7. Jane Schaberg, *The Resurrection of Mary Magdalene: Legends, Apocrypha, and the Christian Testament* (New York: Continuum, 2002), 85. Though John does not use the term "love" for Mary's encounter with Jesus, it seems to represent her intended care of his dead body. Her weeping also indicates a loving disciple.

15. Kunder, "Patristic Magdalene," 107. Neither does Origen according to Kunder: "Like Irenaeus and Tertullian, the passage is used to comment on an issue regarding the nature of Jesus's death, resurrection, and ascension, and there is little comment on the character of Mary Magdalene" (108–9).

16. Origen, *Against Celsus* 2.70 (*ANF* 4:460). Origen was responding to the idea that Jesus was secretive in his resurrection appearance according to the criticism of Celsus. Schaberg concludes from Origen's response that Mary Magdalene may already have been subjected to disrepute at this early stage. Schaberg, *Resurrection of Mary Magdalene*, 85. However, the issue seems to have revolved around the number and quality of witnesses rather than Mary Magdalene per se, whom Celsus does not even recognize by name but maligns as a "half-frantic woman." Origen, *Against Celsus* 2.55, 59 (*ANF* 4:453, 455). Origen points to other Gospel accounts, specifically Matthew, that include Mary Magdalene but name other witnesses as well.

17. Tertullian, *Five Books against Marcion* 4.19.1: "The fact that certain rich women clave to Christ, 'which ministered unto Him of their substance,' amongst whom was the wife of the king's steward, is a subject of prophecy. By Isaiah *the Lord* called these wealthy ladies—'Rise up, ye women that are at ease, and hear my voice'—that He might prove them first as disciples, and then as assistants and helpers: 'Daughters, hear my words in hope; this day of the year cherish the memory of, in labour with hope.' For it was 'in labour' that they followed Him, and 'with hope' did they minister to Him" (*ANF* 3:376).

18. Tertullian offers this interpretation in his work *On the Apparel of Women* 2.1.1 (*ANF* 4:14): ". . . walking about as Eve mourning and repentant, in order that by every garb of penitence she might the more fully expiate that which she derives from Eve,—the ignominy, I mean, of the first sin, and the odium (attaching to her as

the cause) of human perdition. 'In pains and in anxieties dost thou bear (children), woman; and toward thine husband (is) thy inclination, and he lords it over thee.' And do you not know that you are (each) an Eve? The sentence of God on this sex of yours lives in this age: the guilt must of necessity live too. You are the devil's gateway: you are the unsealer of that (forbidden) tree: you are the first deserter of the divine law: you are she who persuaded him whom the devil was not valiant enough to attack. You destroyed so easily God's image, man. On account of your desert—that is, death—even the Son of God had to die."

19. For more on how Eve has been understood in church history, see Amanda W. Benckhuysen, *The Gospel according to Eve: A History of Women's Interpretation* (Downers Grove, IL: IVP Academic, 2019), esp. chaps. 3, 5.

20. Yancy Smith, *The Mystery of Anointing: Hippolytus' Commentary on the Song of Songs in Social and Critical Contexts: Texts, Translations, and Comprehensive Study*, Gorgias Studies in Early Christianity and Patristics 62 (Piscataway, NJ: Gorgias Press, 2015), 116–17, 126.

21. Ambrose, *On the Holy Spirit* 3.11.74: "Mary worshipped Christ, and therefore is appointed to be the messenger of the Resurrection to the apostles, loosening the hereditary bond, and the huge offence of womankind. For this the Lord wrought mystically, 'that where sin had exceedingly abounded, grace might more exceedingly abound'" (*NPNF*[2] 10:145).

22. Ambrose, *On the Holy Spirit* 3.11.74 (*NPNF*[2] 10:145).

23. Prior to Ambrose, Irenaeus claimed that the Virgin Mary was the patroness to the Virgin Eve (*Against Heresies* 5.19). Virginity was a point of connection from his standpoint. Irenaeus writes, "And thus also it was that the knot of Eve's disobedience was loosed by the obedience of Mary. For what the virgin Eve had bound fast through unbelief, this did the virgin Mary set free through faith." *Against Heresies* 3.22.4.

24. Ambrose makes a similar point in his dispute with the Novatians when he claims that Jesus did not demand that Mary not touch him because he was pure and she was not. Ambrose, *Two Books concerning Repentance* 1 (8:38). None of us are pure apart from Christ was Ambrose's point, so he is not merely singling out Mary Magdalene. Jesus was even willing to be baptized by John the Baptist, who was also a sinner (8:39).

25. See references in Kunder, "Patristic Magdalene," 114nn34–35.

26. Ambrose, *Exposition of the Christian Faith* 4.2.25 (*NPNF*[2] 10:265).

27. Ambrose, *Exposition of the Christian Faith* 4.2.25 (*NPNF*[2] 10:265).

28. Ambrose, *Exposition of the Christian Faith* 4.2.26 (*NPNF*[2] 10:265).

29. Ambrose does not mix up Mary Magdalene with Mary of Bethany (or Martha), to whom he pairs Martha and Lazarus in other examples. Ambrose, *Two Books concerning Repentance* 2.7.62.

30. Chrysostom, *Homilies on the Gospel of Saint Matthew*, Homily 6. This becomes an opportunity for him to point to Jesus's tears over Lazarus as well as Paul's tears (*NPNF*[1] 10:38–40).

31. Chrysostom, *Homilies on the Gospel of Saint Matthew*, Homily 6.8 (*NPNF*[1] 10:40).

32. In reference to the Matt. 26 anointing, he writes, "This woman seems indeed to be one and the same with all the evangelists, yet she is not so; but though with the three she doth seem to me to be one and the same, yet not so with John, but another

person, one much to be admired, the sister of Lazarus." Chrysostom, *Homilies on the Gospel of Saint Matthew*, Homily 80 (*NPNF*[1] 10:480); see also Homily 62.

33. Kunder's citations include Origen, Ambrose, and Jerome. Kunder, "Patristic Magdalene," 117n41.

34. Chrysostom, *Homilies on the Gospel of Saint Matthew*, Homily 88 (*NPNF*[1] 10:522).

35. Chrysostom, *Homilies on the Gospel of Saint Matthew*, Homily 88 (*NPNF*[1] 10:522).

36. Chrysostom, *Homilies on the Gospel of St. John and the Epistle to the Hebrews*, Homily 86.1 (*NPNF*[1] 14:323, 324).

37. Chrysostom, *Homilies on the Gospel of St. John and the Epistle to the Hebrews*, Homily 86 (*NPNF*[1] 14:323). Her tears are described as a sign of a "feeble nature" here.

38. Kunder, "Patristic Magdalene," 110.

39. Augustine, *Harmony of the Gospels* 79.154–55: "But my theory is, that it was the same Mary who did this deed on two separate occasions" (*NPNF*[1] 6:301–2).

40. Augustine associates Mary of Bethany with the woman of Luke 7, saying, "Look at the sister of Lazarus herself (if, indeed, it was she who anointed the Lord's feet with ointment, and wiped with her hair what she had washed with her tears), who had a better resurrection than her brother; she was delivered from the mighty burden of a sinful character. For she was a notorious sinner; and had it said of her, 'Her many sins are forgiven her, for she has loved much.'" Augustine, *Tractates on the Gospel of John*, Tractate 49.3 (*NPNF*[1] 7:271).

41. Jerome, Letter 12, To Antony (*NPNF*[2] 6:13). This is probably referring to Mary of Bethany rather than Mary Magdalene, as assumed in the editor's note (13n5).

42. Jerome, Letter 127, To Principia, 5 (*NPNF*[2] 6:255).

43. Mary Magdalene as representative of women and the church is a prominent theme among the early Christian theologians. Kunder, "Patristic Magdalene," 117.

44. Jerome, Letter 39, To Paula, 6 (*NPNF*[2] 6:53). At the same time, Jerome is not concerned by the prostitute or harlot. He believes strongly in the power of the baptismal water to wash away sin and turn the prostitute back into a virgin: "For if there is no difference between a virgin and a widow, both being baptized, because baptism makes a new man, upon the same principle harlots and prostitutes, if they are baptized, will be equal to virgins." Jerome, *Against Jovinianus* 1.33 (*NPNF*[2] 6:370).

45. Jerome, *Jerome: Select Letters*, ed. Jeffrey Henderson, trans. F. A. Wright, Loeb Classical Library 262 (Cambridge, MA: Harvard University Press, 1933), 450–51.

46. For a helpful summary, see Jansen, *Making of the Magdalen*, 32–35.

47. Pope Gregory the Great, *Homilia 33* in *Homiliarum in evangelia*, in *Patrologia Latina* 76:1239, cited in Jansen, *Making of the Magdalen*, 32–33. See also *Epistle to Gregoria* (June 597). Kunder writes, "In addition to the conflation, there is also the trend of Mary as an antitype of Eve, reversing the announcement of sin with her announcement of the loving kindness of God" (123).

48. Joel B. Green reasons, "Undoubtedly, this characterization marks her as a prostitute by vocation, a whore by social status, contagious in her impurity, and probably one who fraternizes with Gentiles for economic purposes." Green, *The Gospel of Luke*, New International Commentary on the New Testament (Grand Rapids: Eerdmans, 1997), 309.

49. Lynn H. Cohick, *Women in the World of the Earliest Christians: Illuminating Ancient Ways of Life* (Grand Rapids: Baker Academic, 2009), 317.

50. Jansen draws attention to the fact that Tertullian identified unbound, female hair with promiscuity. Jansen, *Making of the Magdalen*, 156–57.

51. Marianne Meye Thompson, *John: A Commentary*, New Testament Library (Louisville: Westminster John Knox, 2015), 256.

52. Thompson, *John*, 256.

53. The section from Thompson, *John*, 256–62, on this passage is instructive. The Luke 7 and John 12 washings both use the same Greek verb used for anointing (*aleiphein*), which is not used to convey messianic anointing (*chriein*). Therefore, Mary of Bethany and the woman of Luke 7 are linked not only by the act of foot washing but also by the distinctive verb that is used for the act.

54. Thompson, *John*, 261.

55. Thompson, *John*, 259.

56. Keener, *Gospel of John*, 2:903, 911.

57. Green describes the account in Luke 7 as framed in contrasts. *Gospel of Luke*, 308.

58. Green writes, "Everything about this woman, though, is wrong: she does not belong here and the actions she performs are inappropriate in any setting for someone like Jesus." *Gospel of Luke*, 309.

59. Letting her hair down and rubbing Jesus's feet were considered erotic behaviors. Green, *Gospel of Luke*, 310.

60. Sojourner Truth, "Ain't I a Woman?," available at https://www.learningfor justice.org/classroom-resources/texts/aint-i-a-woman.

61. Green explains that Luke "occasionally introduces persons into the narrative who have already begun the journey of discipleship in some sense though we are never told when or how." *Gospel of Luke*, 313. This rings true for Mary Magdalene's backstory as well.

62. Cohick, *Women in the World of the Earliest Christians*, 316.

63. Green, *Gospel of Luke*, 309.

64. Cohick, *Women in the World of the Earliest Christians*, 284, 282–83.

65. Esther A. de Boer describes the dualism in the Gospel of Mary as "moderate." De Boer, *The Gospel of Mary: Beyond a Gnostic and a Biblical Mary Magdalene* (London: T&T Clark, 2004), 202. Importantly, there is no Gnostic teaching in the text that women must become men in order to be saved. Additionally, the female imagery in the text is not limited to negative examples. De Boer concludes that the Gospel of Mary should not be regarded as Gnostic writing since it does not promote Gnostic teaching (207). Her conclusion confutes the widespread idea that there was a specific Gnostic esteem for Mary Magdalene.

66. Jean-Yves LeLoup, ed. and trans., *The Gospel of Mary Magdalene* (Rochester, VT: Inner Traditions, 2002), 35.

67. LeLoup, *Gospel of Mary Magdalene*, 31.

68. De Boer highlights the points of continuity between the New Testament Gospels and the Gospel of Mary, in this case that she does share what she has learned from Jesus. She concludes that such shared themes indicate the existence of a "first-century tradition about her." De Boer, *Gospel of Mary*, 207.

69. Mark's Gospel does relay how the women were alarmed after encountering an angel at the empty tomb. The text details how they "fled from the tomb, for terror and amazement had seized them, and they said nothing to anyone, for they were afraid" (Mark 16:8). The longer, disputed ending of Mark's Gospel from 16:9 offers further confirmation that Mary Magdalene was the first witness and subsequently shared the good news with Jesus's followers. All the Gospels recognize that the women do indeed share the news with Jesus's followers.

70. LeLoup, *Gospel of Mary Magdalene*, 37.

71. LeLoup, *Gospel of Mary Magdalene*, 37.

72. LeLoup, *Gospel of Mary Magdalene*, 39.

73. For a helpful summary of these dynamics, see Jansen, *Making of the Magdalen*, 25.

74. According to Mark's account, she was instructed by the angel to "tell his disciples and Peter" (Mark 16:7).

75. De Boer concludes, "The Gospel of Mary is significant proof of an early Christian view which considered (at least) Mary Magdalene to be on an equal footing with her brothers (and sisters) in the sense that they all have been made true Human Being[s] and that they all are prepared to preach the gospel of the Kingdom of the Son of Man." De Boer, *Gospel of Mary*, 208.

76. Mary Ann Beavis references the love story narrative structure paired with the martyr character type, in this case the suffering prostitute, present in modern retellings: "Mary Magdalene on Film in Twenty-First Century: A Feminist Theological Critique," *Journal of Religion and Film* 28, no. 1 (April 2024): 1–21. The tendency is noted by Karen L. King, *The Gospel of Mary of Magdala: Jesus and the First Woman Apostle* (Santa Rosa, CA: Polebridge, 2003), 153. See also Jansen, *Making of the Magdalen*, 26.

77. LeLoup, *Gospel of Mary Magdalene*, 31.

78. Grace Hamman, *Jesus through Medieval Eyes: Beholding Christ with the Artists, Mystics, and Theologians in the Middle Ages* (Grand Rapids: Zondervan Reflective, 2023), chap. 3.

79. Hamman, *Jesus through Medieval Eyes*, 64–65.

80. Though the word "friend" too frequently lacks depth in our age, Jesus declares in word and deed that the pinnacle of friendship is to lay down one's life for a friend (John 15:13).

81. Willie James Jennings, *Acts*, Belief: A Theological Commentary on the Bible (Louisville: Westminster John Knox, 2017), 49.

82. For more on Jesus's mother Mary, see Jennifer Powell McNutt and Amy Beverage Peeler, "The First Christian," *Christianity Today*, November 22, 2019, https://www.christianitytoday.com/ct/2019/december/first-christian-virgin-mary.html. See also Scot McKnight, *The Real Mary: Why Evangelicals Can Embrace the Mother of Jesus* (Brewster, MA: Paraclete, 2006); and Beverly Gaventa and Cynthia Rigby, eds., *Blessed One: Protestant Perspectives on Mary* (Louisville: Westminster John Knox, 2002).

83. Keener, *Gospel of John*, 2:1191.

84. Thompson, *John*, 400. The idea of family or kin was not limited to father, mother, and naturally born children in the ancient Mediterranean context.

85. Amy Peeler, *Hebrews*, Commentaries for Christian Formation (Grand Rapids: Eerdmans, 2024), 86.

86. Consider the findings of Reidar Aasgaard, *"My Beloved Brothers and Sisters!":* *Christian Siblings in Paul* (London: T&T Clark, 2004). Aimee Byrd has appealed to the relational paradigm of "sacred siblingship" in her book *Recovering from Biblical Manhood and Womanhood: How the Church Needs to Rediscover Her Purpose* (Grand Rapids: Zondervan Reflective, 2020), 216–23.

87. Aasgaard, *"My Beloved Brothers and Sisters!,"* 59. See source for further details about the brother-sister bond in the New Testament era.

88. Keener, *Gospel of John*, 2:1191.

Chapter 3   Mary Magdalene and Her Church Interpreters

1. "Apollo 8's Christmas Eve 1968 Message," YouTube video, 2:01, posted by NASA Video on May 19, 2013, https://youtu.be/ToHhQUhdyBY.

2. Katherine Ludwig Jansen, *The Making of the Magdalen: Preaching and Popular Devotion in the Later Middle Ages* (Princeton: Princeton University Press, 2000), 37. Mary of Egypt is included in the *Vitae Patrum*, a collection pertaining to eastern desert saints written between the fourth and seventh centuries. For an English translation of Mary of Egypt's life, see Alice-Mary Talbot, ed., *Holy Women of Byzantium: Ten Saints' Lives in English Translation*, trans. Maria Kouli (Washington, DC: Dumbarton Oaks, 1996), 65–93.

3. Jacobus de Voragine, *The Golden Legend* (Princeton: Princeton University Press, 2012), 227. The epitaph echoes Luke 7. Mary is depicted as crying tears of penance, which also identifies her with/as Mary Magdalene (228).

4. See, e.g., Dunois Master, *Saint Mary of Egypt, Covered with Hair, Stretches Out Her Hand to Zosimas, the Priest*, 1436–50, Hours of Jean Dunois, British Library, London, Yates Thompson MS 3, F.287, https://en.wikipedia.org/wiki/Mary_of_Egypt#/media/File:Mary_of_Egypt_british_library.jpg, reprinted in Diane Apostolos-Cappadona, *Mary Magdalene: A Visual History* (New York: T&T Clark, 2023), 37, see also 41, 94–95. Other images include Giovanni Pietro Birago's *St. Mary Magdalene Borne Aloft by Angels* from circa 1490.

5. Jansen, *Making of the Magdalen*, 38.

6. Mary Ann Beavis, "Mary Magdalene," *Encyclopedia of the Bible and Its Reception*, 22 vols., ed. Christine Helmer et al. (Berlin: de Gruyter, 2019), 17:1210.

7. Apostolos-Cappadona, *Mary Magdalene*, 26, 65, 119–21. See painting by Sergei Ivanov, *Mary Magdalene Preaching to Emperor Tiberius*, ca. 1886, Russian Orthodox Church of Saint Mary Magdalene, Gethsemane. For an exploration of the emergence of images from the thirteenth century depicting holy women boldly teaching rulers in the vita icons, see Paraskevi Papadimitriou, "Depictions of Holy Women as Preachers in Vita Icons," *Zograf* 45 (2021): 65–78.

8. Jacobus de Voragine, *Golden Legend*, 219.

9. Jacobus de Voragine, *Golden Legend*, 220.

10. Jacobus de Voragine, *Golden Legend*, 221.

11. For Ambrose on Mary Magdalene, see Ambrose, *De spiritu sancto*, ed. Otto Faller, Corpus Scriptorum Ecclesiasticorum Latinorum 79 (Hölder-Pichler-Tempsky, 1964), 181, quoted in Jansen, *Making of the Magdalen*, 32. References to Ambrose appear in Jacobus de Voragine, *Golden Legend*, 221, 376.

12. Jansen, *Making of the Magdalen,* 59–62.

13. Jacobus de Voragine, *Golden Legend,* 376.

14. Jacobus de Voragine, *Golden Legend,* 220.

15. Jacobus de Voragine, *Golden Legend,* 220, 378.

16. Jacobus de Voragine, *Golden Legend,* 375. The text further explains that "Magdalene" also means "armed, or unconquered, or magnificent."

17. Jacobus de Voragine, *Golden Legend,* 375.

18. Jacobus de Voragine, *Golden Legend,* 220.

19. Jacobus de Voragine, *Golden Legend,* 220.

20. Corine Schleif and Volker Schier, *Katerina's Windows: Donation and Devotion, Art and Music, as Heard and Seen through the Writings of a Birgittine Nun* (University Park: Penn State University Press, 2009), 8.

21. Jacobus de Voragine, *Golden Legend,* 375.

22. Beth Allison Barr explores the dissonance between how Martha is often domesticated today in modern readings while the medieval readings identified her with bold agency and visibility. Barr, *The Making of Biblical Womanhood: How the Subjugation of Women Became Gospel Truth* (Grand Rapids: Brazos, 2021), 83.

23. Jacobus de Voragine, *Golden Legend,* 376.

24. For a recent biography, see Crystal Downing, *Subversive: Christ, Culture, and the Shocking Dorothy L. Sayers* (Minneapolis: Broadleaf, 2020).

25. Dorothy L. Sayers, letter to Val Gielgud, March 3, 1941, Marion E. Wade Center, Wheaton College, Wheaton, Illinois, quoted in Dorothy L. Sayers, *The Man Born to Be King,* ed. Kathryn Wehr (Downers Grove, IL: IVP Academic, 2022), 240.

26. Dorothy L. Sayers, letter to James Welch, February 16, 1942, Marion E. Wade Center, Wheaton College, Wheaton, Illinois, folder 434b, quoted in Sayers, *Man Born to Be King,* 115.

27. Dorothy L. Sayers, "The Human-Not-Quite-Human," in *Are Women Human? Penetrating, Sensible, and Witty Essays on the Role of Women in Society* (Grand Rapids: Eerdmans, 2005), 68.

28. Buzz Aldrin, *Magnificent Desolation: The Long Journey Home from the Moon* (New York: Harmony, 2009), 26.

29. A reassessment is happening through the work of scholar Elizabeth Schrader (now Polczer). See her important article, "Was Martha of Bethany Added to the Fourth Gospel in the Second Century?," *Harvard Theological Review* 110, no. 3 (July 2017): 360–92.

30. Margaret Arnold, *The Magdalene in the Reformation* (Cambridge, MA: Belknap, 2018).

31. Jacques Lefèvre d'Étaples, *De Maria Magdalena* (Paris: Stephani, 1517). For an English translation, see Sheila M. Porrer, trans. and ed., *Jacques Lefèvre d'Étaples and the Three Maries Debates,* Travaux d'Humanisme et Renaissance 451 (Geneva: Librairie Droz, 2009).

32. See Franciscan priest François Demoulins de Rochefort's *The Life of Mary Magdalene* (1517). See the response from bishop of Rochester, John Fisher, in Arnold, *Magdalene in the Reformation,* 40–42. For a summary of events, see Jansen, *Making of the Magdalen,* 11.

33. Martin Luther, "Sermons from the Year 1529" (Weimarer Ausgabe 29:272–73), cited in Susan C. Karant-Nunn and Merry E. Wiesner-Hanks, eds., *Luther and Women: A Sourcebook* (Cambridge: Cambridge University Press, 2003), 83.

34. Luther, "Table Talk 6100" (Weimarer Ausgabe TR 5:488), cited in Karant-Nunn and Wiesner-Hanks, *Luther and Women*, 87.

35. Luther engages with Bonaventure in his "Sermon on Marriage, 1525" (Weimarer Ausgabe 17/1:17), cited in Karant-Nunn and Wiesner-Hanks, *Luther and Women*, 54.

36. Luther, "Sermon on the Day of Mary Magdalene, 1544 (Luke 7:36–50)" (Weimarer Ausgabe 52:664–70, 673), cited in Karant-Nunn and Wiesner-Hanks, *Luther and Women*, 85. Luther identifies her as the woman in Luke 7 in his "Sermon on Indulgence and Grace," in *Annotated Luther: The Roots of Reform*, ed. Timothy Wengert (Minneapolis: Fortress, 2015), 1:61, 146.

37. Luther, "Sermon on the Day of Mary Magdalene," in Karant-Nunn and Wiesner-Hanks, *Luther and Women*, 85.

38. Calvin, *Institutes of the Christian Religion* 1.14.18, ed. John T. McNeill, trans. Ford Lewis Battles, Library of Christian Classics (Philadelphia: Westminster, 1960), 1:176.

39. Calvin, *Institutes* 1.14.15 (1:174).

40. Calvin, *Institutes* 1.14.15 (1:174).

41. Calvin, *Institutes* 1.14.13–14 (1:173).

42. Calvin, *Institutes* 1.14.18 (1:176–78).

43. Luther, "Sermons from the Year 1529" (Weimarer Ausgabe 29:272–73), cited in Karant-Nunn and Wiesner-Hanks, *Luther and Women*, 82.

44. "I am also still a weak disciple of these teachings; I also depend on the container and the salve and the grave, and do not have confidence in or cling to the words, just as the women first were affected; the Lord sustain us." Luther, "Sermons from the Year 1529," in Karant-Nunn and Wiesner-Hanks, *Luther and Women*, 83.

45. Luther, "Sermons from the Year 1529," in Karant-Nunn and Wiesner-Hanks, *Luther and Women*, 82.

46. Luther, "Sermons from the Year 1529," in Karant-Nunn and Wiesner-Hanks, *Luther and Women*, 82–83.

47. My reading of Calvin on Mary Magdalene differs from what is presented in Arnold, *Magdalene in the Reformation*, 167–68.

48. John Calvin, *Commentary on a Harmony of the Evangelists* (Grand Rapids: Baker, 2009), 3:338.

49. John Calvin, "The Lord's Day Service with the Lord's Supper," in *John Calvin: Writings on Pastoral Piety*, ed. and trans. Elsie Anne McKee (New York: Paulist Press, 2001), 114–15. The translation is odd—"to school to women"—so I have adjusted it.

50. Calvin, *Commentary on a Harmony of the Evangelists*, 3:339.

51. Calvin, *Commentary on a Harmony of the Evangelists*, 3:338–39.

52. Calvin, *Commentary on a Harmony of the Evangelists*, 3:347.

53. Calvin, *Commentary on a Harmony of the Evangelists*, 3:347.

54. Karant-Nunn and Wiesner-Hanks comment on the practices of Luther when it comes to biblical women: "This is, in fact, the most important function of all Biblical women [for Luther] . . . (nearly every discussion of a Biblical woman mentions women's weakness), their triumphs could always be attributed directly to the power of God and the faith He created in them." Karant-Nunn and Wiesner-Hanks, *Luther and Women*, 60.

55. Luther, "Sermon on Joel 2:28, 1531" (Weimarer Ausgabe 34:482), in Karant-Nunn and Wiesner-Hanks, *Luther on Women*, 61.

56. Calvin's sermon on Matt. 28:1–10, in McKee, *John Calvin*, 118–19.

57. G. Sujin Pak, "Scripture, the Priesthood of all Believers, and Applications of 1 Corinthians 14," in *The People's Book: The Reformation and the Bible*, ed. Jennifer Powell McNutt and David Lauber, Wheaton Theology Conference Series (Downers Grove, IL: IVP Academic, 2017), 33–51.

58. Marie Dentière's name was added to the wall in 2002 at the request of Rev. Isabelle Graesslé, the first woman moderator of the Reformed Church of Geneva's Company of Pastors and director of the Museum of the Reformation in Geneva.

59. Marie Dentière, *Epistle to Marguerite de Navarre and Preface to a Sermon by John Calvin*, ed. and trans. Mary B. McKinley, The Other Voice in Early Modern Europe (Chicago: University of Chicago Press, 2004), 53.

60. Dentière, *Epistle to Marguerite de Navarre*, 53–54. She talks about how it was not expected that women should understand Scripture or ask questions during her time (79). The fact that women were not encouraged to read the Bible is also mentioned by Argula von Grumbach, "To the University of Ingolstadt," in *Argula von Grumbach: A Woman's Voice in the Reformation*, ed. Peter Matheson (Edinburgh: T&T Clark, 1995), 86.

61. Dentière, *Epistle to Marguerite de Navarre*, 55.

62. Dentière, *Epistle to Marguerite de Navarre*, 55.

63. Dentière, *Epistle to Marguerite de Navarre*, 55–56.

64. Dentière, *Epistle to Marguerite de Navarre*, 79.

65. Dentière, *Epistle to Marguerite de Navarre*, 56. Typically, Protestants during the Reformation emphasized Christ as the one mediator to combat Roman Catholic practices of confession, penance, and intercessory prayer to saints. In this case, Dentière may be emphasizing that Christ is also the sole mediator for women.

66. Dentière, *Epistle to Marguerite de Navarre*, 53, 56. The parable of the talents is cited time and again by women during the Reformation, including Argula von Grumbach's appeal to the passage: "I don't intend to bury my talent, if the Lord gives me grace." Von Grumbach, "To the University of Ingolstadt," in Matheson, *Argula von Grumbach*, 87.

67. Dentière, *Epistle to Marguerite de Navarre*, 56. She uses the terms "preach" (*prescher*) and "woman preacher" (*prescheresse*). Kirsi Stjerna, *Women and the Reformation* (Oxford: Wiley-Blackwell, 2008), 141.

68. For a helpful biographical summary of Marie Dentière, see Mary B. McKinley, "Marie Dentiere (1495–1561): In Defense of Women," in *Women Reformers of Early Modern Europe: Profiles, Texts, and Contexts*, ed. Kirsi I. Stjerna (Minneapolis: Fortress, 2022), 23–34.

69. See Katharina Schütz Zell, *Church Mother: The Writings of a Protestant Reformer in Sixteenth-Century Germany*, ed. and trans. Elsie McKee, The Other Voice in Early Modern Europe (Chicago: University of Chicago Press, 2007). For an overview of her life, see Elsie McKee, "Katharina Schütz Zell (ca. 1498–1562): Passionate Church Mother," in Stjerna, *Women Reformers of Early Modern Europe*, 3–12.

70. Katharina Schütz Zell, "Lament and Exhortation of Katharina Zell to the People at the Grave of Master Matthew Zell," January 11, 1548, funeral oration, in Schütz Zell, *Church Mother*, 98.

71. Schütz Zell, "Lament and Exhortation of Katharina Zell," in Schütz Zell, *Church Mother*, 99. I recognize my former MA student Katherine Goodwin at Wheaton College for stressing the importance of this outlet for Zell in my Reformation class.

72. Schütz Zell, "Lament and Exhortation of Katharina Zell," in Schütz Zell, *Church Mother*, 104.

73. Schütz Zell, "Lament and Exhortation of Katharina Zell," in Schütz Zell, *Church Mother*, 115.

74. Barr highlights how medieval theologians also interpreted Mary Magdalene's preaching as an exception: "The problem wasn't a lack of biblical and historical evidence for women in leadership. . . . The medieval clergy couldn't explain away Mary Magdalene preaching, so they made her an exception." Barr, *Biblical Womanhood*, 87.

75. Jansen, *Making of the Magdalen*, 57.

76. Arnold, *Magdalene in the Reformation*, 237.

77. Erin Vearncombe, "Harriet Livermore," in *Handbook of Women Biblical Interpreters: A Historical and Biographical Guide*, ed. Marion Ann Taylor and Agnes Choi (Grand Rapids: Baker Academic, 2012), 332. See also Harriet Livermore, *Millennial Tidings*, no. 3 (Philadelphia, 1831–1839), 6.

78. For the uncovering of this difficult history, see Frances Finnegan, *Do Penance or Perish: A Study of Magdalene Asylums in Ireland* (Oxford: Oxford University Press, 2004). The Magdalen house was established in London during the mid-eighteenth century by Jonas Hanway. Joelle Mellon, *The Virgin Mary in the Perceptions of Women: Mother, Protector and Queen since the Middle Ages* (Jefferson, NC: McFarland, 2016), 175. See Jonas Hanway, *Thoughts on the Plan for a Magdalen-House for Repentant Prostitutes* (London: James Waugh, 1758).

79. Arnold, *Magdalene in the Reformation*, 41.

80. "One might assume that given all the sanctions against women preaching . . . sensible preachers would not have bothered incorporating Mary Magdalen's problematic preaching apostolate in Gaul into their sermons," but this was not the case in the late medieval context. Jansen, *Making of the Magdalen*, 57.

81. Arnold, *Magdalene in the Reformation*, 41.

82. Congregation for Divine Worship and the Discipline of the Sacraments, "Saint Mary Magdalene," Prot. N. 257/16, June 3, 2016, available at https://www.liturgyoffice.org.uk/Calendar/Sanctoral/July/Jul22-Missal-Eng.pdf.

83. Congregation for Divine Worship and the Discipline of the Sacraments, "Decree on the Celebration of Saints Martha, Mary and Lazarus in the General Roman Calendar," Prot. N. 35/21, January 26, 2021, https://www.vatican.va/roman_curia/congregations/ccdds/documents/rc_con_ccdds_doc_20210126_decreto-santi_en.html.

84. Allie M. Ernst shares her critique, stating, "It is ironic that in feminist research, which explicitly recognises the marginalisation of women in androcentric texts, Martha has consequently remained on the margins and in the shadow of the Magdalene." Ernst, *Martha from the Margins: The Authority of Martha in Early Christian Tradition*, Supplements to Vigiliae Christianae (Leiden: Brill, 2009), 8.

85. This section is based on the groundbreaking research of Ernst, *Martha from the Margins*.

86. In addition to the *Epistula Apostolorum* and Hippolytus's commentary, Ernst points to early Christian hymns such as the Greek Easter hymn and an Ethiopic hymn,

a sermon of Severian of Gabala, and a number of liturgical texts (the Ambrosian Missal and Syrian Catholic Fenqitho, and the Synaxarion of Constantinople) as well as a number of images. Ernst, *Martha*, 294.

87. For a helpful summary of the sources and their significance, see Ernst, *Martha*, 294.

88. See Ernst, *Martha*, chap. 3. The text takes the form of a dialogue between the risen Lord and the disciples after resurrection and before ascension and preserved in Coptic and Ethiopic. The goal of the text is to refute Gnosticism. Ernst, *Martha*, 68.

89. The complexity of these matters is well explained by Ernst, *Martha*, 76–77, 294–95. Ernst includes a translation of the Ethiopic and Coptic versions of the *Epistula* (303–5).

90. Ernst, *Martha*, 293.

91. Yancy Smith, *The Mystery of Anointing: Hippolytus' Commentary on the Song of Songs in Social and Critical Contexts: Texts, Translations, and Comprehensive Study*, Gorgias Studies in Early Christianity and Patristics 62 (Piscataway, NJ: Gorgias Press, 2015), 49. Smith provides the first English translation of the Georgian text of the commentary on 419–561.

92. Hippolytus, *Commentary on the Song of Songs* 24.2, 25.2. Smith repeats the point on several occasions that the women are honored and recognized without granting them official standing, let alone ordination in the leadership of the church. Smith, *Mystery of Anointing*, 414–15.

93. Smith, *Mystery of Anointing*, 130.

94. Hippolytus, *Commentary on the Song of Songs* 2.29, 25.6.

95. Hippolytus, *Commentary on the Song of Songs* 25.9.

96. Ernst raises the point that scholarship too easily assumes the primacy of Mary Magdalene. Ernst, *Martha*, 299.

97. Ernst, *Martha*, 95. Smith's book also weighs the historiography on these matters, citing Ernst. Contrary to popular thought, there is evidence of mixing the Marys in the Eastern tradition. A fifth-century hymn emerging out of Constantinople that conflates Mary of Bethany with Mary Magdalene is one example (Ernst, *Martha*, 57). The hymn focuses on the raising of Lazarus, and its authorship is identified with the name Romanus Melodus, a deacon in Constantinople during the early fifth century.

98. Elizabeth Schrader Polczer's work claims that the oldest, near-complete manuscript of the Gospel of John, Papyrus 66 (a twelfth-century Greek manuscript), erased the number of times Mary is mentioned by adding Martha's name instead. Her reconstruction of John 11 is based on Codex Alexandrinus before correction (John 11:1–2), Papyrus 66 before correction (John 11:3–4), and Codex Colbertinus (John 11:5), which is uncorrected. John 11 becomes, by this reasoning, a statement made by Mary Magdalene. The implications of her work for our understanding of the text and the familial dynamics at Bethany are yet to be sorted out, though they are important for continued reflection and attention. See Polczer, "Was Martha of Bethany Added to the Fourth Gospel in the Second Century?," *Harvard Theological Review* 110, no. 3 (July 2017): 360–92.

99. Ernst, *Martha*, 56.

100. Ernst surveys the history of interpretation and highlights her treatment with Origen and Chrysostom. Ernst, *Martha*, 49–65, esp. 53. In the history of biblical interpretation, Martha has been susceptible to a multitude of interpretations, as both

faithful and faithless. Sometimes her significance has been diminished over the account of her rushing to Jesus over Lazarus and mentioning Lazarus's smell.

101. For a helpful summary, see Apostolos-Cappadona, *Mary Magdalene*, chap. 3.

102. It is a live question whether Paul was aware of Mary Magdalene given her omission from his account of the resurrection in 1 Cor. 15. Considering the popularity of the name Mary also raises valid questions about the identity of Paul's reference in Rom. 16:6.

103. Sergei Ivanov's painting, *Mary Magdalene Preaching to Emperor Tiberius* (ca. 1886), is located in the Russian Orthodox Church of Saint Mary Magdalene, Gethsemane.

104. Greek Orthodox Archdiocese of America, "Saints and Feasts: Mary Magdalene, Myrrhbearer & Equal-to-the-Apostles," accessed May 3, 2024, https://www.goarch.org/chapel/saints?contentid=136.

105. This historical account of the Byzantine tradition of Mary Magdalene is drawn from the work of Vassiliki A. Foskolou, "Mary Magdalene between East and West: Cult and Image, Relics and Politics in the Late Thirteenth-Century Eastern Mediterranean," *Dumbarton Oaks Papers* 65–66 (2011–12): 271–96.

106. Foskolou cites *Synaxarium ecclesiae Constantinopolitanae*, ed. Hippolyte Delehaye (Brussels, 1920).

107. Jacobus de Voragine, *Golden Legend*, 382.

108. Luther identifies this reading with Bonaventure in "Sermon on Marriage" (1525) (Weimarer Ausgabe 17:17–18), in Karant-Nunn and Wiesner-Hanks, *Luther on Women*, 45. Instead he sides with Nicephorus of Constantinople that the bridegroom was Jesus's cousin, the son of his mother's sister.

109. See Susan Haskins, *Mary Magdalen: Myth and Metaphor* (New York: Harcourt, Brace, 1994), 106–7.

110. These details from the *Synaxarion* are repeated by the *Menologion of Basil II* and the *Imperial Menologion* of the mid-eleventh century and is considered hagiography. Foskolou, "Mary Magdalene," 281.

111. Details drawn from Foskolou, "Mary Magdalene," 282.

112. Foskolou, "Mary Magdalene," 284.

113. Foskolou, "Mary Magdalene," 288.

114. During the same century that Pope Gregory in Rome linked Mary Magdalene's name to the sinful woman of Luke 7, Gregory of Antioch (an ancient center of Christianity) affirmed Mary Magdalene as apostle. See Gregory of Antioch, *Sermon on the Bearers of Ointment* 11, cited by Beavis, "Mary Magdalene," 17:1210. Similarly, the Ethiopian church (part of the Oriental Orthodox branch of the church), one of the most ancient forms of Christianity, did not associate Mary Magdalene's story with prostitution and instead elevated her apostolic commission. Beavis, "Mary Magdalene," 17:1216–17.

115. Foskolou, "Mary Magdalene," 289, points also to Gerard of Nazareth as a parallel example of this approach.

116. Apostolos-Cappadona, *Mary Magdalene*, 27.

Chapter 4 France's Beloved Preacher and Evangelist

1. I am grateful to the American College of the Mediterranean in Aix-en-Provence for the Faculty Research Fellowship that enabled me to visit these historic Christian sites.

2. For Irenaeus of Lyon's teaching on apostolic tradition, see *Against Heresies*. The apostle Paul also writes to the church at Corinth about handing on traditions (1 Cor. 11:2). He declares, "For I received from the Lord what I also handed on to you" (11:23).

3. Jennifer Powell McNutt and David W. McNutt, *Know the Theologians* (Grand Rapids: Zondervan Academic, 2024), 15; see also chap. 1.

4. In response to Waldensian women preaching, Mary Magdalene's example was reinterpreted by clerical leaders from preaching to simply relaying a message. Katherine Ludwig Jansen, *The Making of the Magdalen: Preaching and Popular Devotion in the Later Middle Ages* (Princeton: Princeton University Press, 2000), 57.

5. Clarity on this point comes from Amy Beverage Peeler and is represented in our cowritten article, "The First Apostle's Unlikely Witness," *Christianity Today*, March 18, 2024, https://www.christianitytoday.com/ct/2024/april/mary-magdalene-first -apostle-mcnutt-peeler.html.

6. Beverly Roberts Gaventa, *Acts*, Abingdon New Testament Commentaries (Nashville: Abingdon, 2003), 68.

7. *The Golden Legend* connects her departure to the aftermath of the martyrdom of Stephen and expulsion of the disciples from Judea so that "the disciples went off into the lands of the various nations and there sowed the word of the Lord." Jacobus de Voragine, *The Golden Legend* (Princeton: Princeton University Press, 2012), 376.

8. Origen, *Against Celsus* 2.55, 59 (ANF 4:453, 455).

9. Jansen, *Making of the Magdalen*, 35; and Susan Haskins, *Mary Magdalen: Myth and Metaphor* (New York: Harcourt, Brace, 1994), 108.

10. See Margaret Arnold, *The Magdalene in the Reformation* (Cambridge, MA: Belknap, 2018), esp. 20–21.

11. Arnold, *Magdalene*, 21. Vézelay's Romanesque Basilica of St. Magdalene is a UNESCO World Heritage Site today.

12. Both Peter Abelard and Bernard of Clairvaux described Mary Magdalene as apostle to the apostles. Jansen, *Making of the Magdalen*, 62–63.

13. Arnold, *Magdalene*, 18–19.

14. Jansen, *Making of the Magdalen*, part 1, esp. section "Mendicant Magdalen."

15. Arnold, *Magdalene*, 18.

16. Jacobus de Voragine, *Golden Legend*, 381–82, discusses the moving of the relics.

17. Allie M. Ernst mentions the Ethiopic tradition's inclusion of a Sarah as surprising. Ernst, *Martha from the Margins: The Authority of Martha in Early Christian Tradition* (Leiden: Brill, 2009), 73. Interestingly, the name also pops up in the French tradition as well, though the explanation is elusive. Perhaps the repeat is an indication that cross-influences are more common than we realize.

18. Recounted in Jacobus de Voragine, *Golden Legend*, 376–77.

19. Jacobus de Voragine, *Golden Legend*, 380.

20. The details are reflected in her early biographies, a genre known as *vita* for "life": *Vita apostolico-eremetica* (ninth century) and *Vita apostolica Mariae Magdalenae* (tenth century). See Victor Saxer, *Le dossier vézelien de Marie-Madeleine . . . Subsidia hagiographica* (Brussels: Société des Bollandistes, 1975), note 57.

21. The beauty of the walk is captured in the pastel by Pierre Petit, *Montée sur le Chemin des Rois, vers la grotte de Marie-Madeleine*, reproduced in Jean-Marc Thenoux, ed., *7 hommages à Marie-Madeleine: Les vitraux de la grotte sainte Marie-Madeleine a la Sainte-Baume*, 3rd ed. (Sainte-Baume: Écomusée de la Sainte-Baume, 2012), 10.

22. The Benedictine abbey in Vézelay has also played an important role in serving as the caretakers of Mary Magdalene's relics and memory.

23. This was a gift from the parish of la Madeleine de Paris. For more details on the artwork on site at la grotte sainte Marie-Madeleine à la Sainte-Baume, see Thenoux's brochure, *7 hommages à Marie-Madeleine*.

24. Another example of the Pietà that includes Mary Magdalene comes from the Italian Renaissance sculptor Michelangelo, called *The Deposition* (also called the Bandini Pietà or the Lamentation over the Dead Christ), ca. 1547–1555, Opera del Duomo Museum, Florence, Italy. Annibale Carracci's *Pietà with Saints Clare, Francis and Mary Magdalene* is a 1585 oil on canvas painting, now in the Galleria nazionale di Parma.

25. Vassiliki A. Foskolou, "Mary Magdalene between East and West: Cult and Image, Relics and Politics in the Late Thirteenth-Century Eastern Mediterranean," *Dumbarton Oaks Papers* 65–66 (2011–12): 293.

26. Catharina Regina von Greiffenberg, *On the Supremely Holy and the Supremely Salvific Suffering of Jesus: First Meditation* 12–13, cited in *Luke*, ed. Beth Kreitzer, Reformation Commentary on Scripture NT 3 (Downers Grove, IL: IVP Academic, 2015), 3:163. See also Joy A. Schroeder, "The Prenatal Theology of Catharina Regina von Greiffenberg," *Lutheran Forum* 46, no. 3 (2012): 50–56.

27. This particular exchange has led to varying interpretations in Christian history, including insinuations that Jesus is rebuffing romantic or erotic touch. Jane Schaberg, *The Resurrection of Mary Magdalene: Legends, Apocrypha, and the Christian Testament* (New York: Continuum, 2002), 330–35. Tertullian contrasts Mary Magdalene's touch with Thomas's touch, pointing out that the former was out of love and the latter out of doubt. Schaberg, *Resurrection of Mary Magdalene*, 85.

28. This story is depicted in the striking altarpiece of Mary Magdalene in the Chapel of Saint-Pilon at the summit of Sainte-Baume, shown in Apostolos-Cappadona, *Mary Magdalene*, xvii.

29. The tooth of Mary Magdalene, meanwhile, is housed at the Metropolitan Museum of Art in New York. See "Reliquary of Mary Magdalene," The Met, accessed January 19, 2024, https://www.metmuseum.org/art/collection/search/464469.

30. Calvin, *Treatise on Relics*, trans. Valerian Krasinski, 2nd ed. (Edinburgh: Johnstone, Hunter, 1870), 224, available at https://ccel.org/ccel/calvin/treatise_relics/treatise_relics.v.html?queryID=33968534&resultID=121236.

31. Calvin, *Treatise on Relics* (trans. Krasinski, 265–66).

Chapter 5 A Woman Possessed—and Healed

1. Scandal surrounded the Christian bestseller by Kevin Malarkey and Alex Malarkey, *The Boy Who Came Back from Heaven* (Carol Stream, IL: Tyndale, 2010), which was exposed as a fabrication years later.

2. This comes from the Niceno-Constantinopolitan Creed that was embraced in 381 CE at Constantinople, but it is commonly called the Nicene Creed.

3. Tish Harrison Warren, *Prayer in the Night: For Those Who Work or Watch or Weep* (Downers Grove, IL: IVP Academic, 2021), 25.

4. For more on this topic, see Jennifer Powell McNutt, "What Is the Meaning of Evil and Suffering?," in *Theology Questions Everyone Asks: Christian Faith in Plain*

Language, ed. Gary Burge and David Lauber (Downers Grove, IL: InterVarsity, 2014), 80–94.

5. Philip Jenkins, "Believing in the Global South," *First Things* 168 (December 2006), https://www.firstthings.com/article/2006/12/believing-in-the-global-south. In the same article, Jenkins recognizes that "precious little is left of the New Testament after we purge all mentions of angels, demons, and spirits."

6. Mark 16:9 offers another reference, but this is likely a later addition rather than original to the text.

7. C. S. Lewis, *Screwtape Letters*, in *The Complete C. S. Lewis Signature Classics* (San Francisco: HarperSanFrancisco, 2002), 183. Lewis describes the unbearable experience of writing that book: "The world into which I had to project myself while I spoke through Screwtape was all dust, grit, thirst and itch. Every trace of beauty, freshness and geniality had to be excluded. It almost smothered me before I was done" (283).

8. In New Testament times, illness was blamed on evil spirits. James F. McGrath, *The A to Z of the New Testament: Things Experts Know That Everyone Else Should Too* (Grand Rapids: Eerdmans, 2023), 137.

9. This account reflects other patterns of suffering from demon possession, such as shrieking (Acts 8:7), which is attributed in the New Testament to the tormenting of unclean spirits (Acts 5:16).

10. This summary of Jewish understandings of demonology is drawn from Craig Keener, *The IVP Bible Background Commentary: New Testament*, 2nd ed. (Downers Grove, IL: InterVarsity, 2014), 201, 209–10.

11. Discussion primarily revolves around his use of prayer. Richard H. Bell, "Demon, Devil, Satan," in *Dictionary of Jesus and the Gospels*, 2nd ed., ed. Joel B. Green (Downers Grove, IL: IVP Academic, 2013), 197–98.

12. Jesus is so good at exorcism that he is accused of working for Beelzebul (a common Jewish name for the devil), since the demons know him and obey him (Matt. 12:24; Mark 3:22; Luke 11:15).

13. Bell, "Demon, Devil, Satan," 198.

14. See Keener, "Luke 8:33," and "Luke 11:21–23," in *IVP Bible Background Commentary*, 201, 210.

15. Craig Keener writes, "Most scholars believe that Jesus historically gained a reputation as an exorcist" (Keener, *Miracles* [Grand Rapids: Baker Academic, 2011], 2:784). See also McGrath, *A to Z of the New Testament*, 140; and Graham H. Twelftree, *Jesus the Exorcist: A Contribution to the Study of the Historical Jesus* (Tübingen: Mohr Siebeck, 1993).

16. Bell, "Demon, Devil, Satan," 198.

17. See Tertullian and Origen, cited in Keener, *Miracles*, 2:785. Patristic sources report that Christianity spread because of successful exorcisms.

18. Pope Gregory the Great, *Homily* 33, cited in Katherine Ludwig Jansen, *The Making of the Magdalen: Preaching and Popular Devotion in the Later Middle Ages* (Princeton: Princeton University Press, 2000), 33.

19. During the fifteenth century, the idea that women were more susceptible to demons than men and that demons were attracted to sinful people was advanced by a dangerous document titled *Malleus Maleficarum (The Hammer of the Witches)* by Heinrich Kramer.

20. Keener, *Miracles*, 2:785.

21. Heiko Oberman, *Luther: Man between God and the Devil* (New Haven: Yale University Press, 1989), 310, 319–20.

22. Jesus breaks Sabbath restrictions because "the Son of Man is lord of the sabbath" (Matt. 12:8).

23. See also Mark 6:34; 8:2; 9:22; Luke 7:13; 10:33; 15:20.

24. A version of the story that follows was published in Jennifer Powell McNutt, "No Simple Story: How Women's Roles Changed in the Sixteenth Century," *Christian History Magazine* 131, Women of the Reformation: Lesser-Known Stories (August 2019), 6–10.

25. Martin Luther, "Consolation for Women Whose Pregnancies Have Not Gone Well," in *The Annotated Luther: Pastoral Writings*, ed. Mary Jane Haemig (Minneapolis: Fortress, 2016), 4:426.

26. Using this same familial imagery, Jesus contrasts the children of the kingdom with the children of the evil one (Matt. 13:38). This contrast is evident in other parts of the New Testament (1 John 3:10).

27. According to 1 John 3:8, "The Son of God was revealed for this purpose: to destroy the works of the devil."

28. Some texts indicate that seventy-two were sent.

29. Richard Bauckham, *Gospel Women: Studies of the Named Women in the Gospels* (Grand Rapids: Eerdmans, 2002), 112.

30. See Robin M. Jensen, *Living Water: Images, Symbols, and Settings of Early Christian Baptism* (Leiden: Brill, 2010). Alongside the anchor, early Christian artifacts paired the symbol of the fish (or IXTHUS), which was an acrostic for the terms Jesus Christ, God's Son, and Savior in Greek. To those who knew, a powerful sermon was proclaimed through just two ordinary symbols. An example can be found on the funerary stele of Licinia Amias, an ancient Christian inscription, at Epigraphical Museum, Athens, Greece, available at https://en.m.wikipedia.org/wiki/File:Stele_Licinia_Amias_Terme_67646.jpg.

31. John Calvin, *Institutes of the Christian Religion* 3.17.1, ed. John T. McNeill, trans. Ford Lewis Battles, Library of Christian Classics (Philadelphia: Westminster, 1960), 1:803.

32. In Orthodox art, sixteenth- and seventeenth-century depictions of Mary Magdalene's seven demons focus on her healing, while nineteenth-century depictions focus on her possession: Ralitsa Rousseva, "The Scene *Christ Expels Seven Demons from Mary Magdalene* in Post-Byzantine Art," *Scripta* 22 (2022): 221–32. In this chapter, I invite us to focus on her healing.

Chapter 6 The "Certain Women" in Jesus's Inner Circle

1. Director Christian Stückl also went to some lengths to remove anti-Semitic elements that existed in the play prior to 2010.

2. Matt. 21:1–11; Mark 11:1–11; Luke 19:28–44; John 12:12–19.

3. Indeed, Jesus taught that they are the "greatest in the kingdom of heaven" (Matt. 18:4).

4. For those interested in tracing this journey, I recommend Peter Walker, *In the Steps of Jesus: An Illustrated Guide to the Places of the Holy Land* (Grand Rapids: Zondervan, 2007).

5. Amanda Lehr, "Selected Negative Teaching Evaluations of Jesus Christ," McSweeney's Internet Tendency, March 2, 2022, https://www.mcsweeneys.net/articles/selected-negative-teaching-evaluations-of-jesus-christ.

6. Nijay K. Gupta, *Tell Her Story: How Women Led, Taught, and Ministered in the Early Church* (Downers Grove, IL: IVP Academic, 2023), 62.

7. Gupta writes, "Mary Magdalene is a good example of a Jesus follower who was given direct instruction by Jesus and followed through. If she is not a disciple, it is hard to make a case for anyone, male or female." *Tell Her Story*, 65.

8. Craig Keener, *The IVP Bible Background Commentary: New Testament*, 2nd ed. (Downers Grove, IL: InterVarsity, 2014), 200. Keener explains, "While a small number of philosophers had women disciples, many criticized this practice; we know of no other women disciples among Jewish teachers in this period" (200). For a nuanced view, see Lynn H. Cohick, *Women in the World of the Earliest Christians: Illuminating Ancient Ways of Life* (Grand Rapids: Baker Academic, 2009), 309–10.

9. Cohick, *Earliest Christians*, 310.

10. Robert C. Tannehill explains it as "shocking" in its time. Tannehill, *Luke*, Abingdon New Testament Commentaries (Nashville: Abingdon, 1996), 140.

11. Others have critiqued the series for not moving well enough beyond the idea of Mary Magdalene as the "thirteenth disciple" to highlight the way in which she is one of many women traveling with Jesus. Mary Ann Beavis, "Mary Magdalene on Film in Twenty-First Century: A Feminist Theological Critique," *Journal of Religion and Film* 28, no. 1 (April 2024): 15.

12. Richard Bauckham, *Gospel Women: Studies of the Named Women in the Gospels* (Grand Rapids: Eerdmans, 2002), 113.

13. Matt. 27:55–56 references Mary Magdalene, Mary the mother of James and Joseph, and the (unnamed) mother of the sons of Zebedee. Mark 15:40–41 references Mary Magdalene, Mary the mother of James the younger and of Joses, and Salome.

14. The Greek root for "cared for" is *diakonos* (as in "these women had followed him and cared for his needs," Mark 15:41), which is also used to describe Phoebe in Rom. 16:1. There is no reason to assume that this implies low social status. Cohick, *Earliest Christians*, 313.

15. Keener, *IVP Bible Background Commentary*, 200. See also Bauckham, *Gospel Women*, 121–35.

16. Caryn A. Reeder, *The Samaritan Woman's Story: Reconsidering John 4 after #ChurchToo* (Downers Grove, IL: IVP Academic, 2022), 133.

17. Reeder, *Samaritan Woman's Story*, 142.

18. Cohick, *Earliest Christians*, 311.

19. Susan E. Hylen, *Finding Phoebe: What New Testament Women Were Really Like* (Grand Rapids: Eerdmans, 2023), 13.

20. Cohick, *Earliest Christians*, 311. See also Hylen, *Finding Phoebe*, 31.

21. Cohick, *Earliest Christians*, 311.

22. This information is primarily drawn from Cohick, *Earliest Christians*, chap. 9.

23. Cohick, *Earliest Christians*, 308.

24. For a helpful overview of Junia as apostle, see Gupta, *Tell Her Story*, chap. 9.

25. Bauckham, *Gospel Women*, chap. 5.

26. Bauckham, *Gospel Women*, 119. According to Bauckham, if she had left a husband who was not a follower of Jesus, the text would not have bothered naming him.

27. Cohick, *Earliest Christians*, chap. 7.

28. Hylen, *Finding Phoebe*, 37.

29. John Bunyan, *The Pilgrim's Progress*, ed. W. R. Owens (Oxford: Oxford University Press, 2003), 243–44.

30. Bunyan, *Pilgrim's Progress*, 244.

31. Bauckham, *Gospel Women*, 114. Bauckham cites Peter's declaration in Luke 18:28: "We have left our homes and followed you." He writes, "The twelve who abandon everything and the women who give their material resources for the common support of the community of disciples exemplify in different ways the teaching of Luke's Jesus about possessions" (115).

32. In John's Gospel, it is revealed that Judas was in charge of the money for the poor but was actually stealing from that fund (John 12:6).

33. Katelyn Beaty, *Celebrities for Jesus: How Personas, Platforms, and Profits Are Hurting the Church* (Grand Rapids: Brazos, 2022), 109–12. For full disclosure, Beaty is also my editor.

34. See Carmen Joy Imes, *Being God's Image: Why Creation Still Matters* (Downers Grove, IL: IVP Academic, 2023).

35. This well-known, polished epigram, paraphrased here, was not written by Chesterton in that exact form, though versions of the concept are found in his various works. Quoted in Émile Cammaerts, *The Laughing Prophet: The Seven Virtues and G. K. Chesterton* (London: Methuen, 1937).

36. Bauckham, *Gospel Women*, 112, 216–17. Bauckham suggests, based on Elisabeth Schüssler Fiorenza's work *In Memory of Her*, that even pairs of men and women, such as the married couples that served as coworkers with Paul (Priscilla and Aquilla, Andronicus and Junia), were possibly among the seventy. See also Gupta, *Tell Her Story*, 66.

Chapter 7 Go and Tell like Mary Magdalene

1. Nijay K. Gupta, *Tell Her Story: How Women Led, Taught, and Ministered in the Early Church* (Downers Grove, IL: IVP Academic, 2023), 65.

2. The male disciples had dispersed, which was predicted by Jesus (John 16:32; 18:8–9).

3. Beverly Roberts Gaventa, *Acts*, Abingdon New Testament Commentaries (Nashville: Abingdon, 2003), 68.

4. Craig Keener, "Matthew 27:55–56," and "Mark 15:41," in *The IVP Bible Background Commentary: New Testament*, 2nd ed. (Downers Grove, IL: InterVarsity, 2014), 122–23, 173–74.

5. George Eliot, *Middlemarch* (London: Woodsworth Editions, 1994), 688.

6. Keener, *IVP Bible Background Commentary*, 310.

7. There are many versions and iterations of *Weeping Woman* by Picasso. Apostolos-Cappadona is citing Pablo Picasso, *Weeping Woman* 1937, oil on canvas, 55.2 × 46.2 cm, National Gallery of Victoria, Melbourne, https://www.ngv.vic.gov.au/explore/collection/work/4256, cited in Diane Apostolos-Cappadona, *Mary Magdalene: A Visual History*

(New York: T&T Clark, 2023), 90–91. See also Apostolos-Cappadona, "Pablo Picasso, The Weeping Woman," in *Beyond Belief: Modern Art and the Religious Imagination*, ed. Rosemary Crumlin (Melbourne: National Gallery of Victoria, 1998), 66–67.

8. Origen, *Contra Celsus* 2.59, in *The Ante-Nicene Fathers: Translations of the Writings of the Fathers down to A.D. 325*, ed. Alexander Roberts and James Donaldson, 10 vols. (New York: Christian Literature, 1885–1887; repr., Peabody, MA: Hendrickson, 1994), 4:455. Celsus also accused the Virgin Mary of being an adulteress (1.28, in *ANF* 4:408).

9. Origen, *Contra Celsus* 2.70 (*ANF* 4:460).

10. Richard Bauckham, *Gospel Women: Studies of the Named Women in the Gospels* (Grand Rapids: Eerdmans, 2002), 271.

11. See John Calvin, *Commentary on the Gospel of John* 20.11. Calvin described her tears as idle, useless, superstitious, and carnal feelings. For further discussion of this point, see Margaret Arnold, *The Magdalene in the Reformation* (Cambridge, MA: Belknap, 2018), 168. The interpretation of Calvin by Arnold is not exactly correct, since he does permit her a temporary apostleship, as detailed in chap. 3 above.

12. Josette A. Wisman, "Christine de Pizan," in *Handbook of Women Biblical Interpreters: A Historical and Biographical Guide*, ed. Marion Ann Taylor and Agnes Choi (Grand Rapids: Baker Academic, 2012), 127.

13. Christine de Pizan, *The Book of the City of Ladies* 1.10, in Christine de Pizan, *The Book of the City of Ladies and Other Writings*, ed. Sophie Bourgault and Rebecca Kingston, trans. Ineke Hardy (Indianapolis: Hackett, 2018), 39.

14. Pizan, *Book of the City of Ladies* 1.9 (Bourgault and Kingston, 37).

15. Pizan, *Book of the City of Ladies* 1.10 (Bourgault and Kingston, 40). She conflates Mary of Bethany with Mary Magdalene here, which was the understanding at the time. Pizan reframes the tears as those of "devotion." She also cites the examples of the widow of Nain and the Canaanite woman.

16. Gregor Erhart, *Sainte Marie Madeleine*, 1515/1520, Louvre Museum, RF 1338, https://collections.louvre.fr/en/ark:/53355/cl010093565.

17. Holly J. Carey, *Women Who Do: Female Disciples in the Gospels* (Grand Rapids: Eerdmans, 2023), 180.

18. Bauckham, *Gospel Women*, 284, also recognizes this dynamic at work in the text.

19. Keener, *IVP Bible Background Commentary*, 310.

20. Augustine may take this too far with the affirmation *per feminam mors, per feminam vita* (through a woman death, through a woman life) because of his emphasis on original sin and the tradition that gains momentum that women carry original sin in a more inherent way than men. Augustine, Sermon 232, cited in Katherine Ludwig Jansen, *The Making of the Magdalen: Preaching and Popular Devotion in the Later Middle Ages* (Princeton: Princeton University Press, 2000), 31.

21. Eckhard J. Schnabel, "Apostle," in *Dictionary of Jesus and the Gospels*, 2nd ed., ed. Joel B. Green, Jeannine K. Brown, and Nicholas Perrin (Downers Grove, IL: IVP Academic, 2013), 34.

22. N. T. Wright claims that this is the reason Paul does not reference them in 1 Cor. 15: "Rather, the tradition which Paul is quoting, precisely for evangelistic and apologetic use, has carefully taken the women out of it so that it can serve that purpose

within a suspicious and mocking world." Wright, *The Resurrection of the Son of God* (Minneapolis: Fortress, 2003), 607. See also Bauckham, *Gospel Women*, 258–59.

23. Wright, *Resurrection of the Son of God*, 608.

24. Bauckham, *Gospel Women*, 259.

25. We should also notice when Paul uses familial language for fellow believers such as when he describes Phoebe as "our sister" in Rom. 16:1 and greeting "brothers and sisters" in Gal. 6:18.

26. In the longer ending of Mark 16:14, Jesus rebukes the eleven for not believing "those who saw him after he had risen."

27. Bauckham, *Gospel Women*, 282.

28. Luther describes the proclamation that Mary is the mother of the Lord as the "first sermon on earth," in his "Sermon on the Visitation" (1535) (Weimarer Ausgabe 41:353–54), cited in *Luke*, ed. Beth Kreitzer, Reformation Commentary on Scripture NT 3 (Downers Grove, IL: IVP Academic, 2015), 23.

29. Jürgen Moltmann, "2009 Emergent Village Theological Conversation with Jürgen Moltmann: Women, Homosexuality, Antisemitism, Hermeneutics and More," PostBarthian.com, accessed May 6, 2024, https://postbarthian.com/2014/01/09/jurgen -moltmann-on-women.

Chapter 8 The First Apostle Chosen by Christ

1. Mary Elise Sarotte, "The Ordinary People Who Brought Down the Berlin Wall," *Wall Street Journal*, November 8, 2019, https://www.wsj.com/articles/the-ordinary -people-who-brought-down-the-berlin-wall-11573228405. Those involved included Gerhard Lauter and Gunter Schabowski. See Sarotte, *The Collapse: The Accidental Opening of the Berlin Wall* (New York: Basic Books, 2015). The account that follows comes from these sources.

2. Early church father Augustine drew theological parallels between the virgin womb and the virgin tomb. Augustine, "Homilies on the Gospel of John," Tractate 120.5, in *A Select Library of Nicene and Post-Nicene Fathers of the Christian Church*, 1st series, ed. Philip Schaff, 14 vols. (New York: Christian Literature, 1886–1889; repr., Peabody, MA: Hendrickson, 1994), 7:435.

3. Other Gospels include the details "early dawn" (Luke 24:1) or "as the first day of the week was dawning" (Matt. 28:1). Evidently some preparation of the body for burial would have been possible even on the Sabbath. The more elaborate preparations could wait until the Sabbath passed.

4. Tacitus, Suetonius, Josephus, and Philo indicate that Rome willingly punished sympathizers of rebels, including women and children. Jane Schaberg, *The Resurrection of Mary Magdalene: Legends, Apocrypha, and the Christian Testament* (New York: Continuum, 2002), 276–77.

5. For an exploration of the possible readings, see Craig Keener, *The IVP Bible Background Commentary: New Testament*, 2nd ed. (Downers Grove, IL: InterVarsity, 2014), 122. Beverly Gaventa surveys possible interpretations of the text and considers whether the tearing of the temple curtain "is simply an additional sign that the approaching death is the death of someone very great." Gaventa, *Acts*, Abingdon New Testament Commentaries (Nashville: Abingdon, 2003), 345.

6. Craig Keener, *The Gospel of Matthew: A Socio-Rhetorical Commentary* (Grand Rapids: Eerdmans, 2009), 686–87.

7. N. T. Wright, *The Resurrection of the Son of God* (Minneapolis: Fortress, 2003), 667.

8. Eckhard J. Schnabel, "Apostle," in *Dictionary of Jesus and the Gospels*, 2nd ed., ed. Joel B. Green, Jeannine K. Brown, and Nicholas Perrin (Downers Grove, IL: IVP Academic, 2013), 34–45.

9. These terms were not used exclusively for men. Mary of Bethany's act of sitting at Jesus's feet to learn is the meaning of disciple (Luke 10:39–40; see also Acts 22:3). Acts 9:36 describes Tabitha (also called Dorcas) as a "disciple" in Joppa. In Romans, Paul greets the "apostle" Junia, who is likely Joanna, the one who witnessed the empty tomb. For more on women disciples, see Nijay K. Gupta, *Tell Her Story: How Women Led, Taught, and Ministered in the Early Church* (Downers Grove, IL: IVP Academic, 2023), 62–67.

10. There were differing expectations surrounding apostolicity for Luke than for Paul. See Beverly Roberts Gaventa, *Acts*, Abingdon New Testament Commentaries (Nashville: Abingdon, 2003), 71–72.

11. "But it remains the case that the events Matthew describes in 27:51–53, as well as being without parallel in other early Christian sources, are without precedent in second-Temple expectation, and we may doubt whether stories such as this would have been invented simply to 'fulfil' prophecies that nobody had understood this way before. . . . Some stories are so odd that they may just have happened." Wright, *Resurrection of the Son of God*, 636.

12. Robert H. Gundry, *Matthew: A Commentary on His Handbook for a Mixed Church under Persecution*, 2nd ed. (Grand Rapids: Eerdmans, 1994), 576. Wright, *Resurrection of the Son of God*, 633, cites a connection to Ezek. 37:12–13.

13. See also Holly J. Carey, *Women Who Do: Female Disciples in the Gospels* (Grand Rapids: Eerdmans, 2023). She writes, "In a context in which simply being a woman was a disadvantage, the female disciples in Jesus' ministry are portrayed as models of faith. They are people who take initiative. They are disciples who act when all others around them do not. They make good on their commitment to follow Jesus and demonstrate the qualities of discipleship that Jesus demands of his followers" (185).

14. The women disciples stayed and therefore saw what the male disciples did not. Carey, *Women Who Do*, 181–84.

15. "In an era when women were rarely if ever designated in this way that it was common to nickname men, this would have indicated her status in Jesus' estimation." James F. McGrath, *The A to Z of the New Testament: Things Experts Know That Everyone Else Should Too* (Grand Rapids: Eerdmans, 2023), 46. For Jesus's love of puns, see also ibid., 107.

16. Carey, *Women Who Do*, 185–88.

17. Karla Zazueta, "Mary Magdalene: Repainting Her Portrait of Misconceptions," in *Vindicating the Vixens: Revisiting Sexualized, Vilified, and Marginalized Women of the Bible*, ed. Sandra L. Glahn (Grand Rapids: Kregel Academic, 2017), 255–72.

18. Richard Bauckham, *Gospel Women: Studies of the Named Women in the Gospels* (Grand Rapids: Eerdmans, 2002), 278.

19. This has been the work of an American nonprofit known as Advancing Women Artists. See John Hooper, "Centuries Later, a Painter of the Renaissance Gets Her Due,"

Wall Street Journal, October 17, 2019, https://www.wsj.com/articles/a-long-forgotten -renaissance-painter-gets-her-due-11571338663.

20. Bauckham, *Gospel Women*, 285.

Epilogue

1. Augustine, *Confessions* 8.19, ed. Sarah Ruden (New York: Modern Library, 2017), 225–26. For more on Augustine, see Jennifer Powell McNutt and David W. McNutt, *Know the Theologians* (Grand Rapids: Zondervan Academic, 2024), chap. 4.

2. Augustine, *Confessions* 8.25 (Ruden, 232).

3. Augustine, *Confessions* 8.28 (Ruden, 235).

4. Augustine, *Confessions* 8.29 (Ruden, 236). Augustine remembers in that moment how Anthony of Thebes was convicted on hearing a reading from the Gospel.

5. Hebrews 4:12 describes Scripture as a living and active word.

6. In the Ethiopian Orthodox Tewahedo tradition, churches are built encircled by forests and described as mini-gardens of Eden, which looks back to Genesis and ahead to the promised paradise of the eschaton. For more on the church forests of Ethiopia, see Jeremy Seifert, "The Church Forests of Ethiopia," *New York Times*, December 3, 2019, https://www.nytimes.com/video/opinion/100000006808736/the-church-forests -of-ethiopia.html.

7. Augustine, "Homilies on the Gospel of John," Tractate 121.3, in *A Select Library of Nicene and Post-Nicene Fathers of the Christian Church*, 1st series, ed. Philip Schaff, 14 vols. (New York: Christian Literature, 1886–1889; repr., Peabody, MA: Hendrickson, 1994), 7:437.

8. We have been instructed to stay alert and keep watch in the garden, but like the disciples before us, we are prone to falling asleep (Matt. 26:40; Mark 14:37). We may act rashly and hurt others (John 18:10–11) or even deny knowing the gardener at all ("Didn't I see you with him in the garden?" John 18:26).

9. Eugene Peterson, *As Kingfishers Catch Fire: A Conversation on the Ways of God Formed by the Words of God* (Colorado Springs: WaterBrook, 2017), 35–41.

10. Peterson, *As Kingfishers Catch Fire*, 35. He continues, "No single word in Leviticus has been quoted more often or in so many different contexts than this imperative verb in Leviticus 19:18: *love*. The word is threaded all through the rest of the Hebrew Scriptures and embedded on nearly every page of the New Testament" (37).

11. Esau McCaulley, *Reading while Black: African American Biblical Interpretation as an Exercise in Hope* (Downers Grove, IL: IVP Academic, 2020), 165.

12. She uses the phrase on several occasions. Barr, *Biblical Womanhood*, esp. chap. 3.

13. This dynamic is helpfully considered in John Thompson, *Reading the Bible with the Dead: What You Can Learn from the History of Exegesis That You Can't Learn from Exegesis Alone* (Grand Rapids: Eerdmans, 2007), 2.

14. Terran Williams encourages some helpful practical implications for the church that resonate with this point. See Williams, *How God Sees Women: The End of Patriarchy* (Cape Town, South Africa: Spiritual Bakery, 2022), esp. chap. 16.

15. Carolyn Custis James, *Lost Women of the Bible: The Women We Thought We Knew* (Grand Rapids: Zondervan, 2005), 37–38; and James, *Finding God in the*

Margins: The Book of Ruth, Transformative Faith Series (Bellingham, WA: Lexham, 2018), 8.

16. Expanding our attention to the women of the Bible should also extend to the women of theology and biblical studies. These women have insight that needs hearing and seeing as well. The only thing obstructing us from familiarizing ourselves with the biblical interpretations of the women who came before us and the women of the contemporary church and academy is exposure and willingness these days; enriching, authoritative sources are increasingly accessible. For a helpful resource on women theologians in the history of the church, see Marion Ann Taylor, ed., *Handbook of Women Biblical Interpreters* (Grand Rapids: Baker Academic, 2012).

17. Roxanne Stone, "Why Are Women Leaving the Church? The Reasons behind the Exodus," *Christianity Today*, June 10, 2015, https://www.christianitytoday.com/ct/2015/june-web-only/why-are-women-leaving-church.html; Katie Gaddini, "A Large Number of Single Women Are Leaving the Church. Why?," *Relevant Magazine*, January 10, 2023, https://relevantmagazine.com/faith/church/why-are-so-many-single-women-are-leaving-the-church; and Gaddini, *The Struggle to Stay: Why Single Evangelical Women Are Leaving the Church* (New York: Columbia University Press, 2022).

18. Rebecca McLaughlin, *Jesus through the Eyes of Women: How the First Female Disciples Help Us Know and Love the Lord* (Columbia, MO: Gospel Coalition, 2022), 174.

19. McLaughlin, *Jesus through the Eyes of Women*, 21.

20. Terran Williams highlights Jesus's question as an invitation to discover. Williams, *How God Sees Women: The End of Patriarchy* (Cape Town, South Africa: Spiritual Bakery, 2022), 7.

21. For those sensing a call to ministry, I recommend Kristen Padilla's book, *Now That I'm Called: A Guide for Women Discerning a Call to Ministry* (Grand Rapids: Zondervan, 2018).

22. Christine de Pizan, *The Book of the City of Ladies* 1.10, in Christine de Pizan, *The Book of the City of Ladies and Other Writings*, ed. Sophie Bourgault and Rebecca Kingston, trans. Ineke Hardy (Indianapolis: Hackett, 2018), 40–41. She continues, "He commanded the blessed Mary Magdalene, to whom He first appeared on the first day of Easter, to announce it to His Apostles and to Peter. Oh, blessed God, praise be upon You who, with the other infinite gifts and favors You bestowed upon the female sex, chose a woman to be the bearer of such exalted and precious news" (41).

23. Simone Weil, *The Need for Roots* (London: Routledge, 2002), 43.

24. Paul states, ". . . together with all those who in every place call on the name of our Lord Jesus Christ, both their Lord and ours" (1 Cor. 1:2).

25. Fleming Rutledge, *The Undoing of Death* (Grand Rapids: Eerdmans, 2002).

Jennifer Powell McNutt (PhD, The University of St. Andrews) is the Franklin S. Dyrness Chair of Biblical and Theological Studies at Wheaton College and professor of theology and history of Christianity. She is an award-winning author, a fellow in the Royal Historical Society, and an ordained teaching elder in  the Presbyterian tradition. McNutt serves as a parish associate at her church and regularly speaks at universities, seminaries, and churches across the country. She and her husband cofounded McNuttshell Ministries, which serves as a bridge between the academy and the church, and live with their three children in Winfield, Illinois.

Connect with Dr. McNutt:

🌐 jenniferpowellmcnutt.com, www.mcnuttshellministries.com

ⓕ Jennifer Powell McNutt

📷 @jpowellmcnutt

𝕏 @jpowellmcnutt

🧵 @jpowellmcnutt